KidbitS

Kidbits

Illustrated by
Bob Italiano

Text by
Jenny Tesar

Executive Editor
Bruce S. Glassman

BLACKBIRCH PRESS, INC.

WOODBRIDGE, CONNECTICUT

Special thanks to my wife Joan, without whom
this project would not have been possible.
–B.I.

Published by Blackbirch Press, Inc.
260 Amity Road
Woodbridge, CT 06525

©1999 by Blackbirch Press, Inc.
First Edition

e-mail: staff@blackbirch.com
Web site: www.blackbirch.com

All photographs ©PhotoDisc

Printed in Singapore

10 9 8 7 6 5 4 3 2 1

The Kidbits Staff
Executive Editor: Bruce S. Glassman
Production Designer: Calico Harington
Assistant Editor: Lissa Poirot

Library of Congress Cataloging-in-Publication Data
Kidbits: more than 1,500 eye-popping charts, graphs, maps, and visuals that instantly show you
everything you want to know about your world!/ by the editors of Blackbirch Press; illustrated by
Bob Italiano
     p.   cm.
    Includes bibliographical references and index.
    ISBN 1-56711-169-6 (alk. paper)
    1. Handbooks, vade-mecums, etc.—Juvenile literature.
I. Italiano, Bob, ill. II. Blackbirch Press
AG106.K54   1999
031.02—dc21
                                                   98-19623
                                                    CIP
                                                     AC

Table of Contents

Health 102

Recreation 124

Music 134

Television 156

Movies and Videos 182

Pro Sports 204

Batting Averages/Most Career Games • Top RBI Leaders/Base Stealers/Run-Scorers • Top Earners in Major League Baseball • Oldest U.S. Baseball Stadiums • Top Teams in World Series Wins • Hockey's Top Goal Scorers/Points-Scorers • Top Earners in NHL • Fastest Horses in Kentucky Derby • Fastest-Winning Speeds of Indianapolis 500 • Top CART Driver Wins • Tennis Prize Money • Top Wimbledon/U.S. Open/Grand Slam Champions • Top Career Prize Money in Tennis • Teens' Favorite Athletes • Average Salaries • Top Athletes in Endorsement Deals

Who Are We?

By 1995, more than 263 million people lived in the
United States. About 70 million were kids—that is,
under age 18. Their ancestors came from every part of
the world. They represented nearly every race and ethnic
background. Most of them lived in cities and suburbs,
and a growing number lived in the South and West.

Every ten years since 1790, the Census Bureau has made an
official count of the U.S. population. It asks people about their
place of birth, age, race, marital status, home, and other aspects of
their lives. The 1990 census found that 80.3% of the population
was white and 12.1% was black. The population also included
Asians, Pacific Islanders, American Indians, Eskimos, and other
people. According to the Census, Hispanics—people of Spanish or
Spanish-American heritage—can be of any race; they made up 8%
of the 1990 population.

The 1990 population included 21.6 million people who were born
in other countries. About 39% had been born in North and Central
America, 25% in Asia, and 22% in Europe. California had the largest
foreign-born population, followed by New York, Florida, and Texas.

Kidbits Tidbits

- In 1996, there were 95.8 males for every 100 females in the U.S. Among young people, there are more males than females. But men die earlier than women, and among older people there are more women than men.
- In 1900, a newborn baby could expect to live to the age of 45. Today, a newborn can expect to live to age 76.
- About 3.9 million babies were born in the U.S. in 1996.
- Families are getting smaller. In 1970, the average size of a family was 3.58 people. By 1996, it was 3.2 people.

The population is expected to grow during the coming decades. By the year 2010, the Census Bureau predicts the U.S. will have 297.7 million people, including more than 72.5 million under age 18.

Each year, some 2.3 million marriages take place in the U.S. May through October are the most popular months for "getting hitched," with June ranking #1. In 1990, about 10.6% of the women and 4.3% of the men who got married were under age 20.

In 1996, 3.9 million babies were born in the U.S. They included 11,242 babies born to girls under age 15 and 494,272 born to girls ages 15 to 19. Those babies, like all babies born in America, could expect to live to an average age of 76. Most of them will grow up in middle- and upper-class families. But some will live in poverty. Today, about 20% of American children live in poverty. This means their families do not have enough income to buy adequate food and clothing.

There were 69.6 million families in the U.S. in 1996. About 51% of the families did not have any children. About 20% had one child, 19% had two children, and 10% had three or more children. Nearly one third of all families with children were headed by a single parent.

Kidbits Tidbits

- 8.9 million kids (people under age 18) lived in California in 1996—more than in any other state. In comparison, Wyoming only had 133,000 residents under age 18.
- In Mississippi, over 35% of the population is black—more than in any other state.
- More than 25% of the population of California and Texas is Hispanic.
- Most U.S. Hispanics are of Mexican origin.
- In 1995, a total of 14,665,000 Americans under age 18 lived in poverty.
- In 1995, more than 25% of the people in New Mexico lived below the poverty level—more than in any other state.
- In 1790, about 5% of U.S. people lived in cities and 95% lived in rural areas. In 1990, 75% lived in cities and 25% lived in rural areas.

Who Are We?

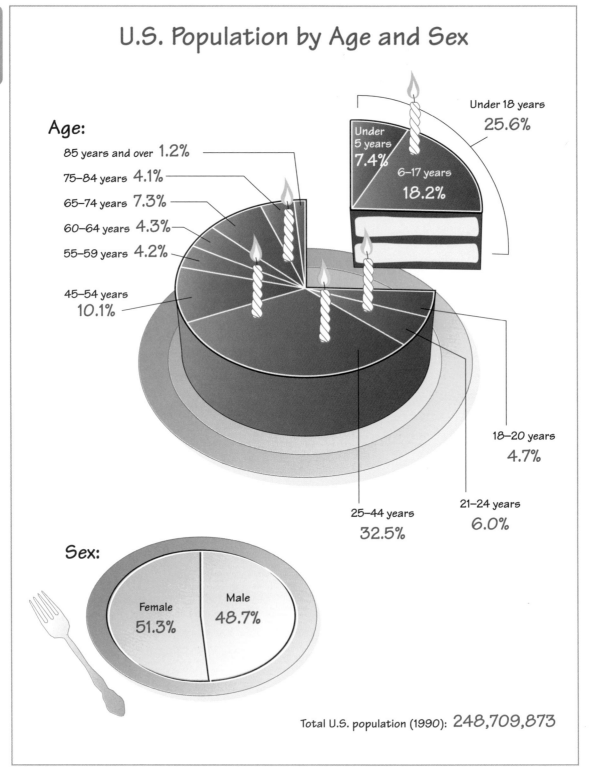

U.S. Population by Age and Sex

Under 18 years
25.6%

Under 5 years
7.4%

6–17 years
18.2%

Age:

85 years and over **1.2%**

75–84 years **4.1%**

65–74 years **7.3%**

60–64 years **4.3%**

55–59 years **4.2%**

45–54 years
10.1%

18–20 years
4.7%

25–44 years
32.5%

21–24 years
6.0%

Sex:

Female
51.3%

Male
48.7%

Total U.S. population (1990): **248,709,873**

SOURCE: Based on data from Bureau of the Census, U.S. Dept. of Commerce; 1990 Census

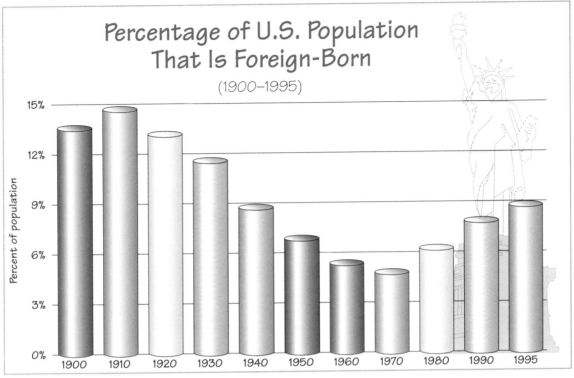

Percentage of U.S. Population That Is Foreign-Born
(1900–1995)

SOURCE: Based on data from Bureau of the Census, U.S. Dept. of Commerce

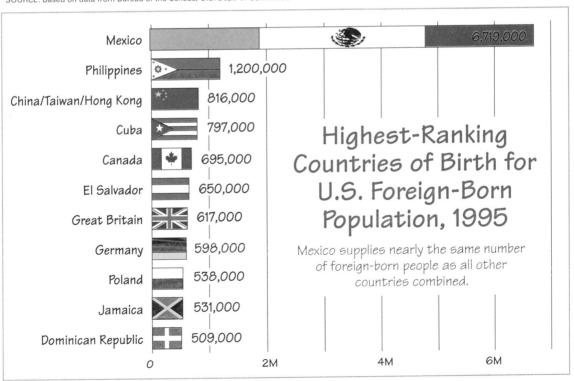

Mexico	6,719,000
Philippines	1,200,000
China/Taiwan/Hong Kong	816,000
Cuba	797,000
Canada	695,000
El Salvador	650,000
Great Britain	617,000
Germany	598,000
Poland	538,000
Jamaica	531,000
Dominican Republic	509,000

Highest-Ranking Countries of Birth for U.S. Foreign-Born Population, 1995

Mexico supplies nearly the same number of foreign-born people as all other countries combined.

SOURCE: Based on data from Bureau of the Census, U.S. Dept. of Commerce

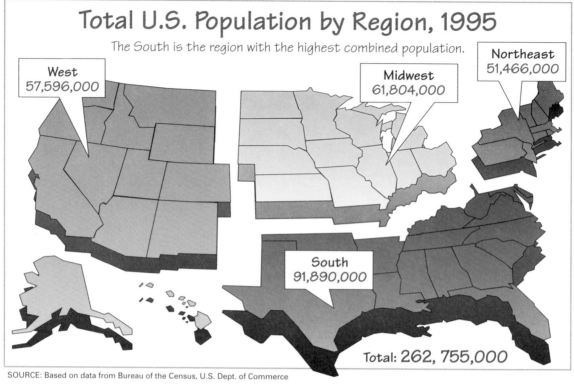

Total U.S. Population by Region, 1995

The South is the region with the highest combined population.

West
57,596,000

Midwest
61,804,000

Northeast
51,466,000

South
91,890,000

Total: 262, 755,000

SOURCE: Based on data from Bureau of the Census, U.S. Dept. of Commerce

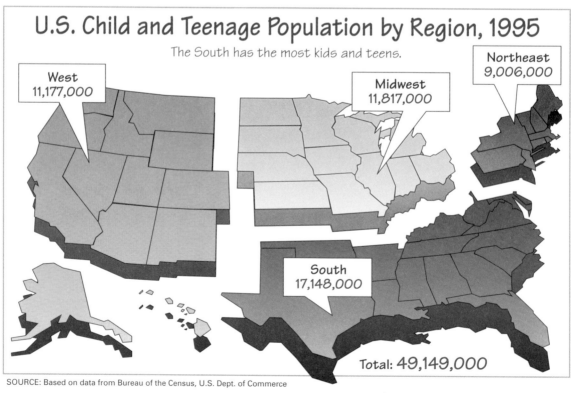

U.S. Child and Teenage Population by Region, 1995

The South has the most kids and teens.

West
11,177,000

Midwest
11,817,000

Northeast
9,006,000

South
17,148,000

Total: 49,149,000

SOURCE: Based on data from Bureau of the Census, U.S. Dept. of Commerce

U.S. Population by Region and Race, 1992

(In millions)

Key

White | Black | American Indian | Asian | Hispanic

Northeast

43.4M
6.0M
.1M
1.5M
4.0M

Midwest

53.5M
6.0M
.4M
.9M
1.9M

West

46.4M
3.1M
1.1M
4.6M
11.0M

South

69.7M
16.6M
.6M
1.3M
7.4M

Who Are We?

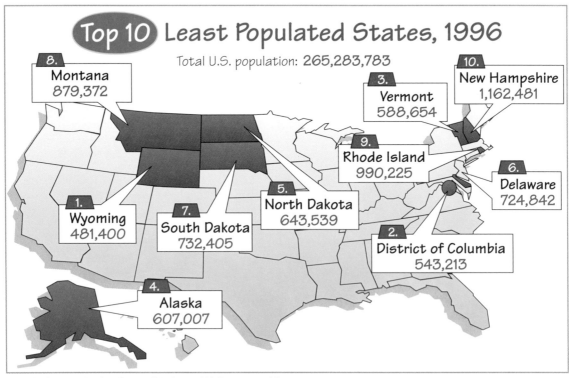

Top 10 Least Populated States, 1996

Total U.S. population: 265,283,783

8. Montana 879,372

3. Vermont 588,654

10. New Hampshire 1,162,481

9. Rhode Island 990,225

6. Delaware 724,842

1. Wyoming 481,400

7. South Dakota 732,405

5. North Dakota 643,539

2. District of Columbia 543,213

4. Alaska 607,007

SOURCE: Based on data from Bureau of the Census, U.S. Department of Commerce

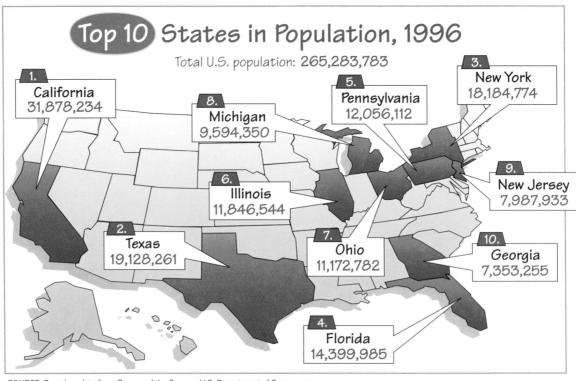

Top 10 States in Population, 1996

Total U.S. population: 265,283,783

1. California 31,878,234

8. Michigan 9,594,350

5. Pennsylvania 12,056,112

3. New York 18,184,774

6. Illinois 11,846,544

9. New Jersey 7,987,933

2. Texas 19,128,261

7. Ohio 11,172,782

10. Georgia 7,353,255

4. Florida 14,399,985

SOURCE: Based on data from Bureau of the Census, U.S. Department of Commerce

English and Non-English Speakers: Total Persons 5 to 17 Years Old

Most kids speak only English.

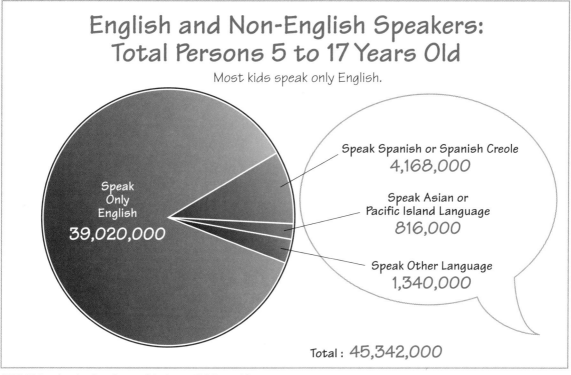

Speak Only English
39,020,000

Speak Spanish or Spanish Creole
4,168,000

Speak Asian or Pacific Island Language
816,000

Speak Other Language
1,340,000

Total : **45,342,000**

SOURCE: Based on data from Bureau of the Census, U.S. Dept. of Commerce

Top 5 Non-English Languages Spoken at Home by Kids

(Persons 5 years old and over who speak language)

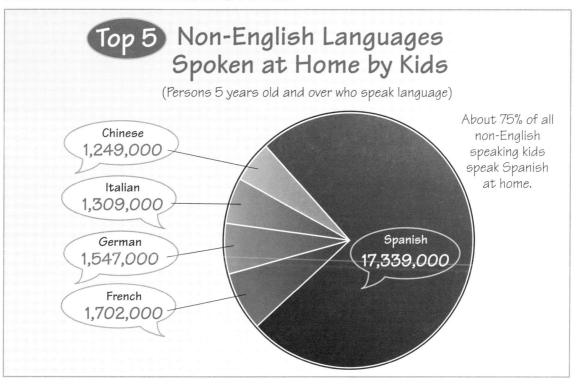

Chinese
1,249,000

Italian
1,309,000

German
1,547,000

French
1,702,000

Spanish
17,339,000

About 75% of all non-English speaking kids speak Spanish at home.

SOURCE: Based on data from Bureau of the Census, U.S. Dept. of Commerce

Households With and Without Kids

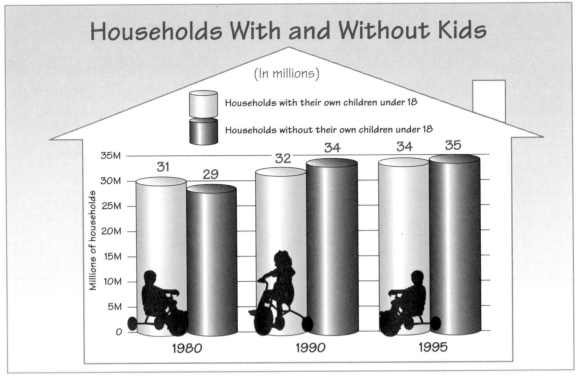

SOURCE: Based on data from Bureau of the Census, U.S. Dept. of Commerce

One-Parent vs. Two-Parent Households

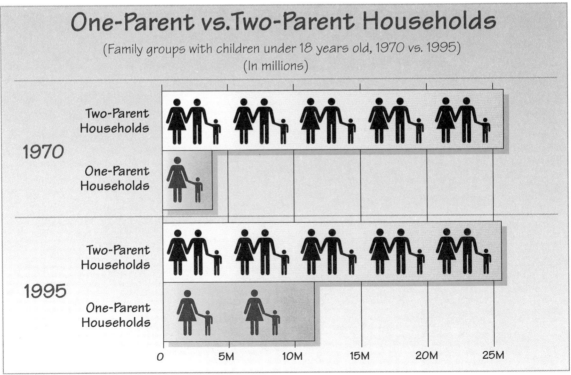

SOURCE: Based on data from Bureau of the Census, U.S. Dept. of Commerce

Size of U.S. Families, 1980 vs. 1995

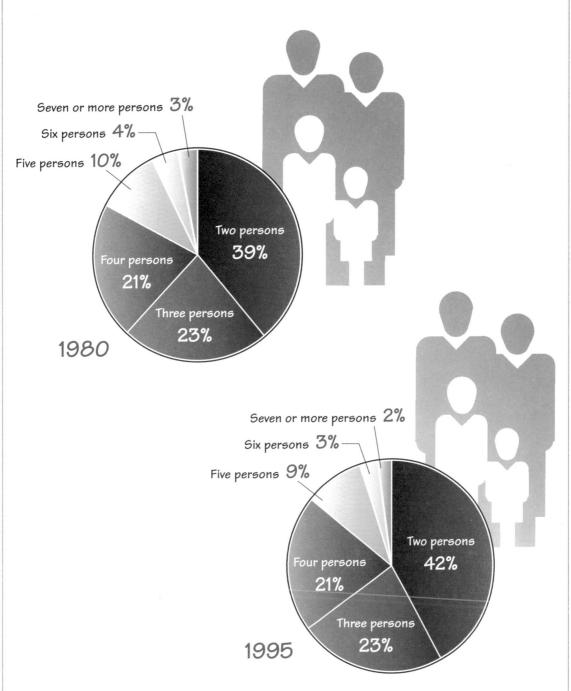

Seven or more persons 3%

Six persons 4%

Five persons 10%

Four persons 21%

Two persons 39%

Three persons 23%

1980

Seven or more persons 2%

Six persons 3%

Five persons 9%

Four persons 21%

Two persons 42%

Three persons 23%

1995

SOURCE: Based on data from Bureau of the Census, U.S. Dept. of Commerce

Religions of the Believers, 1994

(Religions of those who attend services regularly)

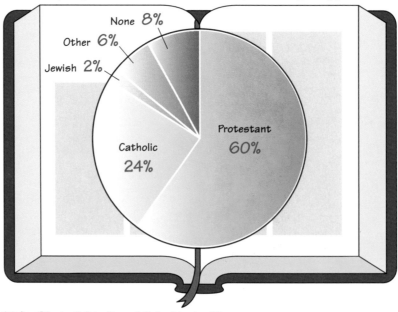

SOURCE: Based on data from Princeton Religion Research Center, Princeton, NJ

Marriage and Divorce Rates: 1950 to 1994

Marriage and divorce have declined since 1980.
(Rate per 1,000 population)

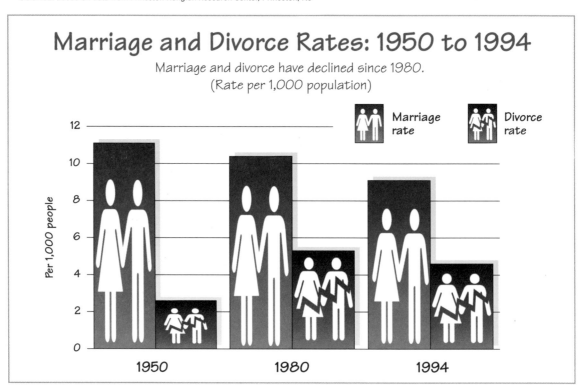

SOURCE: Based on data from U.S. National Center for Health Statistics

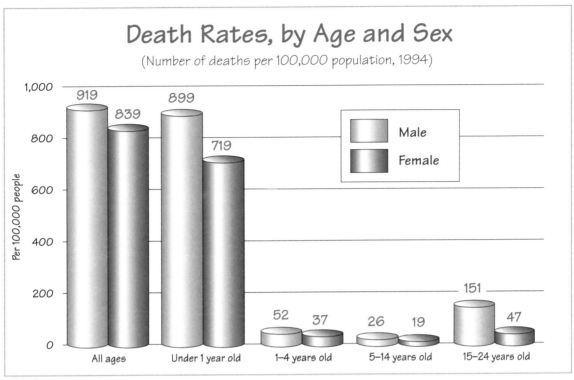

Death Rates, by Age and Sex
(Number of deaths per 100,000 population, 1994)

Legend: Male, Female

- All ages: 919 (Male), 839 (Female)
- Under 1 year old: 899 (Male), 719 (Female)
- 1–4 years old: 52 (Male), 37 (Female)
- 5–14 years old: 26 (Male), 19 (Female)
- 15–24 years old: 151 (Male), 47 (Female)

Per 100,000 people

SOURCE: Based on data from U.S. National Center for Health Statistics

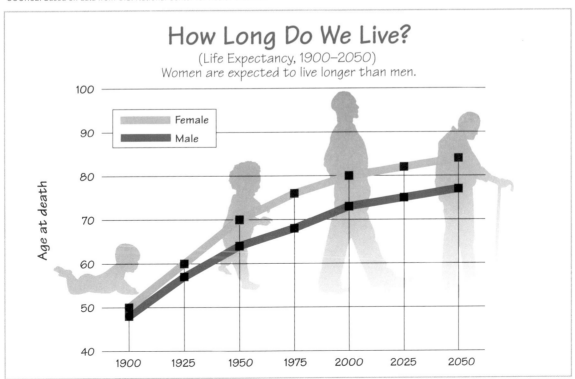

How Long Do We Live?
(Life Expectancy, 1900–2050)
Women are expected to live longer than men.

Legend: Female, Male

Age at death

1900 1925 1950 1975 2000 2025 2050

SOURCE: Based on data from Social Security Administration

Who Are We?

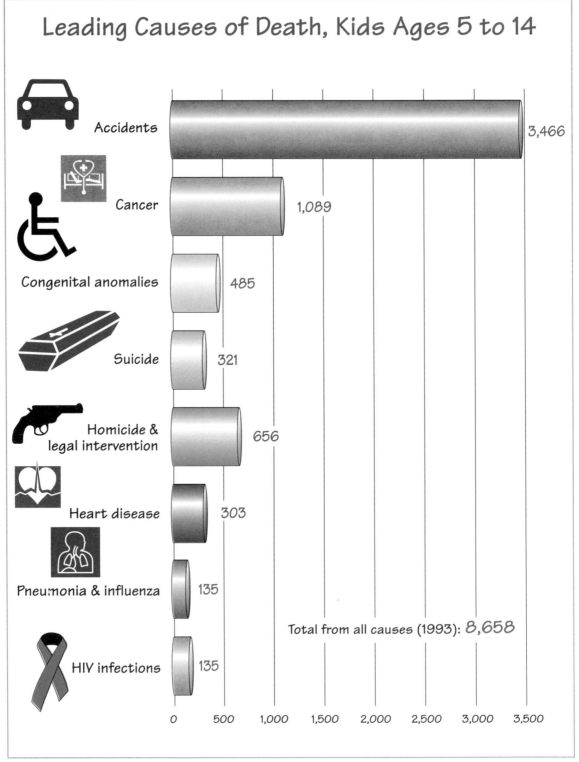

Leading Causes of Death, Kids Ages 5 to 14

Accidents — 3,466

Cancer — 1,089

Congenital anomalies — 485

Suicide — 321

Homicide & legal intervention — 656

Heart disease — 303

Pneumonia & influenza — 135

Total from all causes (1993): 8,658

HIV infections — 135

0   500   1,000   1,500   2,000   2,500   3,000   3,500

SOURCE: Based on data from U.S. National Center for Health Statistics, Monthly Vital Statistics Report, 1996

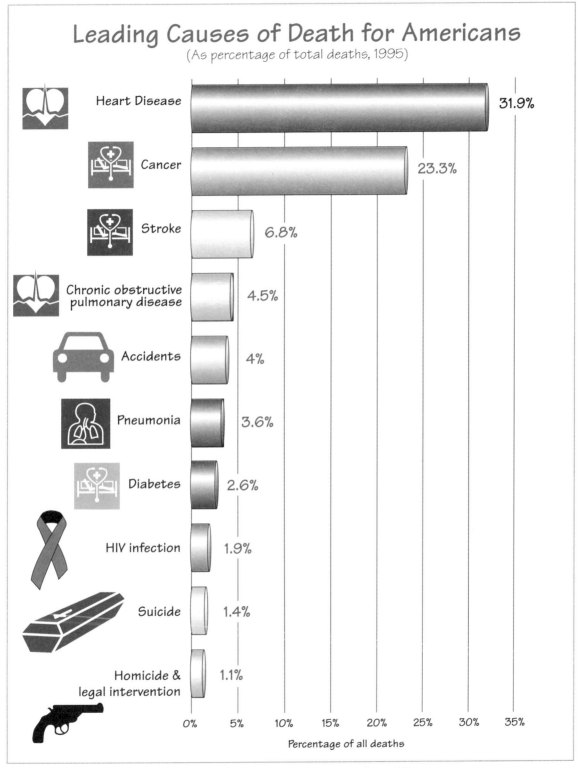

Leading Causes of Death for Americans

(As percentage of total deaths, 1995)

Cause	Percentage
Heart Disease	31.9%
Cancer	23.3%
Stroke	6.8%
Chronic obstructive pulmonary disease	4.5%
Accidents	4%
Pneumonia	3.6%
Diabetes	2.6%
HIV infection	1.9%
Suicide	1.4%
Homicide & legal intervention	1.1%

Percentage of all deaths

SOURCE: Based on data from U.S. National Center for Health Statistics, Monthly Vital Statistics Report, 1997

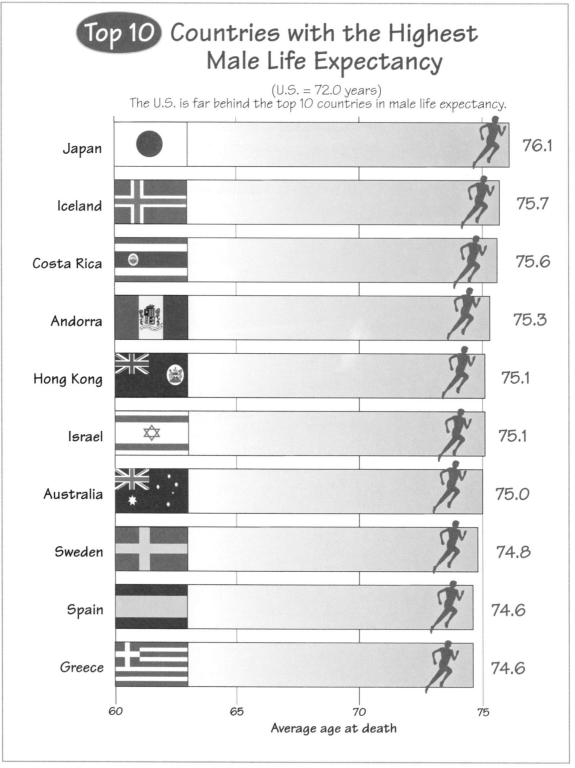

Top 10 Countries with the Highest Male Life Expectancy

(U.S. = 72.0 years)
The U.S. is far behind the top 10 countries in male life expectancy.

Country	Average age at death
Japan	76.1
Iceland	75.7
Costa Rica	75.6
Andorra	75.3
Hong Kong	75.1
Israel	75.1
Australia	75.0
Sweden	74.8
Spain	74.6
Greece	74.6

Average age at death

Source: Based on information given in *The Top 10 of Everything 1997*

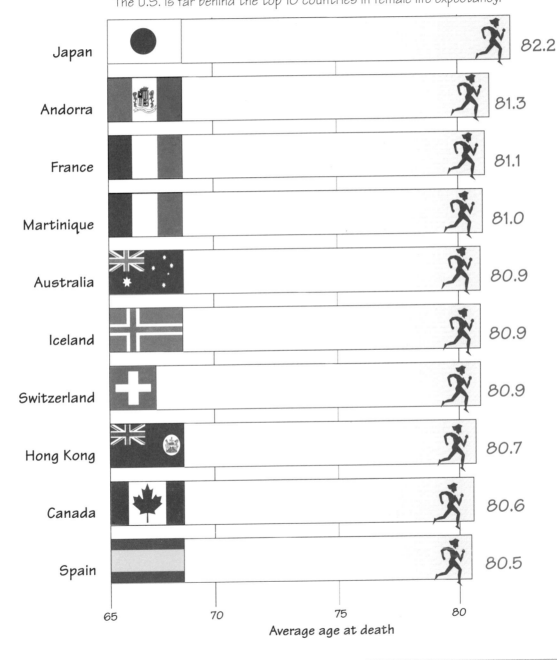

Top 10 Countries with the Highest Female Life Expectancy

(U.S. = 78.9 years)

The U.S. is far behind the top 10 countries in female life expectancy.

Country	Average age at death
Japan	82.2
Andorra	81.3
France	81.1
Martinique	81.0
Australia	80.9
Iceland	80.9
Switzerland	80.9
Hong Kong	80.7
Canada	80.6
Spain	80.5

Average age at death

Source: Based on information given in *The Top 10 of Everything 1997*

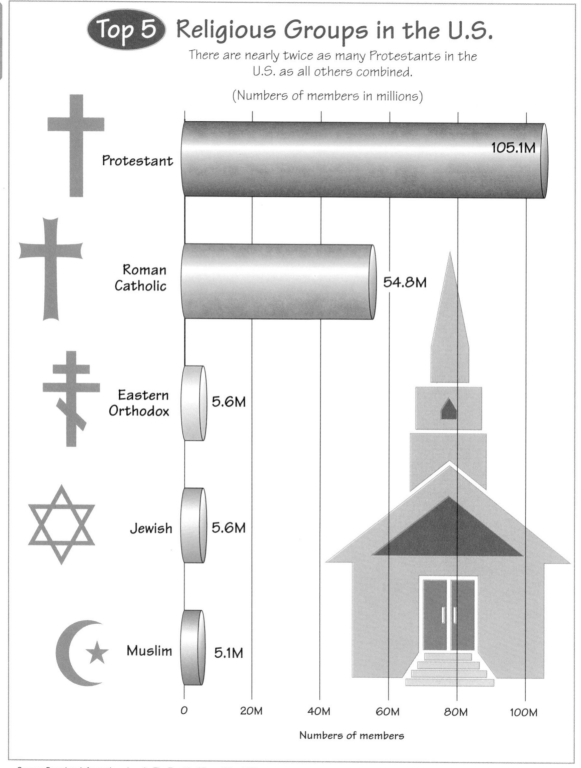

Top 5 Religious Groups in the U.S.

There are nearly twice as many Protestants in the
U.S. as all others combined.

(Numbers of members in millions)

Protestant — 105.1M

Roman Catholic — 54.8M

Eastern Orthodox — 5.6M

Jewish — 5.6M

Muslim — 5.1M

0   20M   40M   60M   80M   100M

Numbers of members

Source: Based on information given in *The Top 10 of Everything 1997*

U.S. Kids Are More Religious

The number of U.S. kids ages 7 - 12 who attend religious services is nearly four times more than the second highest country, the UK.

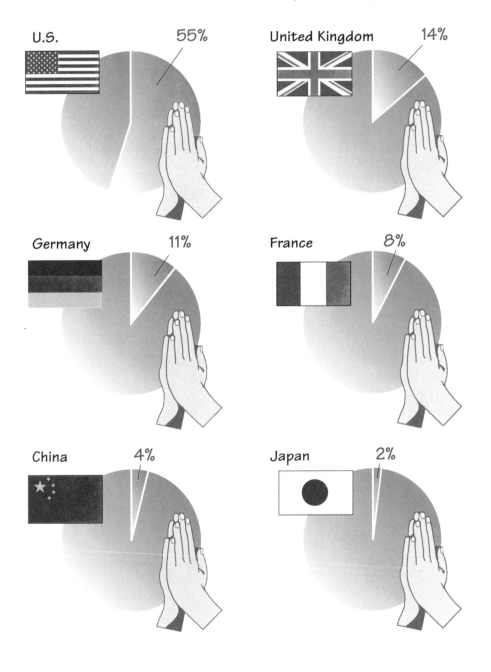

U.S. 55%

United Kingdom 14%

Germany 11%

France 8%

China 4%

Japan 2%

SOURCE: Based on data from Roper Starch Worldwide for A.B.C. Global Kids Study

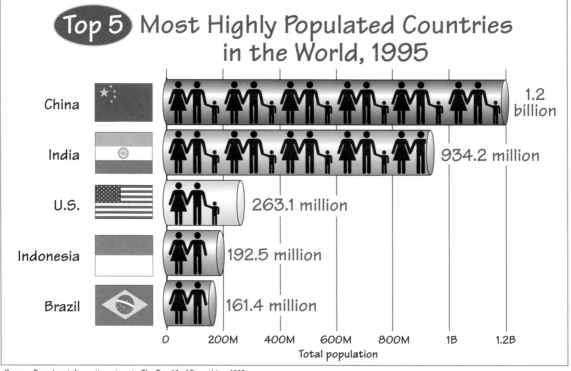

Top 5 Most Highly Populated Countries in the World, 1995

China	1.2 billion
India	934.2 million
U.S.	263.1 million
Indonesia	192.5 million
Brazil	161.4 million

Total population: 0, 200M, 400M, 600M, 800M, 1B, 1.2B

Source: Based on information given in *The Top 10 of Everything 1997*

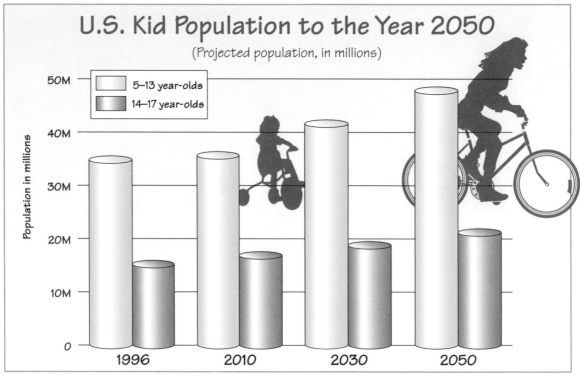

U.S. Kid Population to the Year 2050

(Projected population, in millions)

- 5–13 year-olds
- 14–17 year-olds

Population in millions: 0, 10M, 20M, 30M, 40M, 50M

1996   2010   2030   2050

SOURCE: Based on data from Bureau of the Census, U.S. Dept. of Commerce

Who Are We?

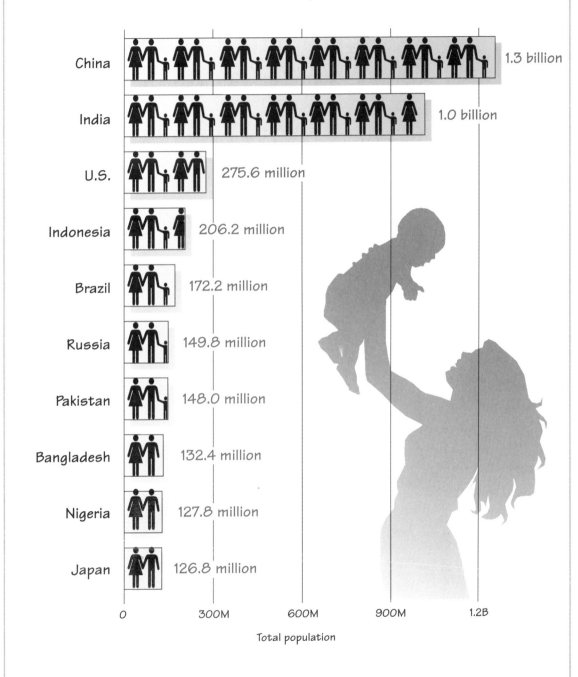

Top 10 Countries with the Highest Estimated Population in 2000

China — 1.3 billion
India — 1.0 billion
U.S. — 275.6 million
Indonesia — 206.2 million
Brazil — 172.2 million
Russia — 149.8 million
Pakistan — 148.0 million
Bangladesh — 132.4 million
Nigeria — 127.8 million
Japan — 126.8 million

0   300M   600M   900M   1.2B

Total population

Source: Based on information given in *The Top 10 of Everything 1997*

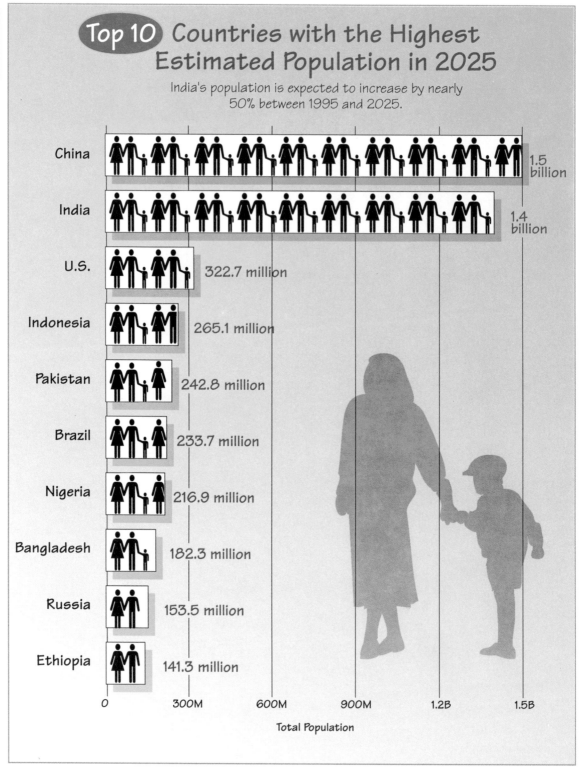

Who Are We?

Top 10 Countries with the Highest Estimated Population in 2025

India's population is expected to increase by nearly 50% between 1995 and 2025.

China — 1.5 billion

India — 1.4 billion

U.S. — 322.7 million

Indonesia — 265.1 million

Pakistan — 242.8 million

Brazil — 233.7 million

Nigeria — 216.9 million

Bangladesh — 182.3 million

Russia — 153.5 million

Ethiopia — 141.3 million

0   300M   600M   900M   1.2B   1.5B

Total Population

Source: Based on information given in *The Top 10 of Everything 1997*

U.S. Doesn't Reach New Heights...
Top 5 Tallest Countries

(Average adult height)
(U.S. = 70.8 inches)

73.0 in.

72.6 in.

72.5 in.

72.2 in.

72.0 in.

71.9 in.

71.8 in.

71.6 in.

71.5 in.

71.0 in.

70.5 in.

70.0 in.

Netherlands   Denmark   Norway   Sweden   Germany

SOURCE: Based on data from Richard Steckel, Ohio State University

Money

Everyone can use money, which is one good reason why people work. Adults aren't the only workers. Many kids work, too. They earn money mowing lawns, babysitting, delivering newspapers, walking dogs, washing cars, and creating computer Web sites. The older they are, the more likely they are to have a job. More than one-quarter of people ages 15 to 18 have part- or full-time jobs. Millions more pick up money doing odd jobs for family, neighbors, and other people.

When the U.S. first set a minimum wage, in 1938, it was 25 cents an hour. By 1997, it had risen to $5.15 an hour! But while wages have increased, so has the cost of living. A comic book, a pair of jeans, a bicycle—they all cost a lot more today then they did when your parents and grandparents were your age.

Of course, jobs aren't the only source of money. Most kids also get money from their parents. Many receive allowances and gifts of money, especially on birthdays and at other special times of the year. Combine all those sources of income and kids have a lot of

Kidbits Tidbits

- In 1995, 26% of teenagers ages 15 to 18 worked; 3% worked full-time and 23% worked part-time. About 62% of college students worked; 32% full-time and 30% part-time.
- In 1998, an *Amazing Fantasy* comic book that included the first appearance of Spider Man, sold for $2,000.
- American consumers owe more than $1 trillion dollars. In 1996, most of this—some $498 billion—was on credit card accounts. Another $390 billion was for automobiles.

spending power! American teenagers alone have more than $100 billion to spend each year!

The #1 item on kid shopping lists is candy. Kids spend their own money on candy more often than on anything else. Other foods also are popular. Surveys show that teenagers visit supermarkets more often than any other kind of store. Convenience stores, which stock tempting arrays of sodas and "junk food," aren't far behind.

Kids also spend lots of money on clothes, sporting goods, music, movies, toys, and books. They like to spend money on collecting stuff, too. Some 32-cent stamps, packs of stickers, or new comic books don't cost very much. But save them for a decade or two and they may be great investments as well as sources of pleasure. Over the years, they

can become very valuable. For instance, a Mickey Mantle rookie-year baseball card is now worth about $30,000!

The main way that kids invest money for the future is to save some of their income. On average, American kids save about 21 cents of every dollar they get. They save it for big purchases, such as a car or a computer. They also save money for college. And they see saving money as a first step toward becoming wealthy. Eighty percent of American kids dream about becoming rich one day!

If you're dreaming about getting rich, you should probably dream about the computer business and related businesses. In 1997, three of America's Top 10 richest people made their billions in the computer industry. Together, the three tycoons are worth an estimated $58 billion!

Kidbits Tidbits

- There are about 10,000 banks in the U.S.
- Almost all the geographical areas expected to have the fastest job growth in the coming decades are in the South. Heading the list are three Florida cities: Punta Gorda, Orlando, and Naples.
- The unemployment rate in 1997 fell below 5%—its lowest rate in 30 years.

Money

Jobs on Teens' Minds

The most common worry for 15- to 18-year-olds around the world is "getting a good job."

Western Europe

Latin America

United States

Eastern Europe

India

China

Asia Pacific

0% 10% 20% 30% 40% 50% 60% 70% 80%

Percentage of teens polled

SOURCE: Based on data from BrainWaves' New World Teen Survey

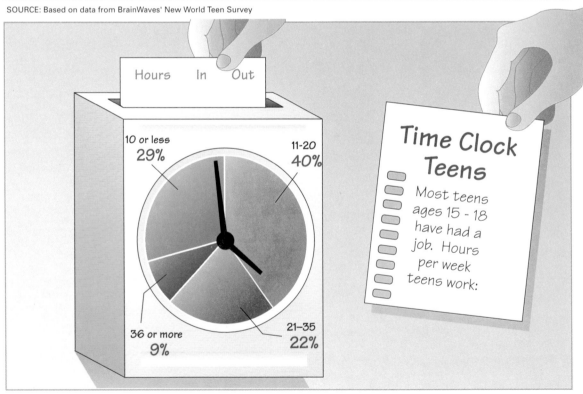

Hours   In   Out

10 or less
29%

11-20
40%

36 or more
9%

21–35
22%

Time Clock Teens

Most teens ages 15 - 18 have had a job. Hours per week teens work:

SOURCE: Based on data from Michaels Opinion Research for MassMutual

Money

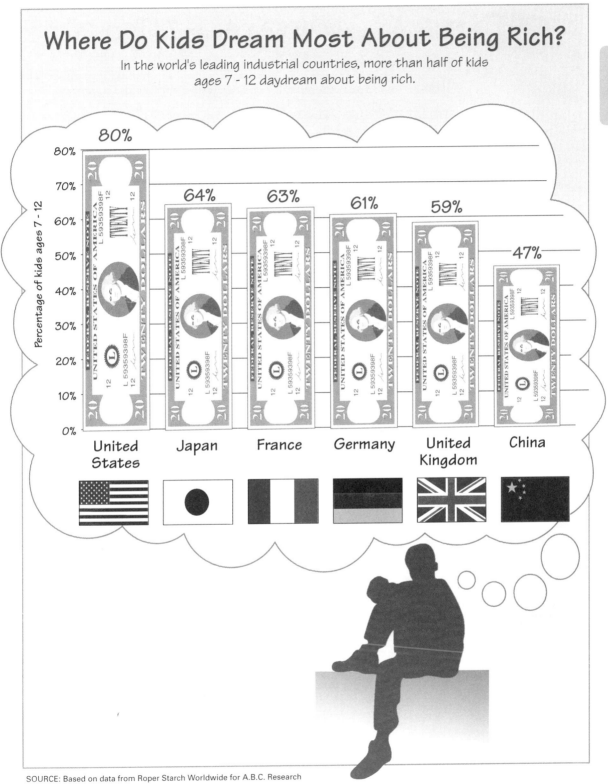

Where Do Kids Dream Most About Being Rich?

In the world's leading industrial countries, more than half of kids ages 7 - 12 daydream about being rich.

Percentage of kids ages 7 - 12

80% — United States
64% — Japan
63% — France
61% — Germany
59% — United Kingdom
47% — China

SOURCE: Based on data from Roper Starch Worldwide for A.B.C. Research

Money

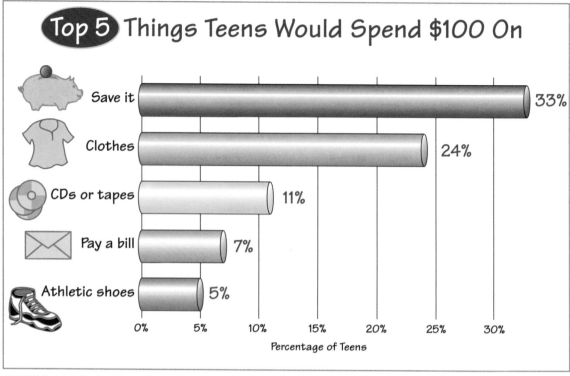

Top 5 Things Teens Would Spend $100 On

- Save it — 33%
- Clothes — 24%
- CDs or tapes — 11%
- Pay a bill — 7%
- Athletic shoes — 5%

Percentage of Teens

SOURCE: Based on data from Teenage Research Unlimited, Inc.

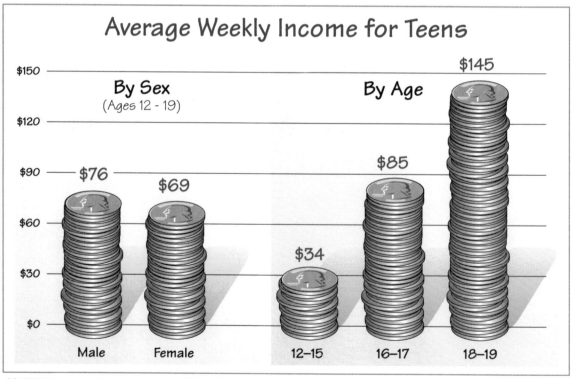

Average Weekly Income for Teens

By Sex
(Ages 12 - 19)

Male — $76
Female — $69

By Age

12–15 — $34
16–17 — $85
18–19 — $145

SOURCE: Based on data from Teenage Research Unlimited, Inc.

Money

Teen Spending Power Grows, 1986–1996

In 1995, teens collectively spent more than $100 billion for the first time.
(In billions)

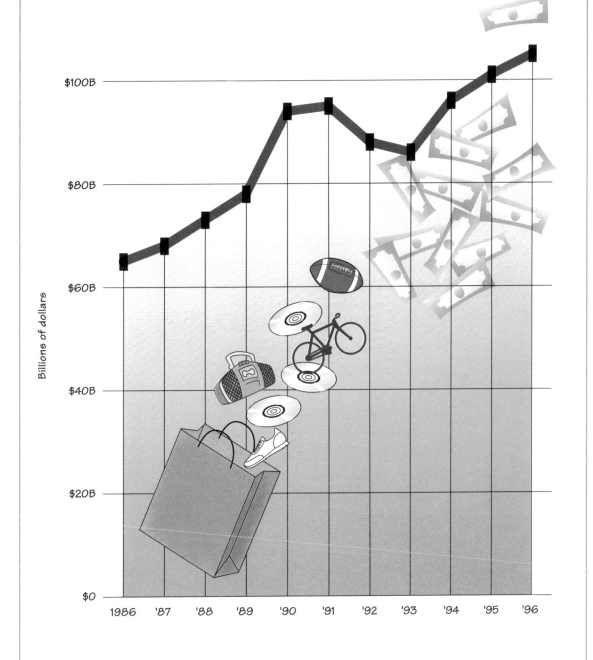

SOURCE: Based on data from Teenage Research Unlimited, Inc.

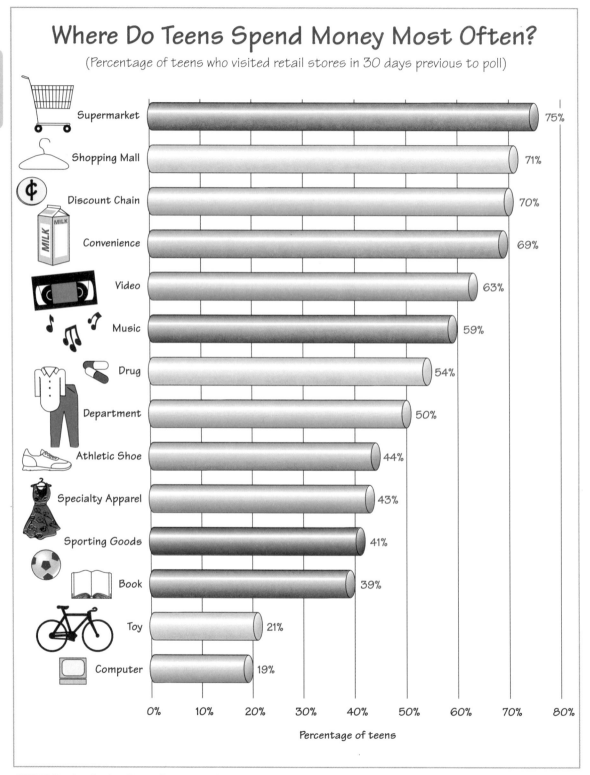

Where Do Teens Spend Money Most Often?

(Percentage of teens who visited retail stores in 30 days previous to poll)

Store	Percentage
Supermarket	75%
Shopping Mall	71%
Discount Chain	70%
Convenience	69%
Video	63%
Music	59%
Drug	54%
Department	50%
Athletic Shoe	44%
Specialty Apparel	43%
Sporting Goods	41%
Book	39%
Toy	21%
Computer	19%

Percentage of teens

SOURCE: Based on data from Teenage Research Unlimited, Inc.

Money

Money

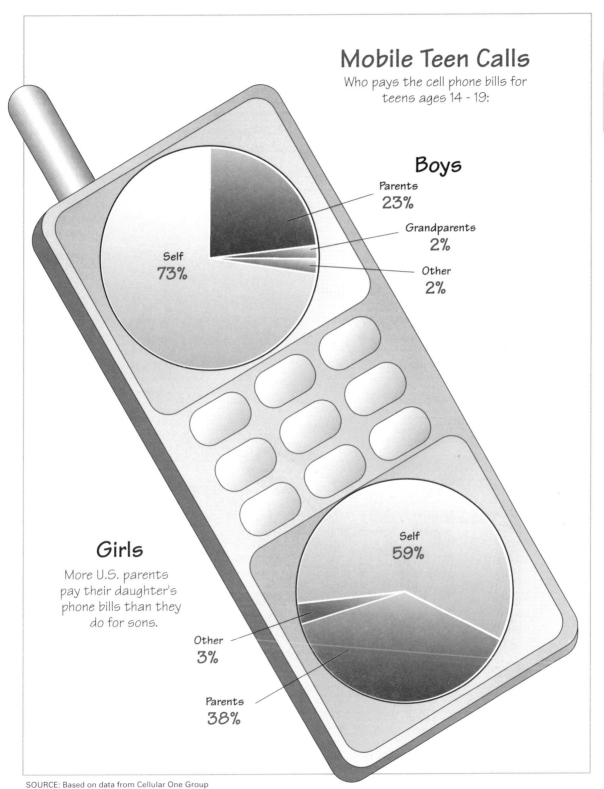

Mobile Teen Calls

Who pays the cell phone bills for teens ages 14 - 19:

Boys

Parents
23%

Grandparents
2%

Other
2%

Self
73%

Girls

More U.S. parents pay their daughter's phone bills than they do for sons.

Other
3%

Self
59%

Parents
38%

SOURCE: Based on data from Cellular One Group

Money

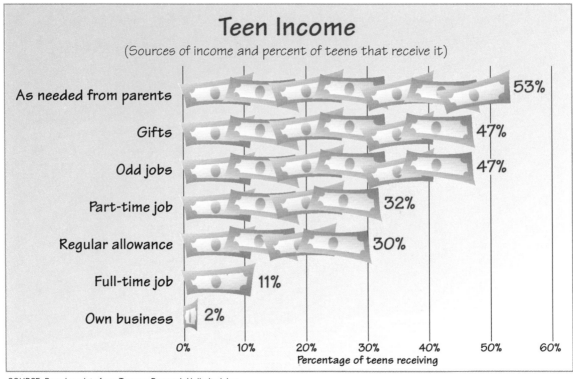

Teen Income
(Sources of income and percent of teens that receive it)

Source	Percentage
As needed from parents	53%
Gifts	47%
Odd jobs	47%
Part-time job	32%
Regular allowance	30%
Full-time job	11%
Own business	2%

Percentage of teens receiving

SOURCE: Based on data from Teenage Research Unlimited, Inc.

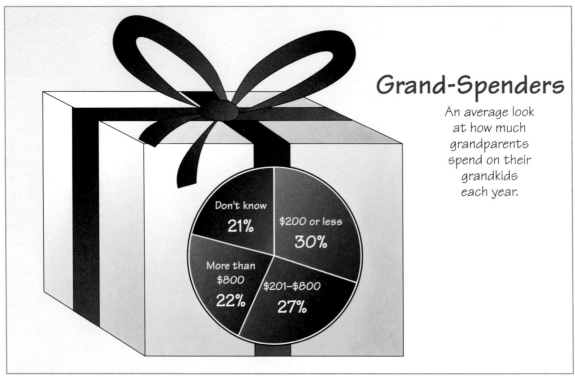

Grand-Spenders

An average look at how much grandparents spend on their grandkids each year.

Don't know 21%

$200 or less 30%

More than $800 22%

$201–$800 27%

SOURCE: Based on data from Roper Starch Worldwide, 1995

Money

Kid Costs

Estimated yearly spending for a child born in 1995, for families in middle-income groups ($33,700 to $56,700).

Cost per year

| $20,000 |
| $15,000 |
| $10,000 |
| $5,000 |
| $0 |

| Age: | Under 1 | 1 | 2 | 3 | 4 | 5 | 6 | 7 | 8 | 9 | 10 | 11 | 12 | 13 | 14 | 15 | 16 | 17 |
| Year: | 1995 | '96 | '97 | '98 | '99 | '00 | '01 | '02 | '03 | '04 | '05 | '06 | '07 | '08 | '09 | '10 | '11 | '12 |

SOURCE: Based on data from Family Economics Research Group, U.S. Dept. of Agriculture

Which Kids Save the Most?

Studies show that Japanese kids save more of every dollar they earn or receive than do kids in the U.S. —about three times more. Here's how various countries stack up:

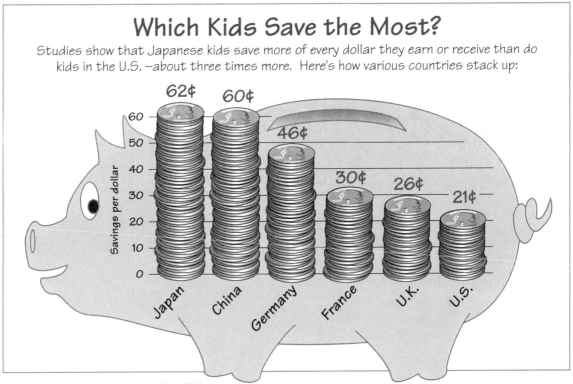

Savings per dollar

62¢ — Japan
60¢ — China
46¢ — Germany
30¢ — France
26¢ — U.K.
21¢ — U.S.

SOURCE: Based on data from Roper Starch/Just Kid Inc.

Money

America's Top 10 Richest People, 1997

Name	Source	Worth in billions of $
William Gates III	Computers	$36.4
Walton Family	Inheritance	$27.6
Warren Buffet	Investment	$23.2
Paul Allen	Computers	$14.1
Haas Family	Retailing	$12.3
Mars Family	Candy, pet food	$12.0
Samuel Newhouse Jr. & Donald Newhouse	Media	$9.0
Cargill Family	Grain	$8.8
Steven Ballmer	Computers	$7.5
John Kluge	Media	$7.2

SOURCE: Based on data from *Forbes*

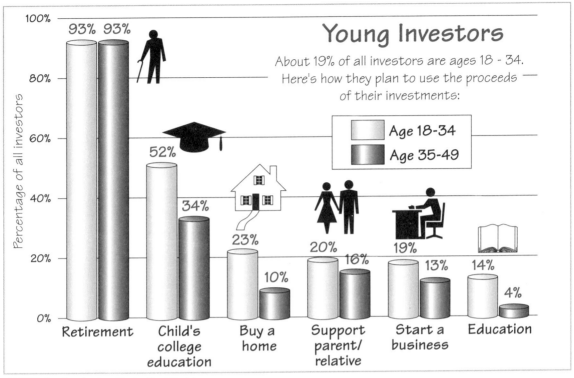

Young Investors

About 19% of all investors are ages 18 - 34.
Here's how they plan to use the proceeds
of their investments:

Age 18-34
Age 35-49

Retirement 93% 93%
Child's college education 52% 34%
Buy a home 23% 10%
Support parent/relative 20% 16%
Start a business 19% 13%
Education 14% 4%

SOURCE: Based on data from Nasdaq Stock Market

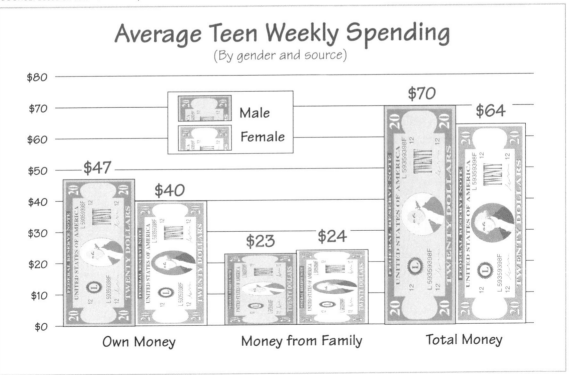

Average Teen Weekly Spending
(By gender and source)

Male
Female

Own Money $47 $40
Money from Family $23 $24
Total Money $70 $64

SOURCE: Based on data from Teenage Research Unlimited, Inc.

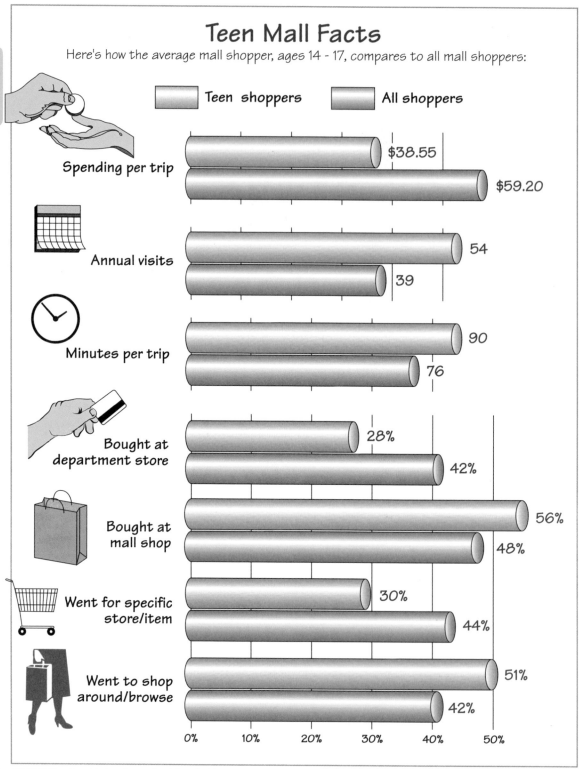

Teen Mall Facts

Here's how the average mall shopper, ages 14 - 17, compares to all mall shoppers:

Money

Teen shoppers | All shoppers

Spending per trip
$38.55
$59.20

Annual visits
54
39

Minutes per trip
90
76

Bought at department store
28%
42%

Bought at mall shop
56%
48%

Went for specific store/item
30%
44%

Went to shop around/browse
51%
42%

0%   10%   20%   30%   40%   50%

SOURCE: Based on data from International Council of Shopping Centers

Money

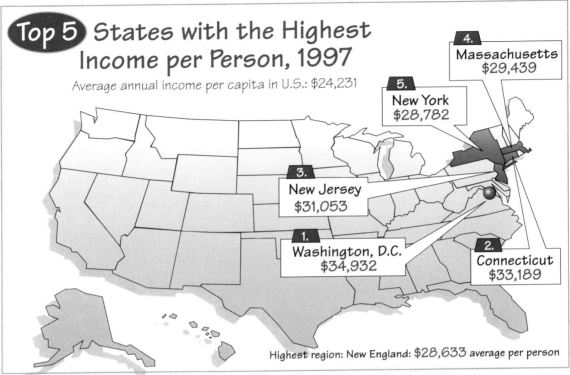

Top 5 States with the Highest Income per Person, 1997

Average annual income per capita in U.S.: $24,231

4. Massachusetts $29,439

5. New York $28,782

3. New Jersey $31,053

1. Washington, D.C. $34,932

2. Connecticut $33,189

Highest region: New England: $28,633 average per person

SOURCE: Based on data from U.S. Commerce Department

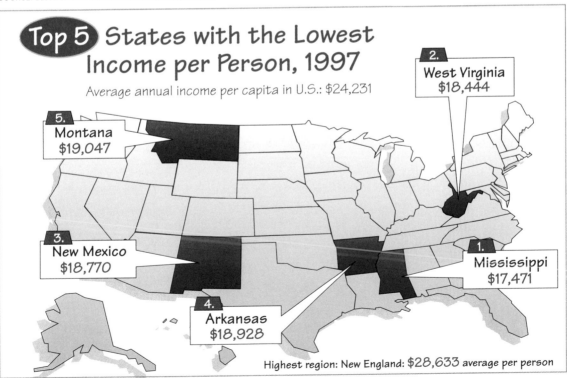

Top 5 States with the Lowest Income per Person, 1997

Average annual income per capita in U.S.: $24,231

2. West Virginia $18,444

5. Montana $19,047

3. New Mexico $18,770

1. Mississippi $17,471

4. Arkansas $18,928

Highest region: New England: $28,633 average per person

SOURCE: Based on data from U.S. Commerce Department

Sports for Fun

Kids are sports crazy! They kick soccer balls, take jump shots, swing bats, tumble, run, swim, and skate. While some prefer team sports such as soccer and basketball, others are into one-on-one sports such as tennis and golf. Activities that can be pursued by oneself, such as running and bicycling, also are popular. And so are new twists on old sports, such as snowboarding, ultimate frisbee, and glow bowling (also called "cosmic bowling" or "xtreme bowling").

As years pass, some sports become more popular among kids while others attract fewer participants. Soccer in America is one sport that has grown in popularity. (It's about time—soccer is by far the most popular sport throughout the rest of the world!) Track and field has declined, in part because many kids prefer to play soccer.

Some kids commit a lot of time to their sports, training to become eligible for national teams and even for professional competitions. Michelle Kwan was only 15 in 1996 when she won

- Basketball is the top high school sport in the U.S. In the '95-96 school year, a total of 991,465 kids played basketball at one time or another. Of these, 45% were girls.
- U.S. high school track and field participation fell 32% for boys and 18% for girls between 1977 and 1997.
- An estimated 35,000 people watched the final game of the 1996 Little League World Series.

Kids play sports because it's fun. But they also want to be physically fit. Sports help kids build muscle strength, improve posture and balance, and develop agility and endurance. But when playing sports, it's important to try to avoid injuries and accidents. Each year, more than 120,000 Americans are injured in and around swimming pools; more than 150,000 are injured playing soccer; and almost 700,000 are injured playing basketball. (In fact, basketball is one of the top causes of injury in America.) So wear a helmet on your bike, a life jacket when in a boat, and use the right equipment when playing sports!

both the U.S. and world women's figure-skating championships. Tiger Woods won his first world golfing title at age 8—and, in 1997, at age 21, he became the youngest person ever to win the Masters. Also in 1997, 16-year-old Martina Hingis became the youngest woman to earn the #1 ranking in tennis. These and other young athletes have become top role models for America's aspiring athletes. They have also greatly increased interest and participation in their sports.

Whether on or off the playing fields, kids like to wear sports attire. For example, people under age 18 account for 57% of all gym shoe and sneaker purchases, and 25% of all jogging and running shoe purchases. They also use 71% of all team sports equipment that is bought each year.

- Americans of all ages list walking as their #1 sports activity. Swimming is #2 and bike riding is #3.
- Americans spent over $57 billion on sporting goods in 1996. This included approximately $10 billion on clothing, $11.8 billion on footwear, $15.7 billion on equipment, and $19.6 billion on transport (boats, bicycles, snowmobiles, etc.).
- It's definitely "cool" to play on the ice and snow. In 1995, a total of 9.3 million Americans reported that they downhill ski. About 7.1 million said they ice or figure skate, and 3.4 million reported cross-country skiing. A total of 2.5 million people play ice hockey, and 2.3 million snowboarded two or more times during the year.

Sports for Fun

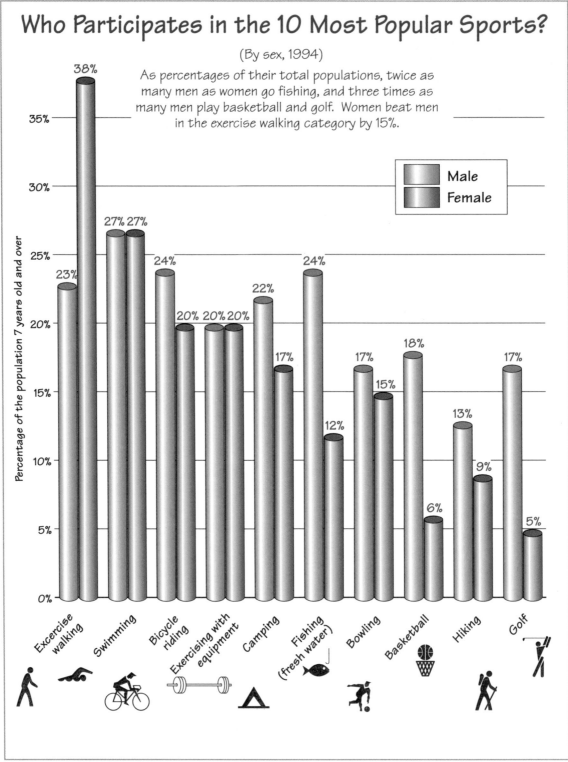

Who Participates in the 10 Most Popular Sports?

(By sex, 1994)

As percentages of their total populations, twice as many men as women go fishing, and three times as many men play basketball and golf. Women beat men in the exercise walking category by 15%.

Male
Female

Percentage of the population 7 years old and over

	Exercise walking	Swimming	Bicycle riding	Exercising with equipment	Camping	Fishing (fresh water)	Bowling	Basketball	Hiking	Golf
Male	23%	27%	24%	20%	22%	24%	17%	18%	13%	17%
Female	38%	27%	20%	20%	17%	12%	15%	6%	9%	5%

SOURCE: Based on data from Bureau of the Census, U.S. Dept. of Commerce

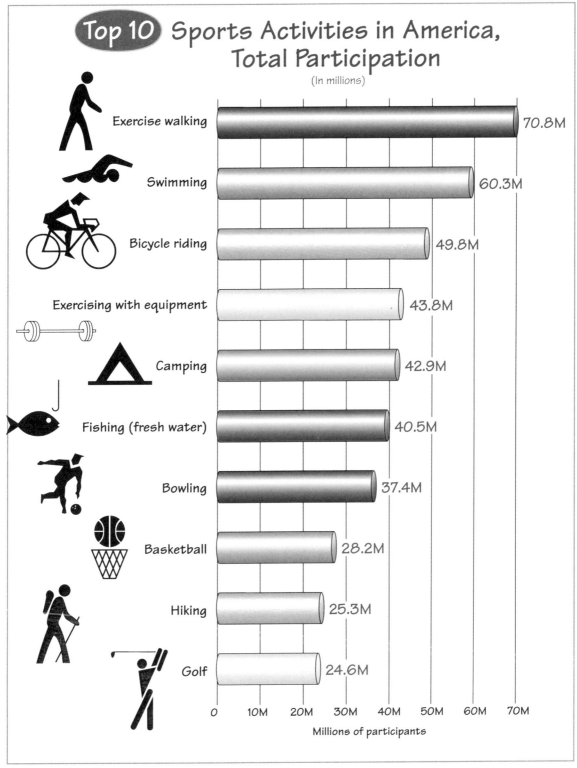

Top 10 Sports Activities in America, Total Participation

(In millions)

Sports for Fun

Activity	Participants
Exercise walking	70.8M
Swimming	60.3M
Bicycle riding	49.8M
Exercising with equipment	43.8M
Camping	42.9M
Fishing (fresh water)	40.5M
Bowling	37.4M
Basketball	28.2M
Hiking	25.3M
Golf	24.6M

0   10M   20M   30M   40M   50M   60M   70M

Millions of participants

SOURCE: Based on data from National Sporting Goods Association, Mt. Prospect, IL

Sports for Fun

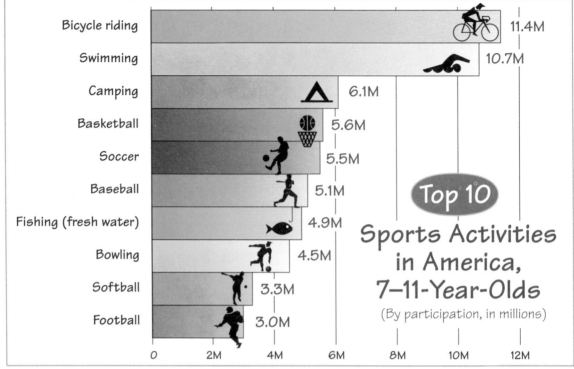

Bicycle riding — 11.4M
Swimming — 10.7M
Camping — 6.1M
Basketball — 5.6M
Soccer — 5.5M
Baseball — 5.1M
Fishing (fresh water) — 4.9M
Bowling — 4.5M
Softball — 3.3M
Football — 3.0M

0   2M   4M   6M   8M   10M   12M

Top 10

Sports Activities in America, 7–11-Year-Olds
(By participation, in millions)

SOURCE: Based on data from National Sporting Goods Association, Mt. Prospect, IL

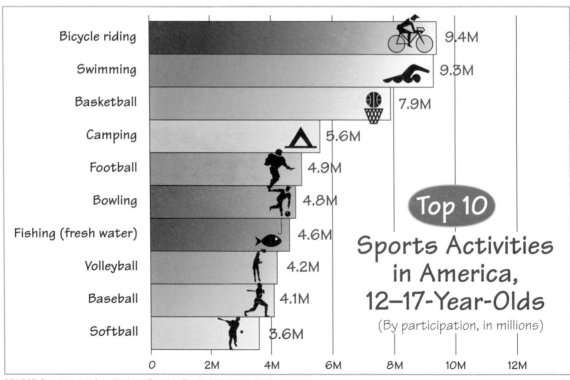

Bicycle riding — 9.4M
Swimming — 9.3M
Basketball — 7.9M
Camping — 5.6M
Football — 4.9M
Bowling — 4.8M
Fishing (fresh water) — 4.6M
Volleyball — 4.2M
Baseball — 4.1M
Softball — 3.6M

0   2M   4M   6M   8M   10M   12M

Top 10

Sports Activities in America, 12–17-Year-Olds
(By participation, in millions)

SOURCE: Based on data from National Sporting Goods Association, Mt. Prospect, IL

Participation in Sports and Activities by Percentage of Total Population, Ages 12–19

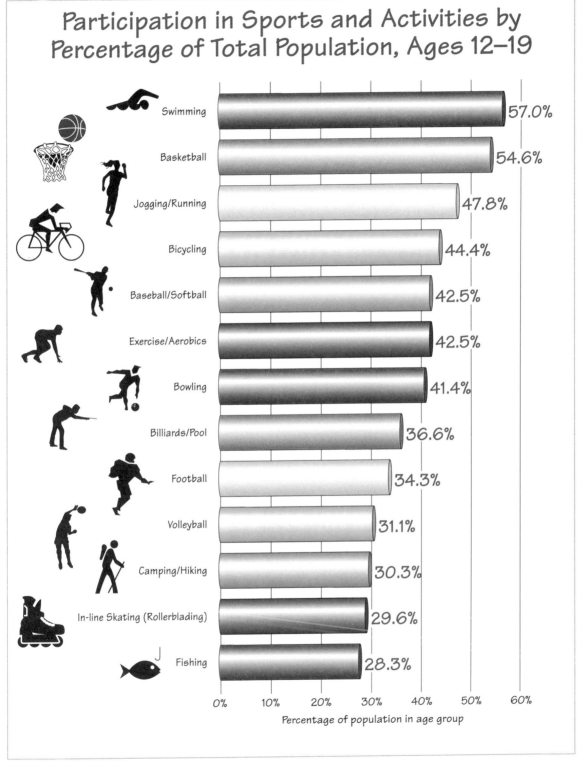

Activity	Percentage
Swimming	57.0%
Basketball	54.6%
Jogging/Running	47.8%
Bicycling	44.4%
Baseball/Softball	42.5%
Exercise/Aerobics	42.5%
Bowling	41.4%
Billiards/Pool	36.6%
Football	34.3%
Volleyball	31.1%
Camping/Hiking	30.3%
In-line Skating (Rollerblading)	29.6%
Fishing	28.3%

Percentage of population in age group

SOURCE: Based on data from Teenage Research Unlimited Inc.

Sports for Fun

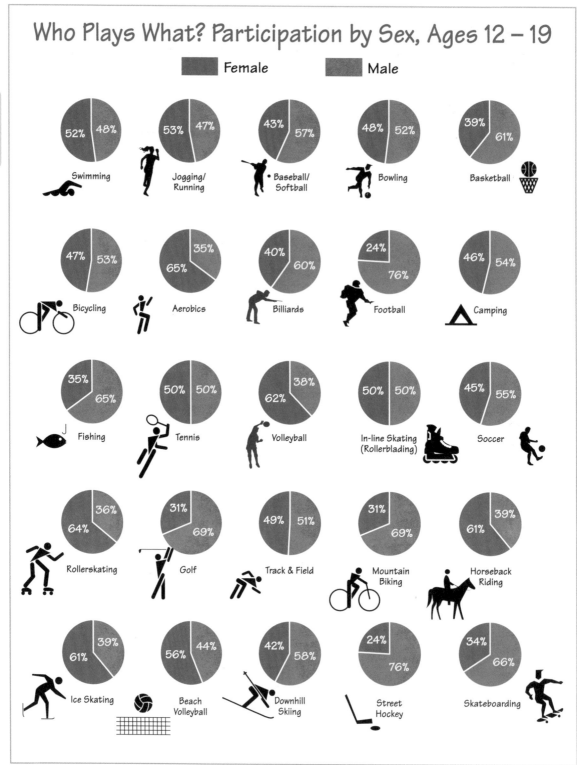

Who Plays What? Participation by Sex, Ages 12 – 19

Female   Male

Swimming — 52% / 48%

Jogging/ Running — 53% / 47%

Baseball/ Softball — 43% / 57%

Bowling — 48% / 52%

Basketball — 39% / 61%

Bicycling — 47% / 53%

Aerobics — 35% / 65%

Billiards — 40% / 60%

Football — 24% / 76%

Camping — 46% / 54%

Fishing — 35% / 65%

Tennis — 50% / 50%

Volleyball — 38% / 62%

In-line Skating (Rollerblading) — 50% / 50%

Soccer — 45% / 55%

Rollerskating — 36% / 64%

Golf — 31% / 69%

Track & Field — 49% / 51%

Mountain Biking — 31% / 69%

Horseback Riding — 39% / 61%

Ice Skating — 39% / 61%

Beach Volleyball — 56% / 44%

Downhill Skiing — 42% / 58%

Street Hockey — 24% / 76%

Skateboarding — 34% / 66%

SOURCE: Based on data from Teenage Research Unlimited Inc.

Who Plays What? Participation by Sex, Ages 12 – 19

Female   Male

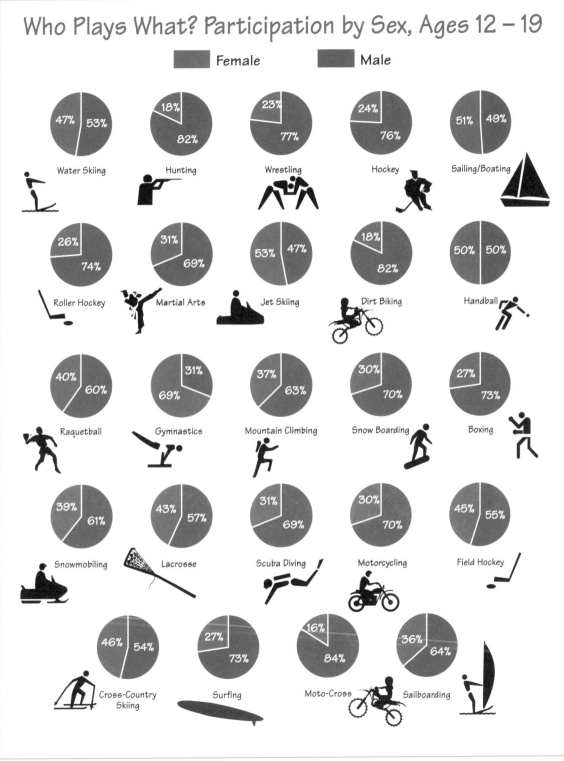

Water Skiing — 47% / 53%
Hunting — 18% / 82%
Wrestling — 23% / 77%
Hockey — 24% / 76%
Sailing/Boating — 51% / 49%

Roller Hockey — 26% / 74%
Martial Arts — 31% / 69%
Jet Skiing — 53% / 47%
Dirt Biking — 18% / 82%
Handball — 50% / 50%

Raquetball — 40% / 60%
Gymnastics — 31% / 69%
Mountain Climbing — 37% / 63%
Snow Boarding — 30% / 70%
Boxing — 27% / 73%

Snowmobiling — 39% / 61%
Lacrosse — 43% / 57%
Scuba Diving — 31% / 69%
Motorcycling — 30% / 70%
Field Hockey — 45% / 55%

Cross-Country Skiing — 46% / 54%
Surfing — 27% / 73%
Moto-Cross — 16% / 84%
Sailboarding — 36% / 64%

SOURCE: Based on data from Teenage Research Unlimited Inc.

Sports for Fun

The Rules "Rule"

Boys and girls claim to understand the most about the rules of basketball.
Percentages of kids, ages 9 - 13, who say they know the rules of the following sports:

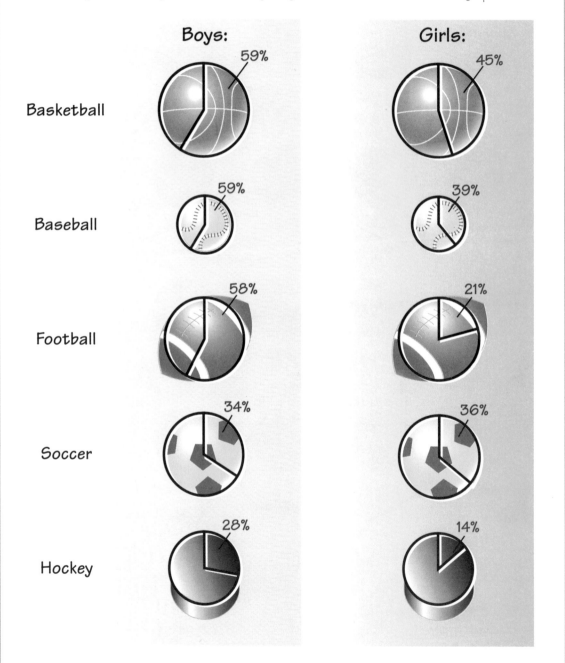

Boys:

Girls:

Basketball — 59% / 45%

Baseball — 59% / 39%

Football — 58% / 21%

Soccer — 34% / 36%

Hockey — 28% / 14%

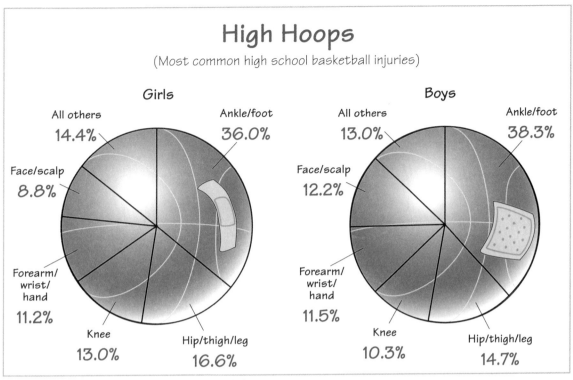

High Hoops

(Most common high school basketball injuries)

Girls

All others
14.4%

Ankle/foot
36.0%

Face/scalp
8.8%

Forearm/
wrist/
hand
11.2%

Knee
13.0%

Hip/thigh/leg
16.6%

Boys

All others
13.0%

Ankle/foot
38.3%

Face/scalp
12.2%

Forearm/
wrist/
hand
11.5%

Knee
10.3%

Hip/thigh/leg
14.7%

SOURCE: Based on data from National Athletic Trainers' Association

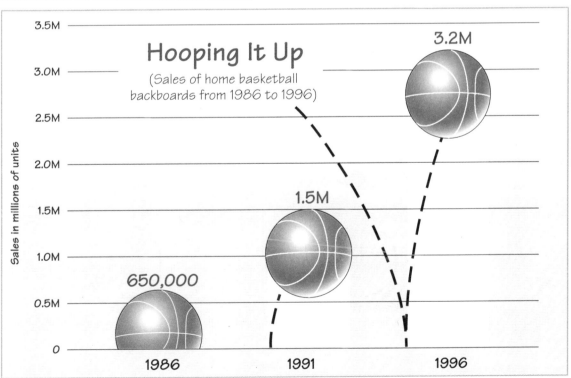

Hooping It Up

(Sales of home basketball backboards from 1986 to 1996)

Sales in millions of units

3.5M
3.0M
2.5M
2.0M
1.5M
1.0M
0.5M
0

3.2M

1.5M

650,000

1986   1991   1996

SOURCE: Based on data from Huffy Sports

Sports for Fun

No Pain, No Gain

In 1995 hospital emergency rooms treated thousands of sports injuries.
Here's a run-down of the top sports by number of E.R. visits:

Sport	Number of injuries
Basketball	693,933
Cycling	599,874
Football	390,180
Snow Skiing	330,289
Skating (all types)	322,311
Baseball	219,023
Soccer	157,251

0   200,000   400,000   600,000

Number of injuries

SOURCE: Based on data from Consumer Product Safety Commission, American Academy of Orthopaedic Surgeons

Sports for Fun

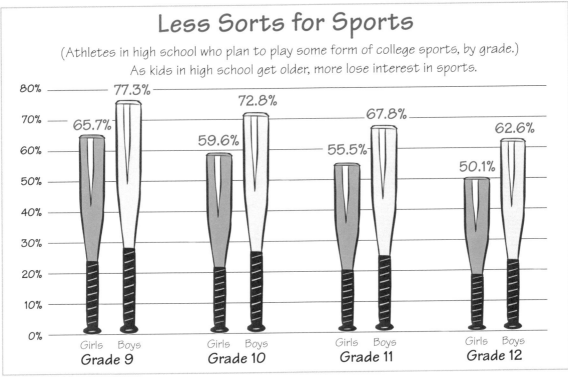

Less Sorts for Sports

(Athletes in high school who plan to play some form of college sports, by grade.)
As kids in high school get older, more lose interest in sports.

- Grade 9: Girls 65.7%, Boys 77.3%
- Grade 10: Girls 59.6%, Boys 72.8%
- Grade 11: Girls 55.5%, Boys 67.8%
- Grade 12: Girls 50.1%, Boys 62.6%

SOURCE: Based on data from The National Athletic Testing Program

Golf Course Cash

Total revenue collected for the four major men's golf championships in 1997. (In millions)

- U.S. Open: $35M
- PGA Championship: $30.5M
- The Masters: $22M
- British Open: $20M

SOURCE: Based on data from *Golf Digest*

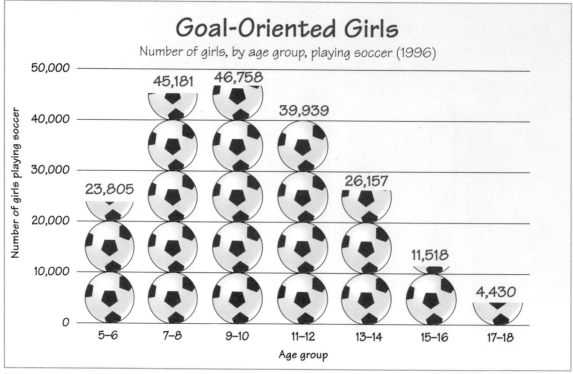

Goal-Oriented Girls

Number of girls, by age group, playing soccer (1996)

SOURCE: Based on data from American Youth Soccer Organization

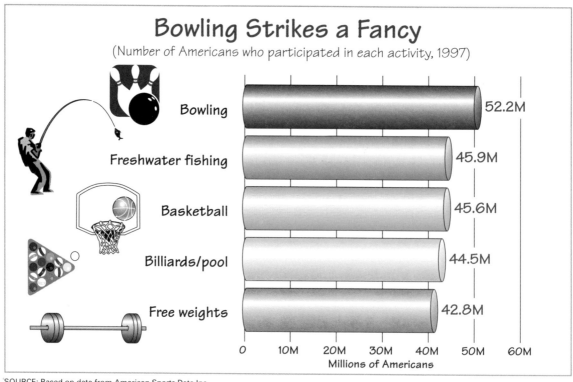

Bowling Strikes a Fancy

(Number of Americans who participated in each activity, 1997)

Bowling — 52.2M
Freshwater fishing — 45.9M
Basketball — 45.6M
Billiards/pool — 44.5M
Free weights — 42.8M

Millions of Americans

SOURCE: Based on data from American Sports Data Inc.

Not Board in the Snow

A total of 3.7 million Americans went snowboarding in 1997. Here's a profile of the snowboarding population:

Age:

18-34
43%

Male
74%

Sex:

Average cost of a snowboard: $309

SOURCE: Based on data from SnowSports Industries America, National Sporting Goods Association

Spending Dough in the Snow

The top-selling kinds of sports equipment for snow sports in 1997-98:
(In millions of dollars)

Shaped Alpine skis — $84M

Snowboards — $71.2M

Straight Alpine skis — $20.4M

Cross-country skis — $9.7M

$0 $20M $40M $60M $80M $100M

SOURCE: Based on data from SnowSports Industries America

Clothes

Mission: wearing stuff that's fashionable, "cool," practical, exactly like everyone else's clothing—except for the fact that it is a part of your unique identity. When it comes to clothing, kids are the ultimate consumers. They know what they like, and they'll spend time and money to get it. They haunt the malls, sneaker superstores, vintage clothing shops, even tag sales and thrift shops. And if they can't find what they want, some kids will buy fabric and sew up their own clothes.

Casual wear such as T-shirts, sweaters, jeans, and sports shoes form the basis of most kids' wardrobes. But not just any T-shirt or sweater will do. Brand names are very important among kids—even for the most ordinary attire. And a brand that's "in" one year may be "out" the next. Kids say that quality is the most important criterion when choosing brand-name clothing. But their parents may question the value of that brand-name label, particularly if it's the parents who are forking over $50 for jeans or $100 for sneakers that are likely to be outgrown in a few months.

Clothes

Kidbits Tidbits

- In 1996 there were more than 42,000 shopping centers in the U.S., with a total of 5.10 billion square feet of retail area.
- More than 10 million people worked in shopping centers in 1996.
- The Mall of America in Bloomington, Minnesota, is the nation's largest mall, with some 500 stores.
- In 1995, the U.S. had 10,781 department stores, 24,769 sporting goods and bicycle shops, 27,487 jewelry stores, and 135,270 apparel and accessory stores.

It's not just what you wear, it's how you wear it. Kids notice who's wearing caps backwards, jeans artfully ripped, or tees too tight. They get inspiration for new trends from their peers, from models in teen magazines, and from their favorite TV, movie, music, and sports personalities.

Some adults feel that kids place too much importance on clothing. They suspect that kids are more interested in what's being worn at school than in what's being taught there. Parochial and private schools have long used school uniforms to provide a more serious approach to learning. They feel this also removes some of the distractions and other problems connected with clothing fashions and fads. Requiring uniforms in public schools is a matter of much debate, though the trend gained momentum during the 1990s. And there was some evidence that wearing uniforms improved students' lives. For example, beginning in 1994, Long Beach, California, required uniforms for its 70,000 students in kindergarten through grade 8. In the first year of the program there was a 43% reduction in suspensions, 54% fewer fights, and more than 20% fewer cases of weapons possession and robbery. Is there a connection? You be the judge.

Kidbits Tidbits

- People spent $20 billion in jewelry stores in 1996.
- Clothing is the third most popular item purchased at yard sales.
- Nike's "Swoosh" logo represents the wing of the Greek goddess Nike.
- Each year, Nike recycles over 2 million athletic shoes into basketball courts and other sports courts.
- Levi Strauss reported record sales of $7.1 billion in 1996.
- December is the busiest shopping month. Americans spent $36.7 billion in department stores in December 1996. They spent a total of $249 billion in these stores during the entire year.
- In a typical month, 185 million adults shop at shopping centers.

Clothes

Yard Sale Shopping

Clothing is the third most popular item purchased at
yard and garage sales, behind books and tools.
(Percentage of purchasers who list item as bought)

Item	Percentage
Books	63%
Tools/hardware	60%
Clothing	51%
Toys	50%
Kitchen items (pots, dishes, utensils)	46%
Sports equipment	35%
Appliances	29%

0%   10%   20%   30%   40%   50%   60%

Percentage of yard sale shoppers

NOTE: May name more than one.

SOURCE: Based on data from Yankelovich for Lutheran Brotherhood

Clothes

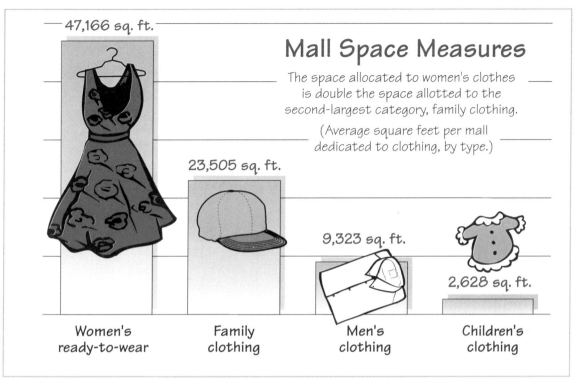

Mall Space Measures

The space allocated to women's clothes is double the space allotted to the second-largest category, family clothing.

(Average square feet per mall dedicated to clothing, by type.)

47,166 sq. ft.

23,505 sq. ft.

9,323 sq. ft.

2,628 sq. ft.

| Women's ready-to-wear | Family clothing | Men's clothing | Children's clothing |

SOURCE: Based on data from Gallup poll for Intl. Council of Shopping Centers

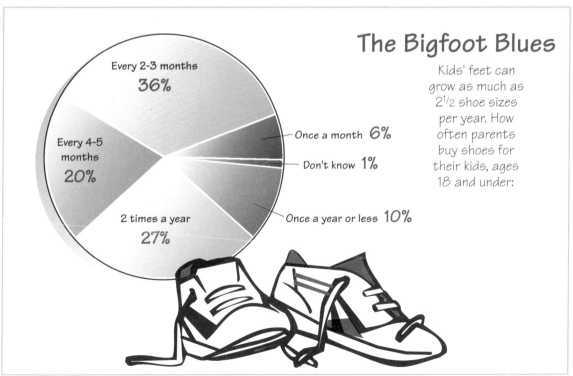

The Bigfoot Blues

Kids' feet can grow as much as $2\frac{1}{2}$ shoe sizes per year. How often parents buy shoes for their kids, ages 18 and under:

Every 2-3 months
36%

Every 4-5 months
20%

2 times a year
27%

Once a month 6%

Don't know 1%

Once a year or less 10%

SOURCE: Based on data from Opinion Research for Payless ShoeSource

Clothes

Sport-Shoe Sales, by Type

Sport shoes account for about $14 billion in sales each year. About 13% of all purchases are made by kids ages 12 and younger.

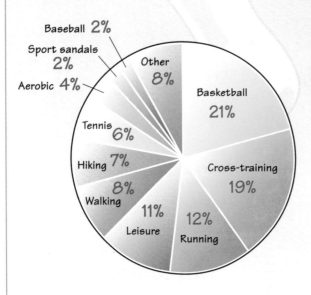

Baseball 2%
Sport sandals 2%
Aerobic 4%
Other 8%
Basketball 21%
Tennis 6%
Hiking 7%
Cross-training 19%
Walking 8%
Leisure 11%
Running 12%

Who Buys Sport-Shoes? By Sex
(Percentage of gender population)

Males   Females

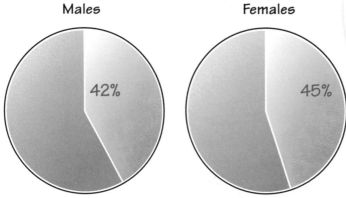

42%   45%

SOURCE: Based on data from NPD Group

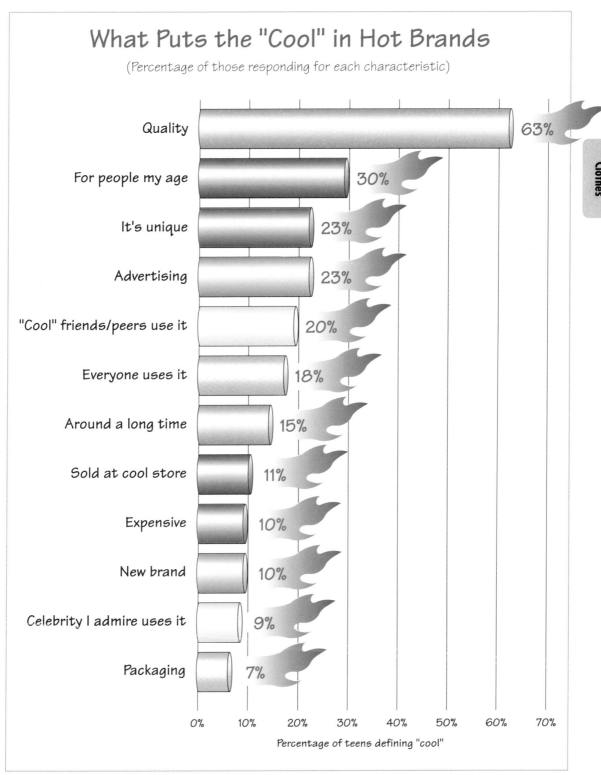

What Puts the "Cool" in Hot Brands

(Percentage of those responding for each characteristic)

Clothes

Quality	63%
For people my age	30%
It's unique	23%
Advertising	23%
"Cool" friends/peers use it	20%
Everyone uses it	18%
Around a long time	15%
Sold at cool store	11%
Expensive	10%
New brand	10%
Celebrity I admire uses it	9%
Packaging	7%

0% 10% 20% 30% 40% 50% 60% 70%

Percentage of teens defining "cool"

SOURCE: Based on data from Teenage Research Unlimited, Inc.

Who Rules Cool?

Top 5 "coolest" brand names, by sex
(Percentage of each gender group that voted it "the coolest")

Clothes

| 1. Nike | 2. Levi's | 3. Calvin Klein | 4. Sony | 5. Pepsi |

Females
38% | 13% | 20% | 8% | 8%

Males
49% | 14% | 5% | 16% | 10%

SOURCE: Based on data from Teenage Research Unlimited, Inc.

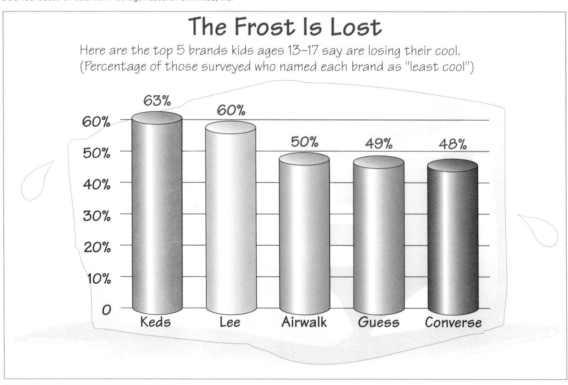

The Frost Is Lost

Here are the top 5 brands kids ages 13–17 say are losing their cool.
(Percentage of those surveyed who named each brand as "least cool")

- Keds 63%
- Lee 60%
- Airwalk 50%
- Guess 49%
- Converse 48%

SOURCE: Based on data from The Zandl Group

Clothes

Clothing "Cool"

Here are the top 5 labels voted the
most "cool" by kids ages 12–19.

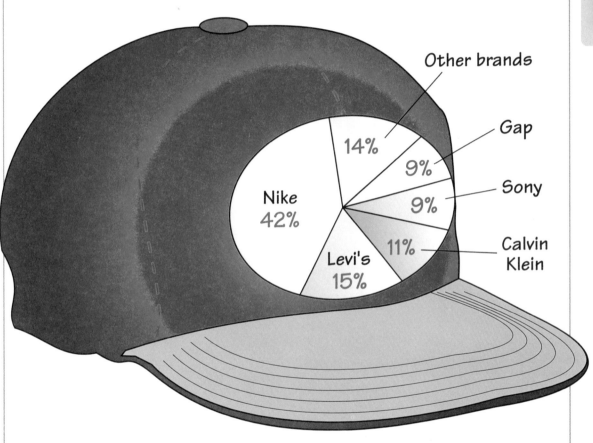

Other brands 14%

Gap 9%

Sony 9%

Calvin Klein 11%

Nike 42%

Levi's 15%

SOURCE: Based on data from Teenage Research Unlimited, Inc.

Clothes

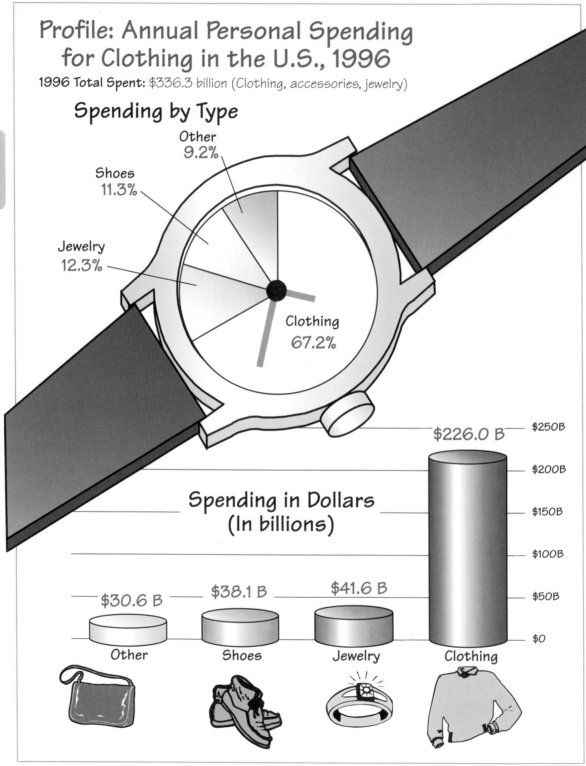

Profile: Annual Personal Spending for Clothing in the U.S., 1996

1996 Total Spent: $336.3 billion (Clothing, accessories, jewelry)

Spending by Type

Other
9.2%

Shoes
11.3%

Jewelry
12.3%

Clothing
67.2%

Spending in Dollars (In billions)

$226.0 B

$250B
$200B
$150B
$100B
$50B
$0

$30.6 B — Other
$38.1 B — Shoes
$41.6 B — Jewelry
Clothing

SOURCE: Based on data from Jupiter Communications

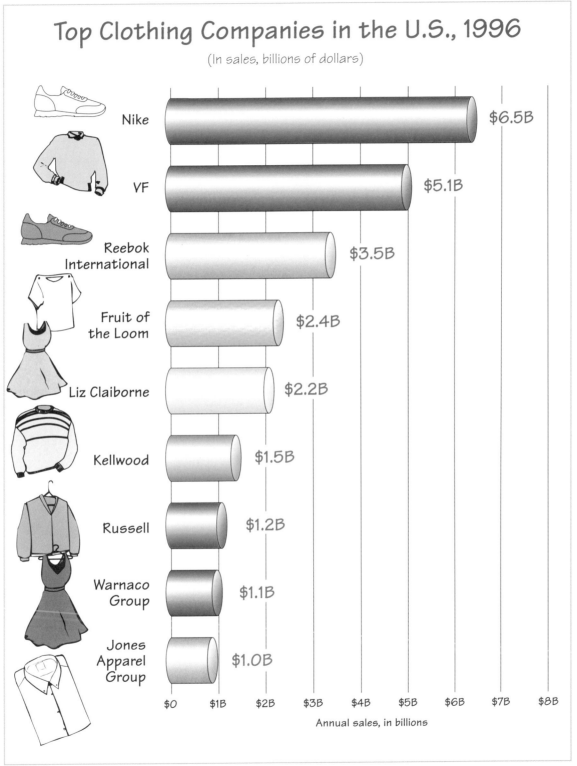

Top Clothing Companies in the U.S., 1996

(In sales, billions of dollars)

Company	Sales
Nike	$6.5B
VF	$5.1B
Reebok International	$3.5B
Fruit of the Loom	$2.4B
Liz Claiborne	$2.2B
Kellwood	$1.5B
Russell	$1.2B
Warnaco Group	$1.1B
Jones Apparel Group	$1.0B

$0 $1B $2B $3B $4B $5B $6B $7B $8B

Annual sales, in billions

Clothes

SOURCE: Based on data from *FORTUNE* Magazine

Entertainment

Screaming on scary rides at the amusement park, checking out the latest models at an auto show, putting together a jigsaw puzzle, attacking aliens in an arcade game, curling up with a good book, visiting a sports hall of fame—the list of ways to be entertained goes on and on!

Video games are especially popular with many young people. They let you fly an airplane, visit spooky caves, battle fierce robots, and maneuver a hang glider through the canyons of a crowded city. Lots of other types of toys and games are popular, too. Some are silly and easy to learn. Others require lots of practice if you want to be really, really good at them. Etienne Bacrot of France started playing the game of chess when he was only four years old. He practiced every day. Determined to be among the world's best players, he got a professional chess coach. In 1997, Etienne became the youngest chess grandmaster ever—he was only 14!

Some kinds of entertainment are fads that are quickly replaced by new pleasures. Others remain popular for many, many years. A

Kidbits Tidbits

- The longest-running musical in history is *Cats*.
- About 1,500 daily newspapers and 7,500 weekly newspapers are published in the U.S.
- The very first newspaper comic strip, "Hogan's Alley," appeared in 1895.
- The world's best-selling fiction author is British mystery writer Agatha Christie, who died in 1976. More than two billion copies of her books have been sold so far.

metal coil called the Slinky was first sold in 1945. By the time it celebrated its 50th birthday in 1995, some 250 million of these bouncy gizmos had been sold. A big hit in 1997 was the electronic cyberpet, which kept signaling its owner to "Feed me!" and "Pet me!" Do you think cyberpets will be around as long as Slinky?

Maybe cyberpets will become collectibles, like Barbie and G.I. Joe dolls. Some collectibles become very valuable—if they are rare and if there is a big demand for them. The hottest toys of 1997 were Beanie Babies, bean-bag animals such as Snort the Bull and Nuts the Squirrel. The first Beanie Babies were introduced in 1994, but they were soon "retired." That is, the company stopped making those designs. By 1997, many

collectors were willing to pay thousands of dollars for retired Beanie Babies, which originally only sold for about $5!

Despite all the new toy and game fads that come and go, a few forms of entertainment remain consistent favorites. Reading, watching television, and listening to music are still the most popular means by which kids and adults entertain themselves. In fact, nearly every home in America has at least one color television and one radio, and 88% of all U.S. households now have aVCR. But, even with all those electronics, the majority of people in America still rank reading as their favorite leisure and entertainment activity.

Kidbits Tidbits

- R. L. Stine's *Goosebumps* books have sold more copies than any other kids' books.
- *People* magazine sold over $525 million worth of advertising in 1996. In second place was *Sports Illustrated*, at $522 million.
- State parks and recreational areas had more than 745 million visitors in 1995. National parks had 64.8 million visitors.
- There are about 900 amusement parks in the U.S. in 1995, they took in $6.4 billion.
- In 1995 there were 10,347 hobby, toy, and game shops in the U.S.

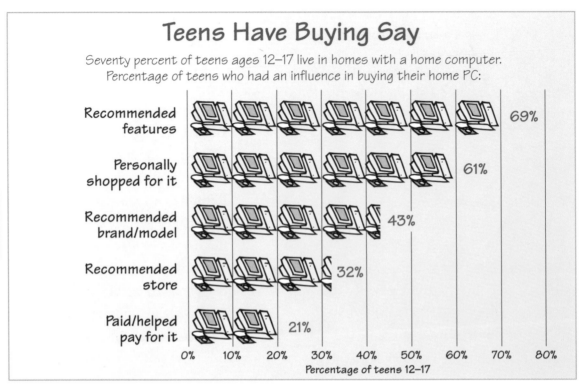

Teens Have Buying Say

Seventy percent of teens ages 12–17 live in homes with a home computer.
Percentage of teens who had an influence in buying their home PC:

Recommended features — 69%
Personally shopped for it — 61%
Recommended brand/model — 43%
Recommended store — 32%
Paid/helped pay for it — 21%

Percentage of teens 12–17

SOURCE: Based on data from Millward Brown for Channel One

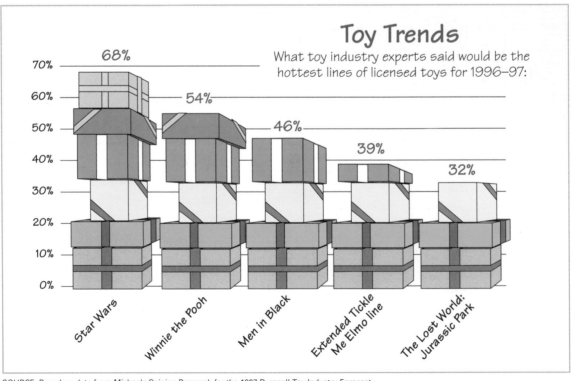

Toy Trends

What toy industry experts said would be the hottest lines of licensed toys for 1996–97:

- Star Wars — 68%
- Winnie the Pooh — 54%
- Men in Black — 46%
- Extended Tickle Me Elmo line — 39%
- The Lost World: Jurassic Park — 32%

SOURCE: Based on data from Michaels Opinion Research for the 1997 Duracell Toy Industry Forecast

Entertainment

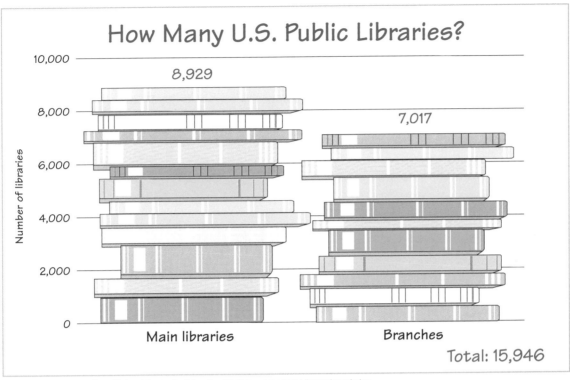

How Many U.S. Public Libraries?

Number of libraries

8,929

7,017

Main libraries

Branches

Total: 15,946

SOURCE: Based on data from National Center for Education Statistics, American Library Association

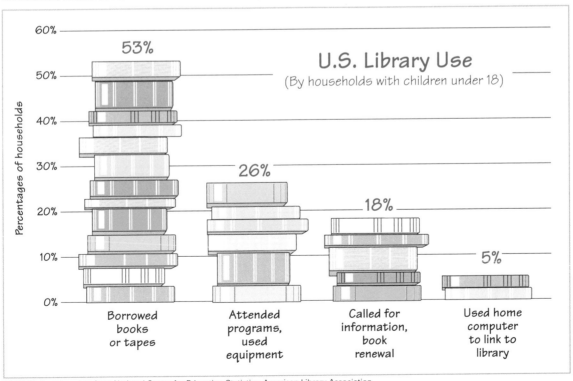

U.S. Library Use
(By households with children under 18)

Percentages of households

53%

26%

18%

5%

Borrowed
books
or tapes

Attended
programs,
used
equipment

Called for
information,
book
renewal

Used home
computer
to link to
library

SOURCE: Based on data from National Center for Education Statistics, American Library Association

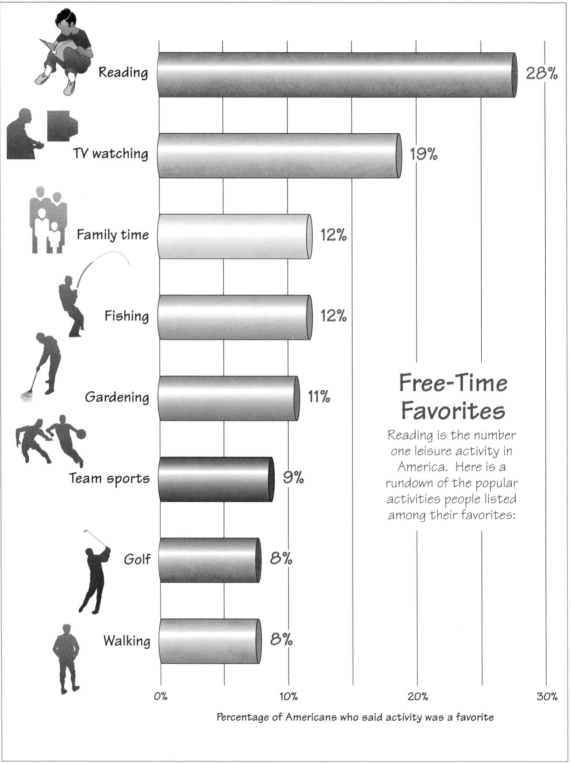

Reading — 28%

TV watching — 19%

Family time — 12%

Fishing — 12%

Gardening — 11%

Team sports — 9%

Golf — 8%

Walking — 8%

Free-Time Favorites

Reading is the number one leisure activity in America. Here is a rundown of the popular activities people listed among their favorites:

0% 10% 20% 30%

Percentage of Americans who said activity was a favorite

Entertainment

SOURCE: Based on data from Louis Harris and Associates

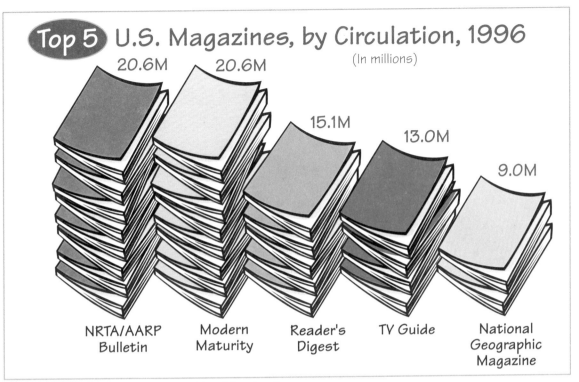

Top 5 U.S. Magazines, by Circulation, 1996

(In millions)

20.6M   20.6M   15.1M   13.0M   9.0M

| NRTA/AARP Bulletin | Modern Maturity | Reader's Digest | TV Guide | National Geographic Magazine |

SOURCE: Based on data from Audit Bureau of Circulations, Schaumberg, IL

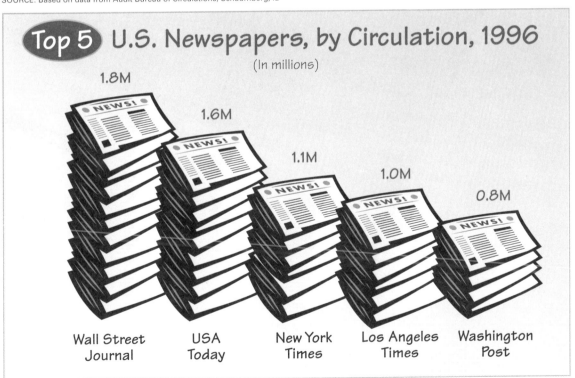

Top 5 U.S. Newspapers, by Circulation, 1996

(In millions)

1.8M   1.6M   1.1M   1.0M   0.8M

| Wall Street Journal | USA Today | New York Times | Los Angeles Times | Washington Post |

SOURCE: Based on data from *Editor & Publisher International Yearbook, 1996*

Entertainment

Books Sold in the U.S., by Type

(Percentage by publisher category)

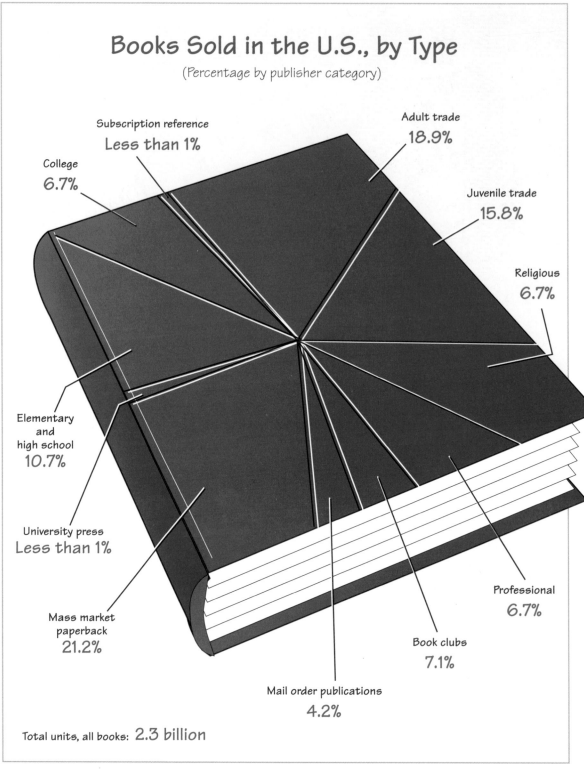

Subscription reference
Less than 1%

College
6.7%

Adult trade
18.9%

Juvenile trade
15.8%

Religious
6.7%

Elementary
and
high school
10.7%

University press
Less than 1%

Mass market
paperback
21.2%

Professional
6.7%

Book clubs
7.1%

Mail order publications
4.2%

Total units, all books: 2.3 billion

SOURCE: Based on data from Book Industry Study Group, Inc.

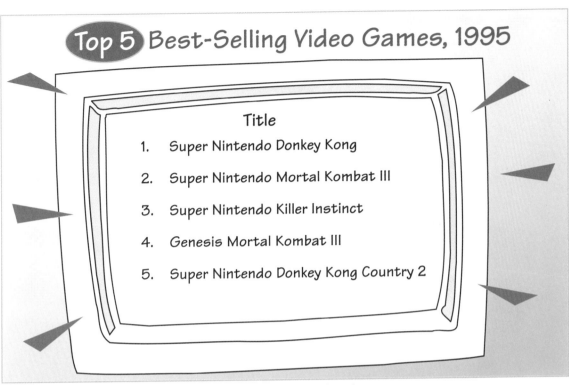

Top 5 Best-Selling Video Games, 1995

Title

1. Super Nintendo Donkey Kong

2. Super Nintendo Mortal Kombat III

3. Super Nintendo Killer Instinct

4. Genesis Mortal Kombat III

5. Super Nintendo Donkey Kong Country 2

SOURCE: Based on data from The NPD TRSTS Video Games Tracking Service, The NPD Group, Inc.

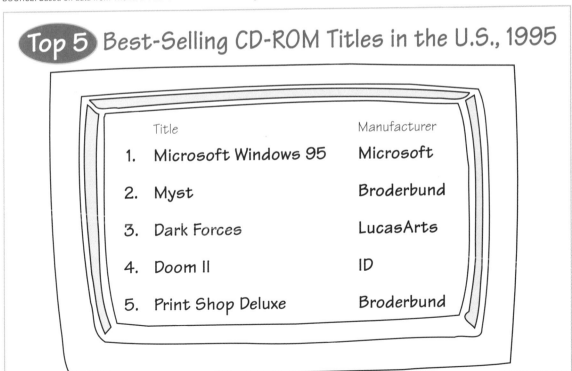

Top 5 Best-Selling CD-ROM Titles in the U.S., 1995

Title	Manufacturer
1. Microsoft Windows 95	Microsoft
2. Myst	Broderbund
3. Dark Forces	LucasArts
4. Doom II	ID
5. Print Shop Deluxe	Broderbund

SOURCE: Based on information given in *The Top 10 of Everything 1997*

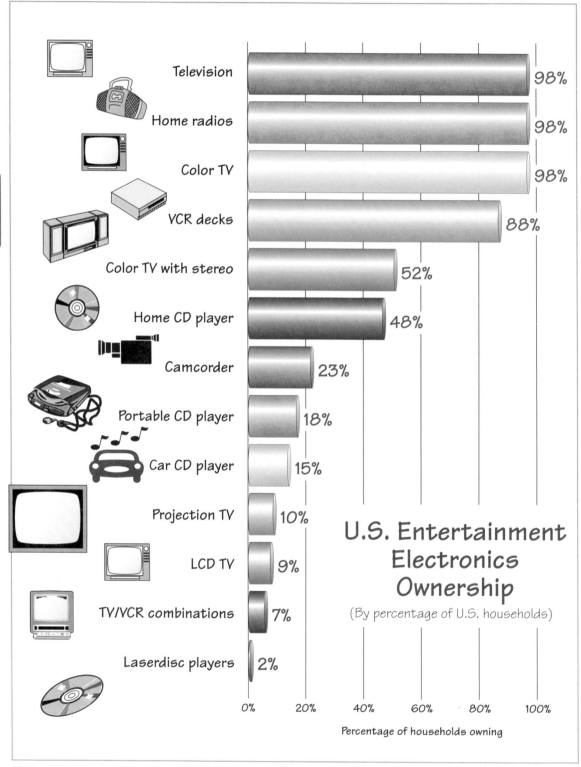

Television — 98%

Home radios — 98%

Color TV — 98%

VCR decks — 88%

Color TV with stereo — 52%

Home CD player — 48%

Camcorder — 23%

Portable CD player — 18%

Car CD player — 15%

Projection TV — 10%

LCD TV — 9%

TV/VCR combinations — 7%

Laserdisc players — 2%

U.S. Entertainment Electronics Ownership

(By percentage of U.S. households)

0%   20%   40%   60%   80%   100%

Percentage of households owning

Entertainment

SOURCE: Based on data from Electronic Industries Association, Market Research Department

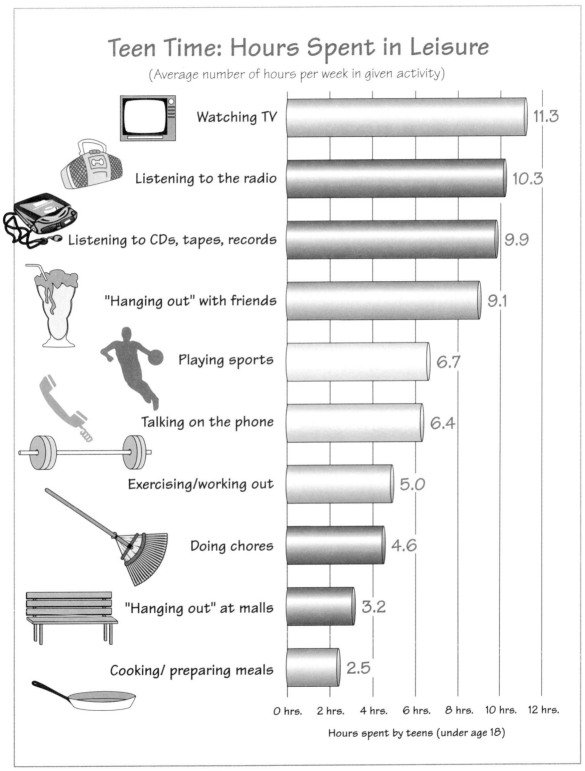

Teen Time: Hours Spent in Leisure

(Average number of hours per week in given activity)

Activity	Hours
Watching TV	11.3
Listening to the radio	10.3
Listening to CDs, tapes, records	9.9
"Hanging out" with friends	9.1
Playing sports	6.7
Talking on the phone	6.4
Exercising/working out	5.0
Doing chores	4.6
"Hanging out" at malls	3.2
Cooking/ preparing meals	2.5

0 hrs.   2 hrs.   4 hrs.   6 hrs.   8 hrs.   10 hrs.   12 hrs.

Hours spent by teens (under age 18)

Entertainment

SOURCE: Based on data from Teenage Research Unlimited, Inc.

Entertainment

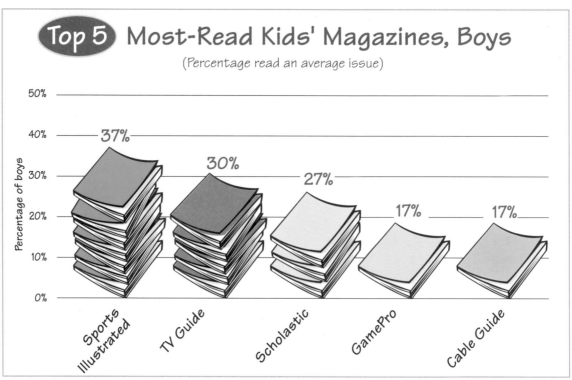

Top 5 Most-Read Kids' Magazines, Boys
(Percentage read an average issue)

Percentage of boys

- Sports Illustrated — 37%
- TV Guide — 30%
- Scholastic — 27%
- GamePro — 17%
- Cable Guide — 17%

SOURCE: Based on data from Teenage Research Unlimited, Inc.

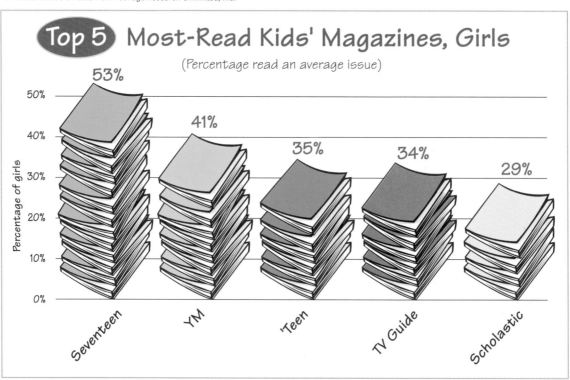

Top 5 Most-Read Kids' Magazines, Girls
(Percentage read an average issue)

Percentage of girls

- Seventeen — 53%
- YM — 41%
- 'Teen — 35%
- TV Guide — 34%
- Scholastic — 29%

SOURCE: Based on data from Teenage Research Unlimited, Inc.

Quality Time Table

How much weekend time do kids, ages 9 to 16, spend with their parents:

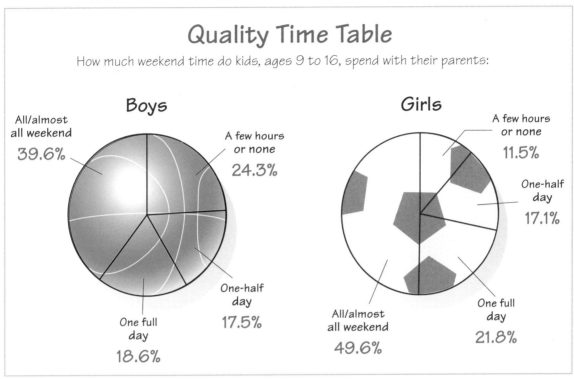

Boys

All/almost all weekend
39.6%

A few hours or none
24.3%

One full day
18.6%

One-half day
17.5%

Girls

A few hours or none
11.5%

One-half day
17.1%

One full day
21.8%

All/almost all weekend
49.6%

SOURCE: Based on data from *KidSpeak* survey

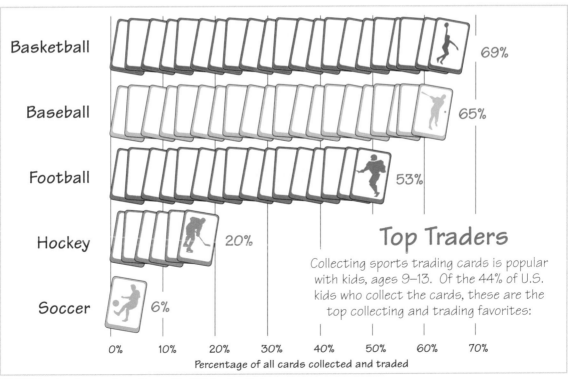

Basketball	69%
Baseball	65%
Football	53%
Hockey	20%
Soccer	6%

Top Traders

Collecting sports trading cards is popular with kids, ages 9–13. Of the 44% of U.S. kids who collect the cards, these are the top collecting and trading favorites:

0%   10%   20%   30%   40%   50%   60%   70%

Percentage of all cards collected and traded

SOURCE: Based on data from *Sports Illustrated for KIDS* Omnibus Study

Entertainment

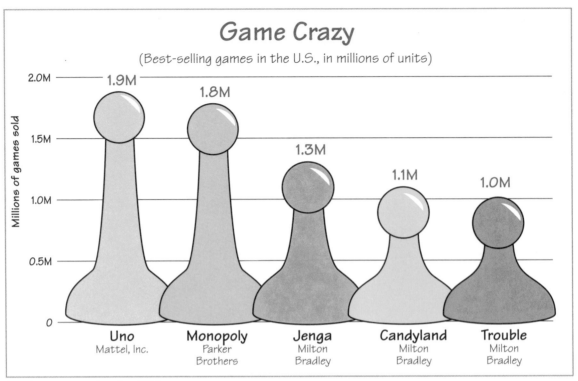

Game Crazy

(Best-selling games in the U.S., in millions of units)

Millions of games sold

2.0M

1.9M — Uno

1.8M — Monopoly

1.5M

1.3M — Jenga

1.1M — Candyland

1.0M — Trouble

1.0M

0.5M

0

Uno	Monopoly	Jenga	Candyland	Trouble
Mattel, Inc.	Parker Brothers	Milton Bradley	Milton Bradley	Milton Bradley

SOURCE: Based on data from *Trsts*, NPD Group

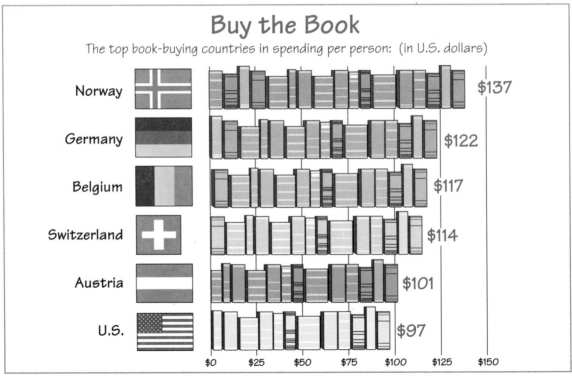

Buy the Book

The top book-buying countries in spending per person: (in U.S. dollars)

Norway	$137
Germany	$122
Belgium	$117
Switzerland	$114
Austria	$101
U.S.	$97

$0 $25 $50 $75 $100 $125 $150

SOURCE: Based on data from Euromonitor

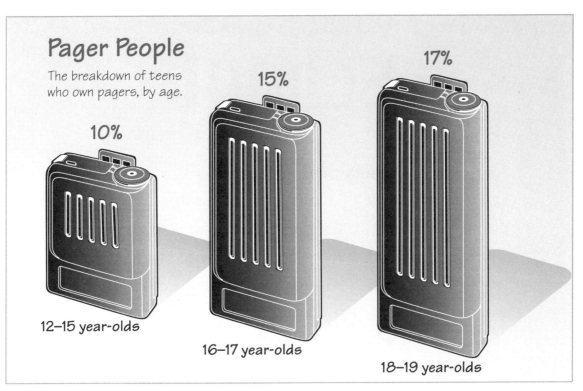

Pager People

The breakdown of teens who own pagers, by age.

10%

15%

17%

12–15 year-olds

16–17 year-olds

18–19 year-olds

Entertainment

SOURCE: Based on data from Teenage Research Unlimited, Inc.

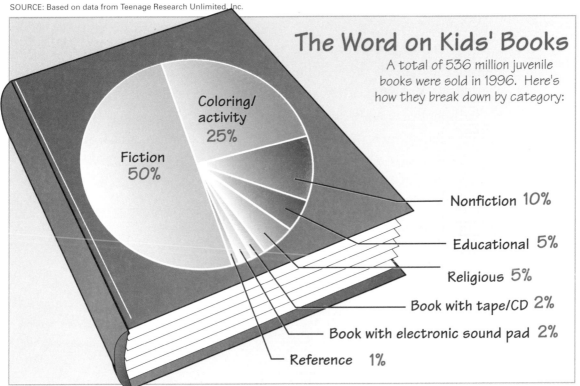

The Word on Kids' Books

A total of 536 million juvenile books were sold in 1996. Here's how they break down by category:

Fiction 50%

Coloring/activity 25%

Nonfiction 10%

Educational 5%

Religious 5%

Book with tape/CD 2%

Book with electronic sound pad 2%

Reference 1%

SOURCE: Based on data from *1996 Consumer Research Study on Book Purchasing*

School

More than 51 million kids attend school—37.3 million in grades K through 9, and 14.3 million in grades 9 through 12. Most of them—45.8 million—attend public schools. About 5.8 million students attend private schools, the majority of which are affiliated with a religion. In 1996, each teacher had an average of 17.1 students per class. In general, elementary school classes were larger than high school classes, and classes in public schools were larger than classes in private schools.

The U.S. has about 76,350 elementary schools, 22,800 high schools, and 10,700 schools that cover grades K through 12. Total spending on K-12 education is more than $300 billion a year! The average spent on each student in the 1995-96 school year was $5,652. The amount varied greatly from state to state, and from one school district to another. New Jersey spent the most—an average of $9,318 per student. Utah spent the least—an average of $3,670 per student.

Kidbits Tidbits

- About 9% of public schools have fewer than 100 students; 9.2% have 1,000 or more students.
- Most private schools are affiliated with a religion.
- In 1996, the average elementary school classroom had 18.7 students. The average high school classroom had 14.6 students.
- 600,000 children eat lunch in school, and 140,000 eat breakfast there.

Most kids graduate from high school, though about 5% of 16- and 17-year-olds are dropouts. Getting a high school degree and doing well in school can pay off in many ways. For example, it makes it easier to get a good job or go to college. It can mean $$$, too! When Rebecca Sealfon won the National Spelling Bee she received a new computer and $5,000 in prize money. Seyi Fayanju got a $25,000 scholarship when he won the National Geography Bee.

Today, a record number of high school graduates continue their education at the college level. More than 14 million people are currently enrolled in college, the great majority of them in public institutions. More women than men are enrolled in college. Attending college can be very expensive.

The average yearly cost of tuition and fees at 4-year colleges in 1997 was $2,966 at public colleges and $12,823 at private colleges. But there's a financial payoff: The greater the amount of education people have, the better their chances of getting jobs—and earning good salaries. In 1996, only 60.2% of people with less than a high school degree had jobs, but 87.8% of college graduates had jobs. The average earnings of people age 18 and older who did not have high school degrees was $14,013. Earnings of people with a bachelor's degree were $36,980; with a master's degree it was $47,609.

Kidbits Tidbits

- College graduates can expect to earn about $600,000 more during their lifetimes than high school graduates can expect to earn.
- 43% of children from low-income families enter college after high school, compared with 83% of children from higher-income families.
- In 1997, the cost of tuition and fees for an average year at a private college was nearly 4.5 times more than a public college.
- In 1997, the average salary of public school teachers was $39,580—up from only $15,913 in 1980.
- A study of 12th graders in 23 countries found that U.S. students scored close to the international average in math, but below average in advanced math and physics.

School

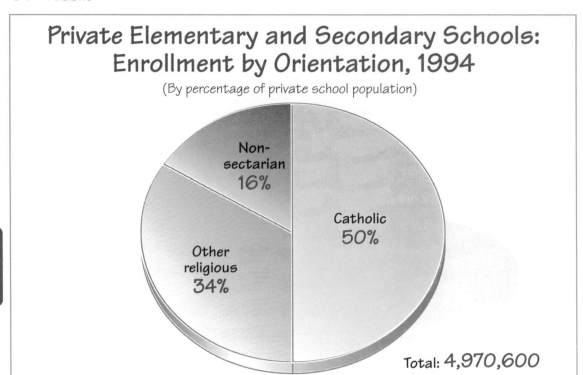

Private Elementary and Secondary Schools: Enrollment by Orientation, 1994

(By percentage of private school population)

Non-sectarian 16%

Catholic 50%

Other religious 34%

Total: 4,970,600

SOURCE: Based on data from U.S. National Center for Education Statistics, *Digest of Educational Statistics*

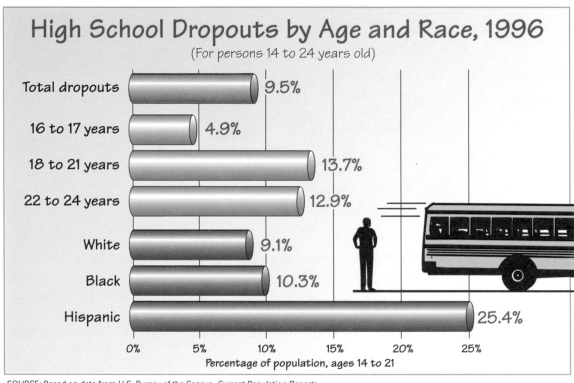

High School Dropouts by Age and Race, 1996

(For persons 14 to 24 years old)

Total dropouts	9.5%
16 to 17 years	4.9%
18 to 21 years	13.7%
22 to 24 years	12.9%
White	9.1%
Black	10.3%
Hispanic	25.4%

0%   5%   10%   15%   20%   25%

Percentage of population, ages 14 to 21

SOURCE: Based on data from U.S. Bureau of the Census, *Current Population Reports*

Average Monthly Income, by Highest Educational Degree Earned

(For persons 18 and over)

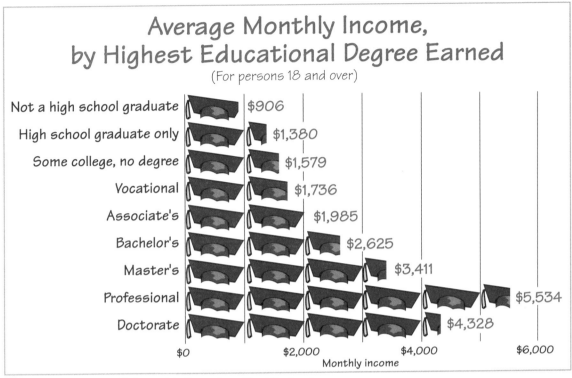

Not a high school graduate	$906
High school graduate only	$1,380
Some college, no degree	$1,579
Vocational	$1,736
Associate's	$1,985
Bachelor's	$2,625
Master's	$3,411
Professional	$5,534
Doctorate	$4,328

$0 $2,000 $4,000 $6,000

Monthly income

SOURCE: Based on data from U.S. Bureau of the Census, *Current Population Reports*

U.S. Public Elementary and Secondary School Enrollment, 1980 to 1995

(In millions)

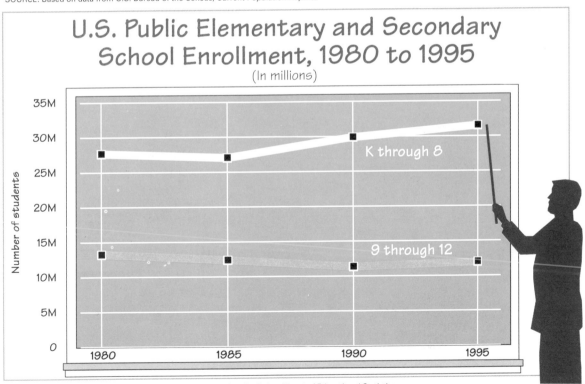

Number of students

K through 8

9 through 12

1980   1985   1990   1995

SOURCE: Based on data from U.S. National Center for Education Statistics, *Digest of Educational Statistics*

School

School

Profile: Student Use of Computers in School

(By average percentage of population per category)

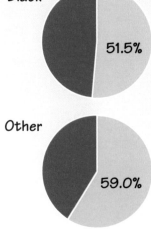

Total student population
59.0%

Prekindergarten and kindergarten
26.2%

Grades 1-8
68.9%

Grades 9-12
58.2%

Male
59.4%

Female
58.7%

White
61.6%

Black
51.5%

Hispanic
52.3%

Other
59.0%

SOURCE: Based on data from U.S. National Center for Education Statistics, *Digest of Educational Statistics*

Profile: Student Use of Computers at Home for School Work

(By average percentage of population per category)

Total student population
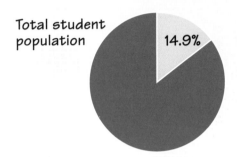
14.9%

Male
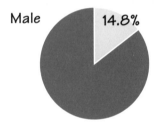
14.8%

Female
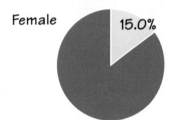
15.0%

White
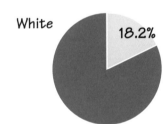
18.2%

Black
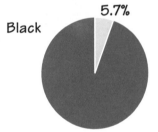
5.7%

Hispanic
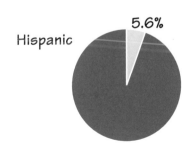
5.6%

Other
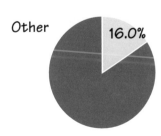
16.0%

School

SOURCE: Based on data from U.S. National Center for Education Statistics, *Digest of Educational Statistics*

School

Profile: Technology in U.S. Public Schools, 1997

(By percentage of total)

Schools with interactive videodisk players

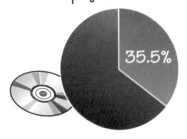

35.5%

Schools with modems

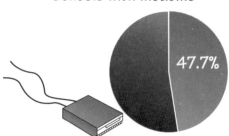

47.7%

Schools with networks

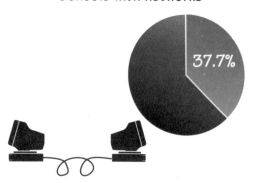

37.7%

Schools with CD-ROM's

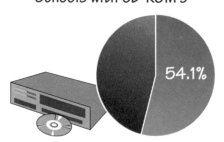

54.1%

Schools with satellite dishes

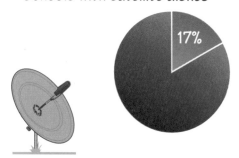

17%

Schools with cable

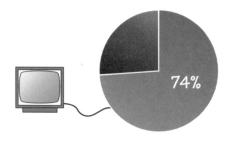

74%

SOURCE: Based on data from Quality Education Data, Inc., Denver, CO., *Technology in Public Schools*

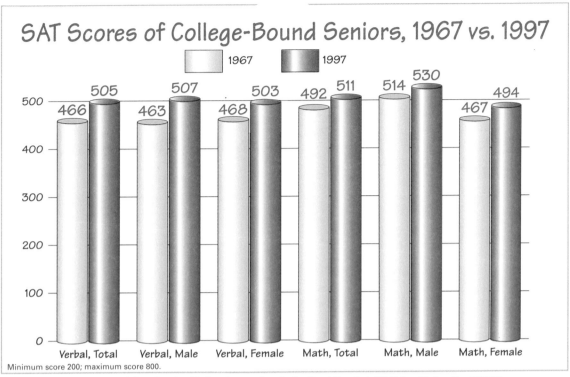

SAT Scores of College-Bound Seniors, 1967 vs. 1997

1967   1997

	Verbal, Total	Verbal, Male	Verbal, Female	Math, Total	Math, Male	Math, Female
1967	466	463	468	492	514	467
1997	505	507	503	511	530	494

Minimum score 200; maximum score 800.

SOURCE: Based on data from the College Board and College Entrance Examination Board, New York, NY, *National College Bound Senior*

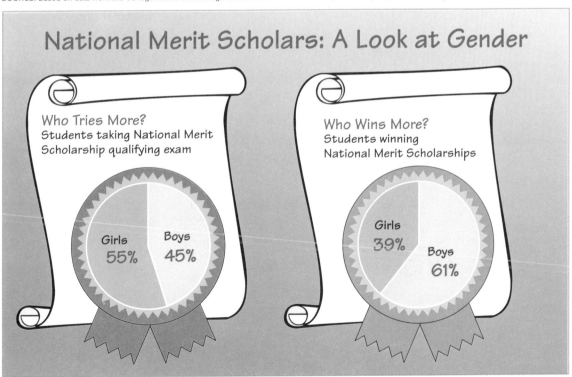

National Merit Scholars: A Look at Gender

Who Tries More?
Students taking National Merit Scholarship qualifying exam

Girls 55%   Boys 45%

Who Wins More?
Students winning National Merit Scholarships

Girls 39%   Boys 61%

SOURCE: Based on data from National Center for Fair & Open Testing

School

A Profile of U.S. College Freshmen

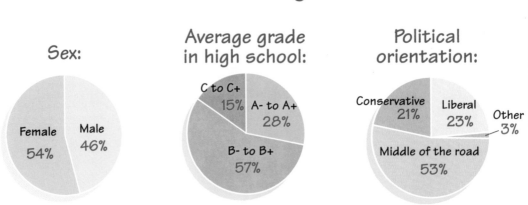

Sex:

Female 54%

Male 46%

Average grade in high school:

C to C+ 15%

A- to A+ 28%

B- to B+ 57%

Political orientation:

Conservative 21%

Liberal 23%

Other 3%

Middle of the road 53%

Probable field of study:

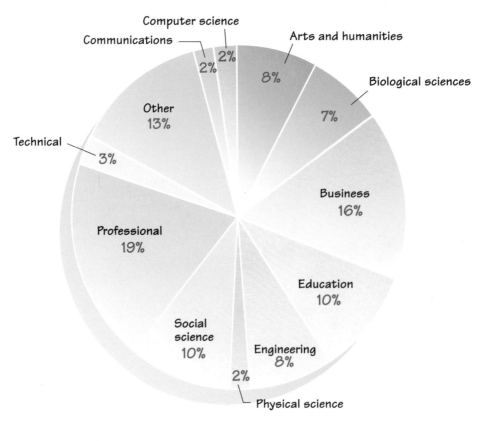

Computer science 2%

Communications 2%

Arts and humanities 8%

Biological sciences 7%

Other 13%

Technical 3%

Business 16%

Professional 19%

Education 10%

Social science 10%

Engineering 8%

Physical science 2%

SOURCE: Based on data from The Higher Education Research Institute, University of California, Los Angeles, CA.
The American Freshman: National Norms

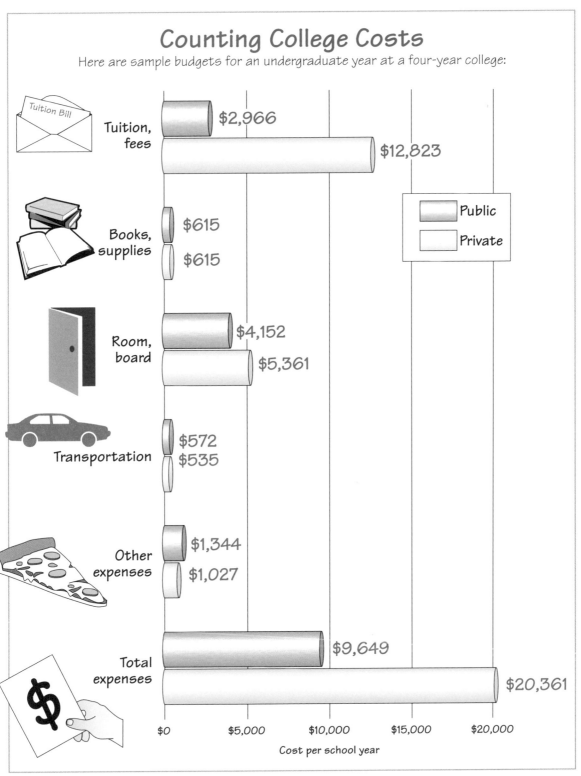

Counting College Costs

Here are sample budgets for an undergraduate year at a four-year college:

Tuition, fees
- $2,966
- $12,823

Books, supplies
- $615
- $615

Room, board
- $4,152
- $5,361

Transportation
- $572
- $535

Other expenses
- $1,344
- $1,027

Total expenses
- $9,649
- $20,361

Public
Private

$0 — $5,000 — $10,000 — $15,000 — $20,000

Cost per school year

School

SOURCE: Based on data from The College Board

School

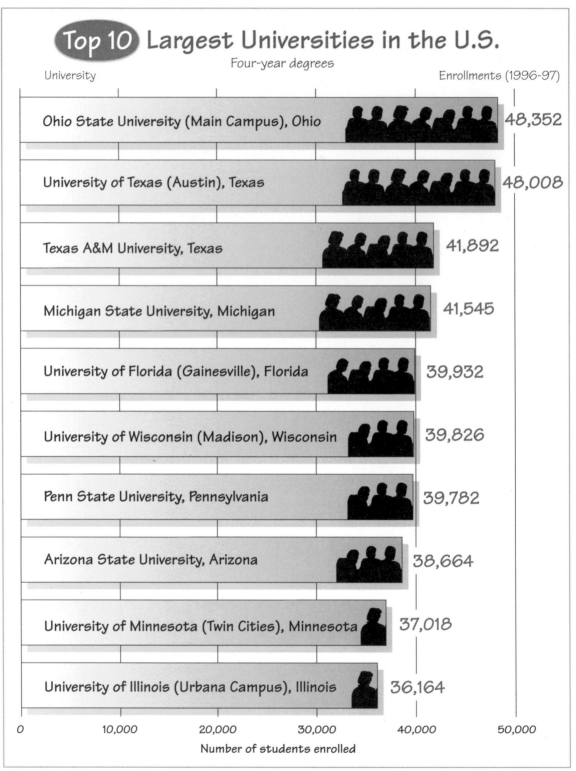

Top 10 Largest Universities in the U.S.

Four-year degrees

University   Enrollments (1996-97)

University	Enrollment
Ohio State University (Main Campus), Ohio	48,352
University of Texas (Austin), Texas	48,008
Texas A&M University, Texas	41,892
Michigan State University, Michigan	41,545
University of Florida (Gainesville), Florida	39,932
University of Wisconsin (Madison), Wisconsin	39,826
Penn State University, Pennsylvania	39,782
Arizona State University, Arizona	38,664
University of Minnesota (Twin Cities), Minnesota	37,018
University of Illinois (Urbana Campus), Illinois	36,164

0   10,000   20,000   30,000   40,000   50,000

Number of students enrolled

SOURCE: Based on data from National Center for Educational Statistics, U.S. Department of Education

Older Grade, Less Play

About 60% of all U.S. high school students are enrolled in physical education classes, but PE enrollment drops (especially with girls) as students get older:

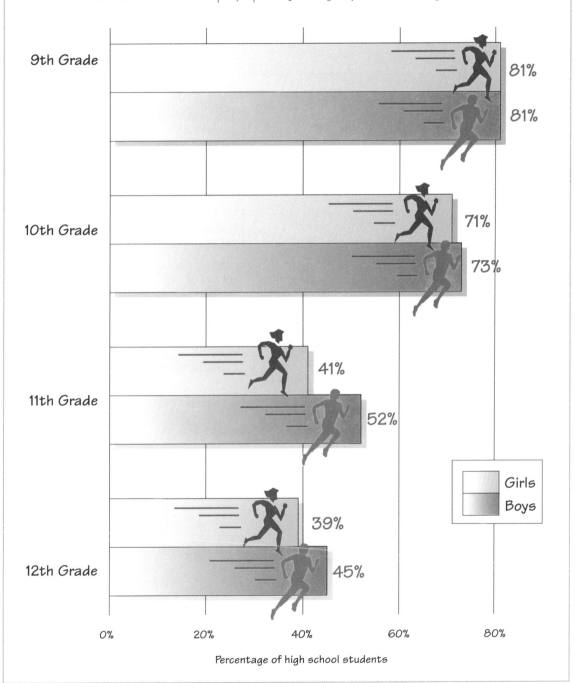

School

SOURCE: Based on data from Department of Health and Human Services for "Girl Power!"

School

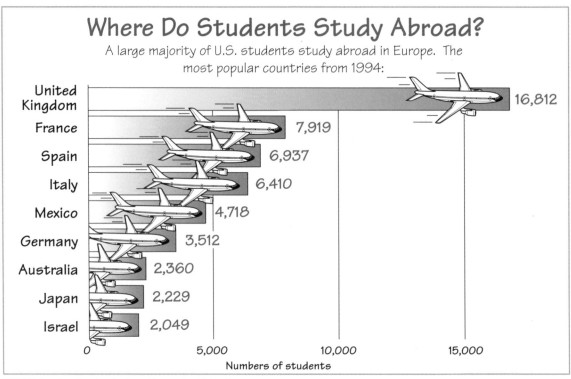

Where Do Students Study Abroad?

A large majority of U.S. students study abroad in Europe. The most popular countries from 1994:

Country	Students
United Kingdom	16,812
France	7,919
Spain	6,937
Italy	6,410
Mexico	4,718
Germany	3,512
Australia	2,360
Japan	2,229
Israel	2,049

Numbers of students

SOURCE: Based on data from Institute of International Education

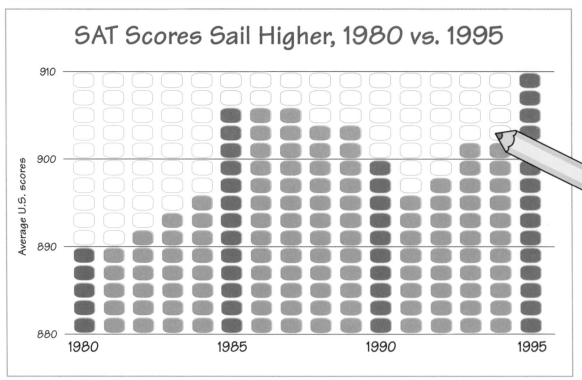

SAT Scores Sail Higher, 1980 vs. 1995

Average U.S. scores

SOURCE: Based on data from The College Board

Comparing Countries: How Do We Stack Up in Math?

Here's a look at how U.S. 13-year-olds compare to their peers in nine other countries for math skills. (By test score averages)

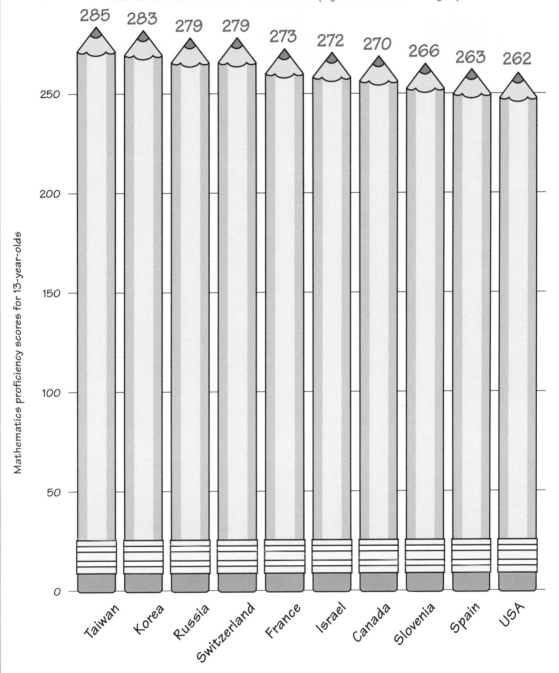

SOURCE: Based on data from National Science Foundation, "Learning Curve" report

House for Homework

Most parents say homework is the first thing kids do when they get home from school. Here's a look at where kids say they do their homework:

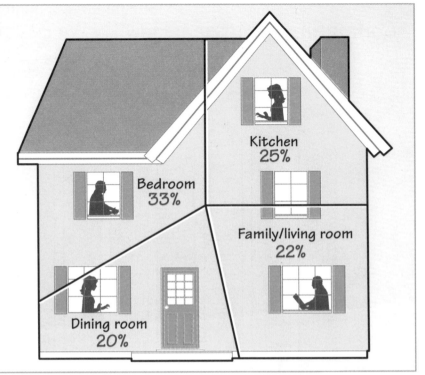

Kitchen
25%

Bedroom
33%

Family/living room
22%

Dining room
20%

SOURCE: Based on data from Federal National Mortgage Association

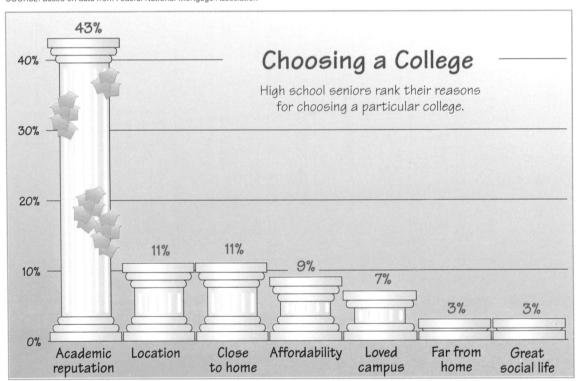

Choosing a College

High school seniors rank their reasons for choosing a particular college.

40%	43%
30%	
20%	
10%	11% 11% 9% 7%
0%	3% 3%

Academic reputation — 43%
Location — 11%
Close to home — 11%
Affordability — 9%
Loved campus — 7%
Far from home — 3%
Great social life — 3%

SOURCE: Based on data from Kaplan Educational Centers

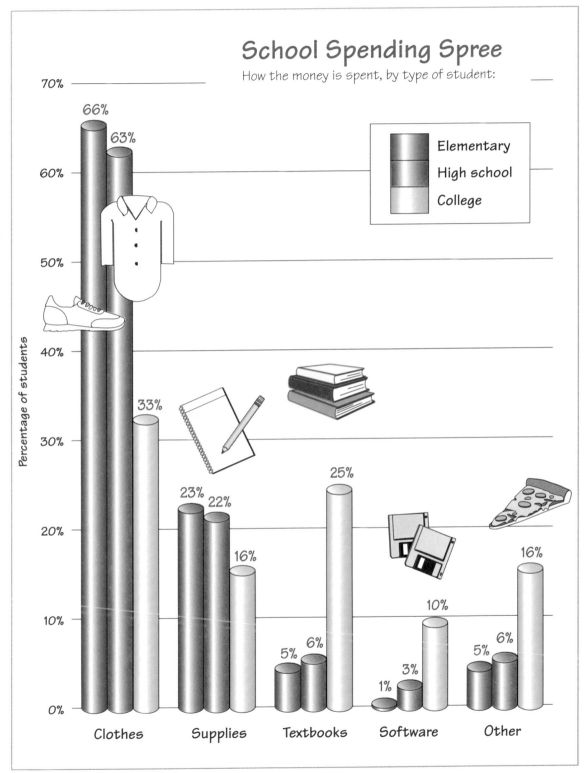

School Spending Spree

How the money is spent, by type of student:

Legend:
- Elementary
- High school
- College

Percentage of students

70%
60%
50%
40%
30%
20%
10%
0%

Clothes: 66%, 63%, 33%
Supplies: 23%, 22%, 16%
Textbooks: 5%, 6%, 25%
Software: 1%, 3%, 10%
Other: 5%, 6%, 16%

SOURCE: Based on data from American Express Retail Index

School

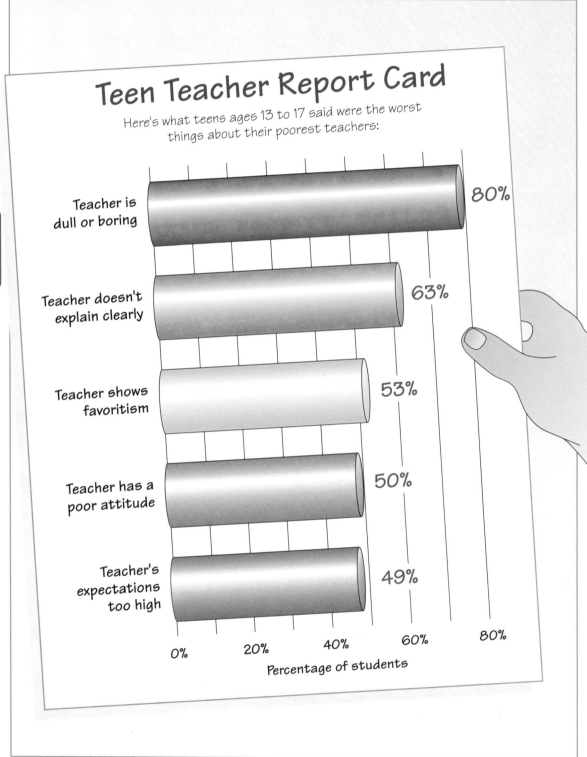

Teen Teacher Report Card

Here's what teens ages 13 to 17 said were the worst things about their poorest teachers:

- **Teacher is dull or boring** — 80%
- **Teacher doesn't explain clearly** — 63%
- **Teacher shows favoritism** — 53%
- **Teacher has a poor attitude** — 50%
- **Teacher's expectations too high** — 49%

0% 20% 40% 60% 80%

Percentage of students

School

SOURCE: Based on data from 1996 *Mood of American Youth* by NFO Research for Horatio Alger Association, National Association of Secondary School Principals

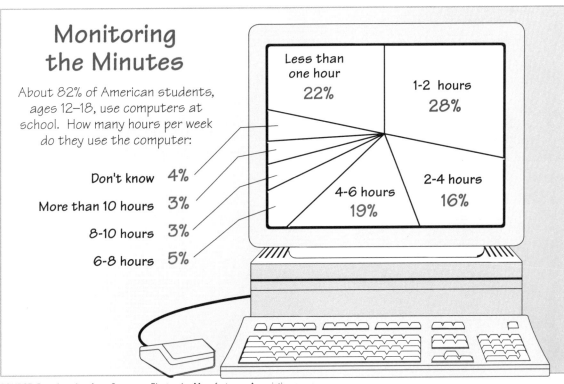

Monitoring the Minutes

About 82% of American students, ages 12–18, use computers at school. How many hours per week do they use the computer:

Don't know **4%**

More than 10 hours **3%**

8-10 hours **3%**

6-8 hours **5%**

Less than one hour **22%**

1-2 hours **28%**

2-4 hours **16%**

4-6 hours **19%**

School

SOURCE: Based on data from Consumer Electronics Manufacturers Association survey

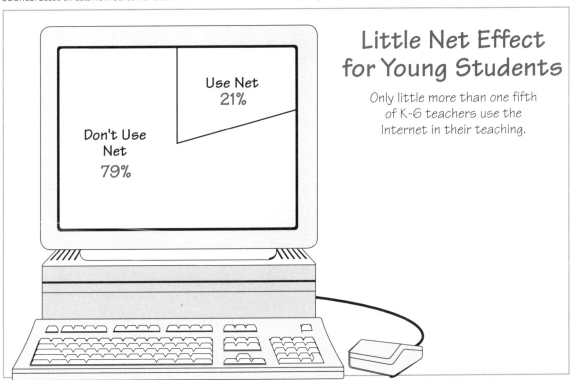

Little Net Effect for Young Students

Only little more than one fifth of K-6 teachers use the Internet in their teaching.

Use Net **21%**

Don't Use Net **79%**

SOURCE: Based on data from 1997 Tenth Planet Teachers & Technology survey

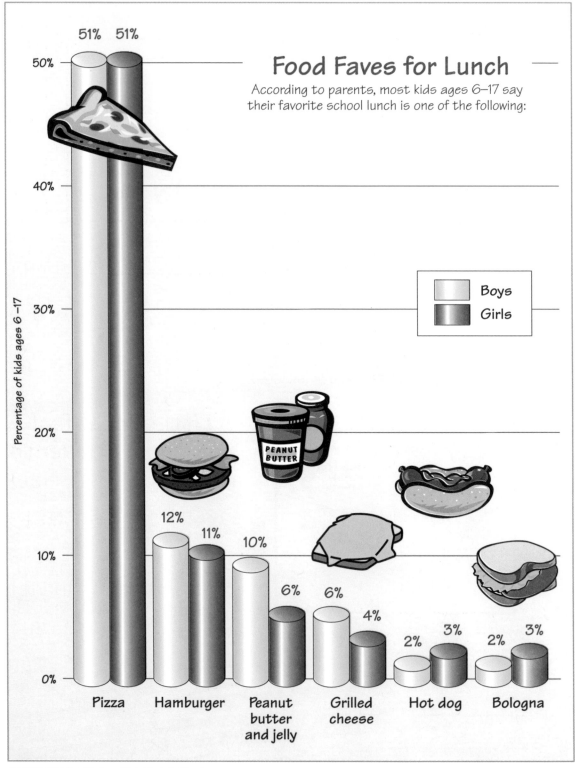

Food Faves for Lunch

According to parents, most kids ages 6–17 say their favorite school lunch is one of the following:

Percentage of kids ages 6–17

| | Boys |
| | Girls |

Pizza: 51%, 51%
Hamburger: 12%, 11%
Peanut butter and jelly: 10%, 6%
Grilled cheese: 6%, 4%
Hot dog: 2%, 3%
Bologna: 2%, 3%

School

SOURCE: Based on data from Market Facts for Shout

Daily Diet in School

The average public school student spends 1,000 hours in the school cafeteria, from first grade to high school graduation. Here's an example of what's served every day in the lunchrooms:

Fresh fruit
4.9 million pounds

Milk
1.9 million gallons

Slices of bread
65 million

Vegetables
375,000 pounds

School

SOURCE: Based on data from American School Food Service Association

Health

To be healthy and physically fit, you need good health habits. These habits include eating properly, exercising regularly, getting enough sleep, and taking precautions to avoid accidents. For example, using safety belts reduces the risk of fatal injury to people riding in the front seat of a car by 45%. Receiving recommended childhood vaccines reduces the risk of contracting polio, hepatitis, and other diseases. Exercising reduces the risk of heart disease, cancer, and diabetes. Following good habits does more than lower your risk of getting sick or injured. It's also the key to living to a healthy old age.

One of the saddest but most serious U.S. health problems is the use of alcohol, tobacco, and illegal drugs. These substances are bad news—they ruin health and often cause death. Teachers, parents, and others try to make sure that kids know about the dangers of using drugs. But many of these substances are easily available, and kids continue to use them. For example, each day about 3,000 kids start smoking cigarettes.

Kidbits Tidbits

- Of the 33 largest cities in the U.S., New Orleans has the highest percentage of fat people. More than 37% of its residents are considered obese.
- At conception, you consisted of one cell. By the time you're an adult, your body will consist of 100 trillion cells.
- The largest organ in your body is your skin. An adult has about 20 square feet of skin.

Another serious problem is weight control. People of all ages are more likely to be overweight than they were 20 years ago. A full one-third of Americans are obese, or seriously overweight. About 300,000 people die each year because their excess weight led to diabetes, heart disease, and other deadly illnesses. Many people try to fight the "battle of the bulge" by dieting. Billions of dollars are spent annually on special foods, diet clubs, and medicines—all in unsuccessful efforts to lose weight. Americans also spend billions of dollars yearly on vitamins and minerals, to try to make up for not eating enough of the proper foods.

Heart disease and cancer are the major causes of death in the United States. Accidents are the fifth-leading cause. Every 10 minutes, 2 people are killed in accidents. Deadly infectious diseases also claim many lives each year. These are illnesses caused by viruses and other germs—they include AIDS, pneumonia, and the flu.

In comparison to many other countries, Americans are very healthy. Excellent medical care, safe food and water, and good sanitation means that Americans can expect to live an average of 76 years. In some countries, the average life expectancy is less than 50 years. In the U.S., 7.6 infants age one year or less die per 1,000 live births. In more than a dozen countries where most people are very poor, over 100 infants die per 1,000 live births.

Kidbits Tidbits

- The U.S. spends more than $1 trillion a year on health care.
- In 1997, Americans spent about $6.5 billion on vitamin and mineral pills.
- Unintentional injuries are the main cause of death for Americans between the ages of 1 and 24.
- Each year, more than 3,000 Americans under age 15 die in motor-vehicle accidents. Almost 11,000 people between the ages of 15 and 24 die in auto accidents.
- Americans consumed 480 billion cigarettes in 1994. That's almost 2,500 for each person in the country.

Health

Who Exercises the Least?

Studies show that people between the ages of 35–44 excercise the least as a group. Percentage of age group that excercises regularly:

Percentage of age group

- 18–24: 21%
- 25–34: 23%
- 35–44: 20%
- 45–54: 27%
- 55 and up: 28%

Age

SOURCE: Based on data from American Sports Data for SGMA, Active and Ageless

Health

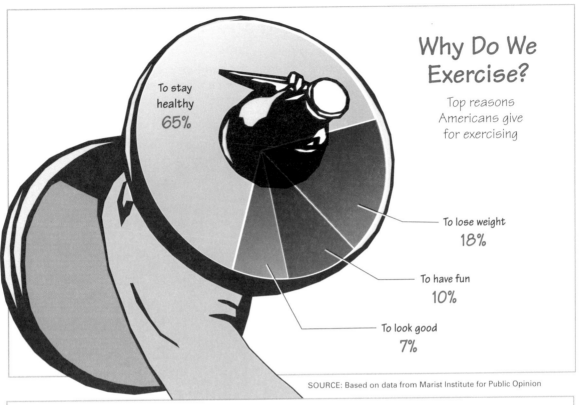

Why Do We Exercise?

Top reasons Americans give for exercising

To stay healthy
65%

To lose weight
18%

To have fun
10%

To look good
7%

SOURCE: Based on data from Marist Institute for Public Opinion

Health

Who Uses Mouthwash the Most?
(By age)

Percentage of age group

60%
50%
40%
30%
20%
10%
0%

18–24   25–34   35–44   45–54   55–64   65+

Age group

SOURCE: Based on data from Mediamark Research

Recommended Daily Dietary Allowances

	Weight (lbs.)	Protein (grams)	Fat soluble vitamins				Water soluble vitamins							Minerals					
			Vitamin A	Vitamin D	Vitamin E	Vitamin K (mcg.)	Vitamin C (mg.)	Thiamine (mg.)	Riboflavin (mg.)	Niacin (mg.)	Vitamin B 6 (mg.)	Folate (mcg.)	Vitamin B 12 (mcg.)	Calcium (mg.)	Phosphorus (mg.)	Magnesium (mg.)	Iron (mg.)	Zinc (mg.)	Iodine (mcg.)
Children																			
1–3	29	16	400	10	6	15	40	0.7	0.8	9	1.0	50	0.7	800	800	80	10	10	70
4–6	44	24	500	10	7	20	45	0.9	1.1	12	1.1	75	1.0	800	800	120	10	10	90
7–10	62	28	700	10	7	30	45	1.0	1.2	13	1.4	100	1.4	800	800	170	10	10	120
Males																			
11–14	99	45	1000	10	10	45	50	1.3	1.5	17	1.7	150	2.0	1200	1200	270	12	15	150
15–18	145	59	1000	10	10	65	60	1.5	1.8	20	2.0	200	2.0	1200	1200	400	12	15	150
Females																			
11–14	101	46	800	10	8	45	50	1.1	1.3	15	1.4	150	2.0	1200	1200	280	15	12	150
15–18	120	44	800	10	8	55	60	1.1	1.3	15	1.5	180	2.0	1200	1200	300	15	12	150

SOURCE: Based on data from the Food and Nutrition Board, National Academy of Sciences–National Research Council; 1989

How Many Calories Do I Need Per Day?

Recommended Daily Dietary Allowances (RDA's)

	Age	Weight (in pounds)	Height (in inches)	Calories needed	Grams of protein needed
Males	11–14	97	63	2,800	44
	15–18	134	69	3,000	54
	19–22	147	69	3,000	54
Females	11–14	97	62	2,400	44
	15–18	119	65	2,100	48
	19–22	128	65	2,100	46

SOURCE: Based on data from *The New York Public Library Desk Reference*

What's the Best Part of Having a Cold?

(Kids ages 7–11)

Pre-teens were asked what they like most about being sick or having a cold.

Something else
3%

Eating ice cream
5%

Sleeping a lot
17%

Being waited on
18%

Watching TV/videos
25%

Missing school
32%

SOURCE: Based on data from *Breathe Right* Stuffy Nose News Survey

Health

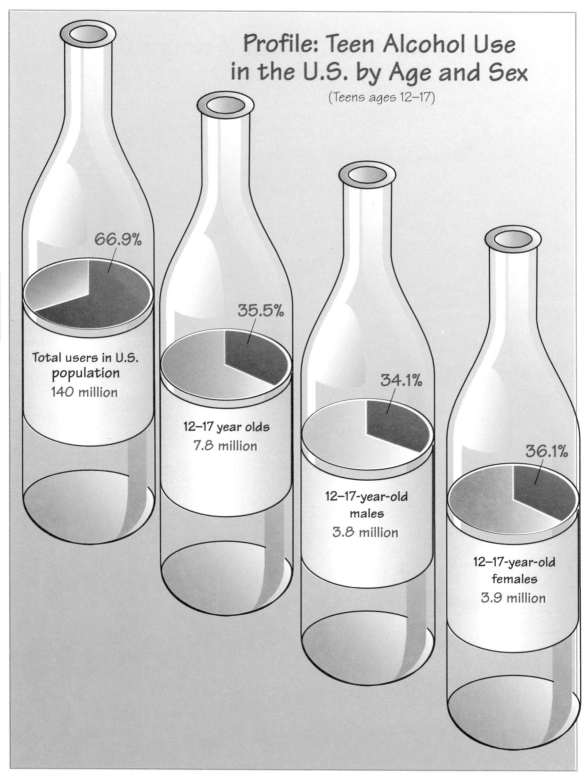

Profile: Teen Alcohol Use in the U.S. by Age and Sex
(Teens ages 12–17)

66.9%

Total users in U.S. population
140 million

35.5%

12–17 year olds
7.8 million

34.1%

12–17-year-old males
3.8 million

36.1%

12–17-year-old females
3.9 million

SOURCE: Based on data from U.S. Dept. of Health and Human Services

How Long Does It Take My Body to Absorb Alcohol?

Drinking and driving is a very dangerous combination. Many states have very strict laws for people who drive while intoxicated. The following chart is intended as a general guideline of how long to wait after drinking before driving a motor vehicle. The time varies, however, from person to person. The best rule is "Never drink and drive." In the following chart, one drink equals 1 1/2 ounces of liquor (86 proof) or 4 ounces of wine or champagne or 12 ounces of beer.

Body weight (in pounds)	1 drink	2 drinks	3 drinks	4 drinks	5 drinks	6 drinks
100–119	30–45 min.	3 hours	6 hours	10 hours	13 hours	16 hours
120–139	30–45 min.	2 hours	5 hours	8 hours	10 hours	12 hours
140–159	30–45 min.	2 hours	4 hours	6 hours	8 hours	10 hours
160–179	30–45 min.	1 hour	3 hours	5 hours	7 hours	9 hours
180–199	30–45 min.	30–45 min	2 hours	4 hours	6 hours	7 hours
200–219	30–45 min.	30–45 min	2 hours	3 hours	5 hours	6 hours
Over 220	30–45 min.	30–45 min	1 hour	3 hours	4 hours	6 hours

SOURCE: Based on data from *The New York Public Library Desk Reference*

U.S. Annual Alcohol Consumption

(Gallons of alcohol per person, 1940–1994)

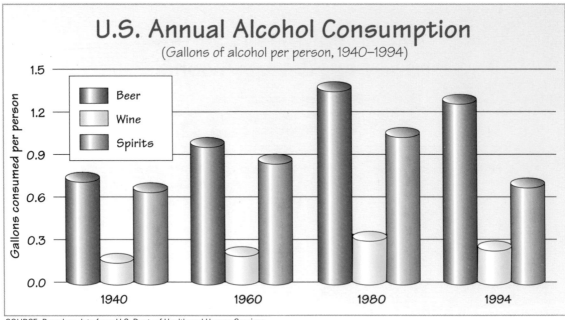

SOURCE: Based on data from U.S. Dept. of Health and Human Services

What Are the Most Commonly Abused Drugs?

Drug	Primary Effect	Popular Names
Alcohol	Depressant	Drink, booze
Amphetamines	Stimulant	Pep pills, uppers; *methamphetamines:* speed, crystal, crank, ice
Amyl or butyl nitrites	Stimulant	Poppers, snappers, rush, locker room
Barbituates	Depressant	Sleeping pills, dolls
Cocaine	Stimulant	Coke, snow, lady; *smokable form:* crack
Ephedra	Stimulant	Ma huang; *brand names:* Herbal Ecstacy, Euphoria, Buzz Tablets, Brain Wash
Heroin	Depressant	Snow, smack; *synthetic form:* China white, Persian heroin, gasoline dope; *combined heroin & cocaine:* speedball
D-lysergic acid diethylamide	Hallucinogen	LSD, acid
Marijuana	Hallucinogen/ depressant	Pot, grass, joint, cannabis, dope, reefer, weed, herb, skunk
MDMA (combination of synthetic mescaline and an amphetamine)	Stimulant/ hallucinogen	Ecstacy, love potion
Mescaline	Hallucinogen	Peyote, cactus
Morphine	Depressant	
PCP (phencyclidine)	Hallucinogen	Angel dust
Tranquilizers	Depressants	Downers, *brand names:* Valium, Librium, Darvon

SOURCE: Based on data from U.S. Dept. of Health and Human Services

Profile: Drug Use by U.S. High School Seniors, 1996

(By percentage of students who ever used)

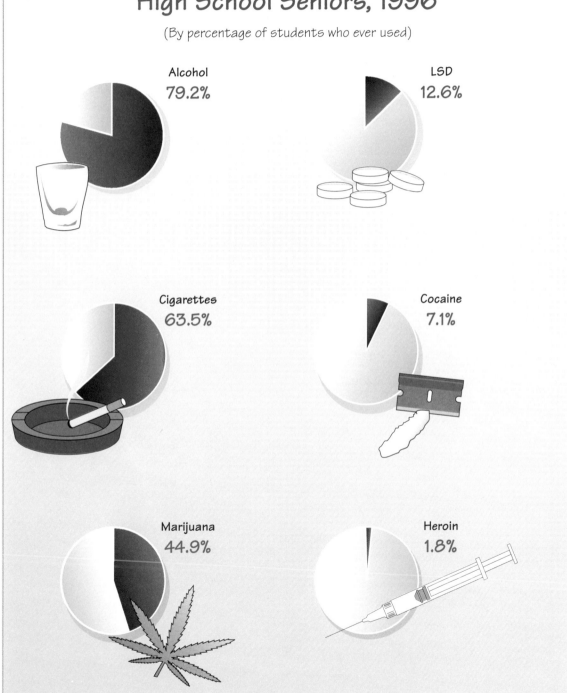

Alcohol
79.2%

LSD
12.6%

Cigarettes
63.5%

Cocaine
7.1%

Marijuana
44.9%

Heroin
1.8%

SOURCE: Based on data from University of Michigan, Institute for Social Research

Health

Health

Smoking: What Does Starting Age Have to Do With Quitting Age?

Adults who start smoking in their early teens are more likely to still be smoking at age 30. Of those who've quit by age 30, the percentage of smokers who:

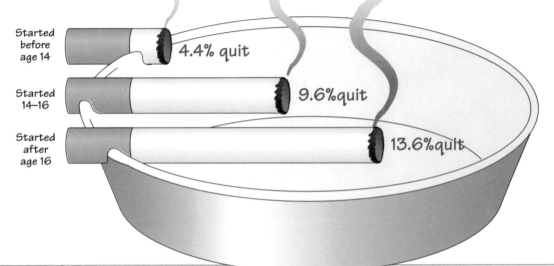

Started before age 14 — 4.4% quit

Started 14–16 — 9.6% quit

Started after age 16 — 13.6% quit

SOURCE: Based on data from *American Journal of Public Health*

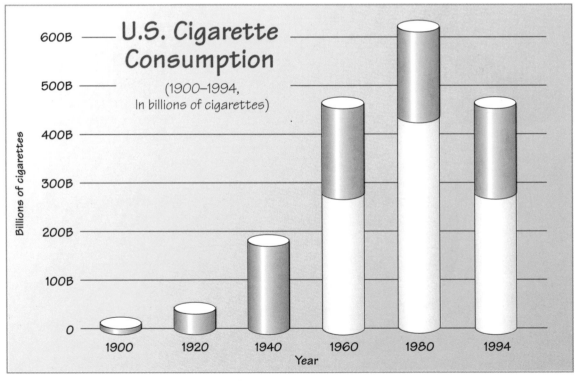

U.S. Cigarette Consumption

(1900–1994, In billions of cigarettes)

Billions of cigarettes

Year: 1900, 1920, 1940, 1960, 1980, 1994

SOURCE: Based on data from U.S. Dept. of Health and Human Services

Profile: Teenage Tobacco Users

Cigarette use is about equal among teen males
and females. Teen males, however, make up the
vast majority of smokeless tobacco users.

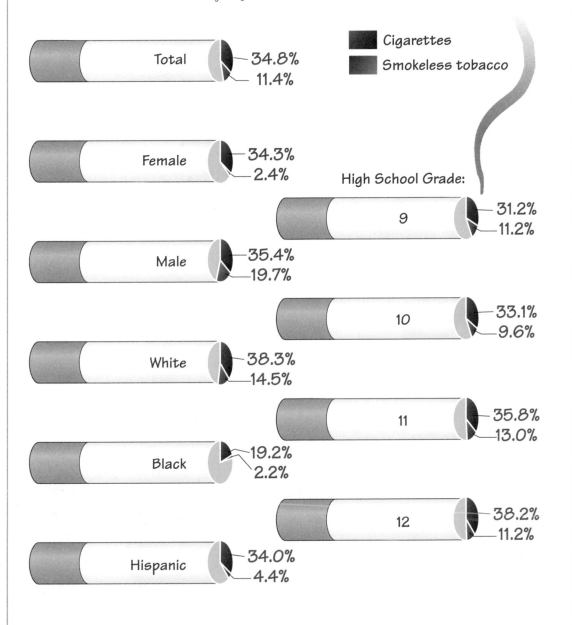

Cigarettes
Smokeless tobacco

Total — 34.8% / 11.4%

Female — 34.3% / 2.4%

Male — 35.4% / 19.7%

White — 38.3% / 14.5%

Black — 19.2% / 2.2%

Hispanic — 34.0% / 4.4%

High School Grade:

9 — 31.2% / 11.2%

10 — 33.1% / 9.6%

11 — 35.8% / 13.0%

12 — 38.2% / 11.2%

Health

SOURCE: Based on data from U.S. Dept. of Health and Human Services

Health

Profile: Where Do Kids Under Age 18 Get Cigarettes?

(By race)

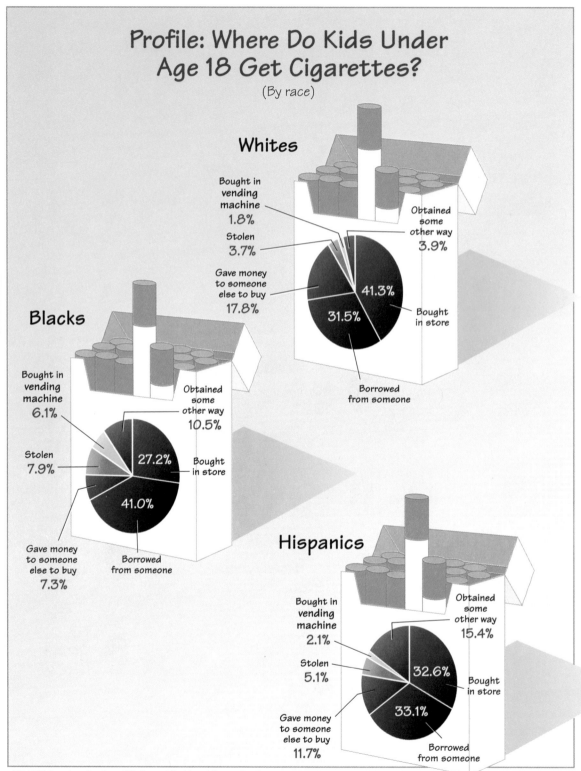

Whites

Bought in vending machine 1.8%

Stolen 3.7%

Gave money to someone else to buy 17.8%

Obtained some other way 3.9%

41.3% Bought in store

31.5%

Borrowed from someone

Blacks

Bought in vending machine 6.1%

Obtained some other way 10.5%

Stolen 7.9%

27.2% Bought in store

41.0%

Gave money to someone else to buy 7.3%

Borrowed from someone

Hispanics

Bought in vending machine 2.1%

Obtained some other way 15.4%

Stolen 5.1%

32.6% Bought in store

33.1%

Gave money to someone else to buy 11.7%

Borrowed from someone

SOURCE: Based on data from U.S. Dept. of Health and Human Services

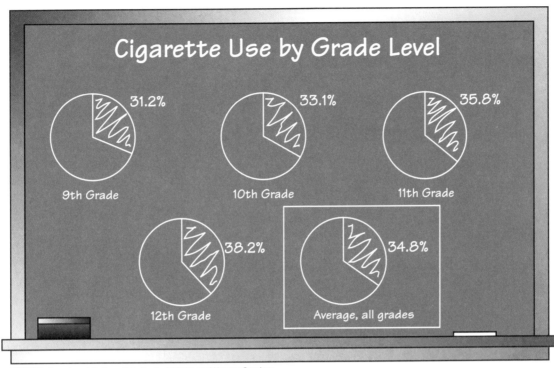

Cigarette Use by Grade Level

31.2% — 9th Grade

33.1% — 10th Grade

35.8% — 11th Grade

38.2% — 12th Grade

34.8% — Average, all grades

SOURCE: Based on data from U.S. Dept. of Health and Human Services

Health

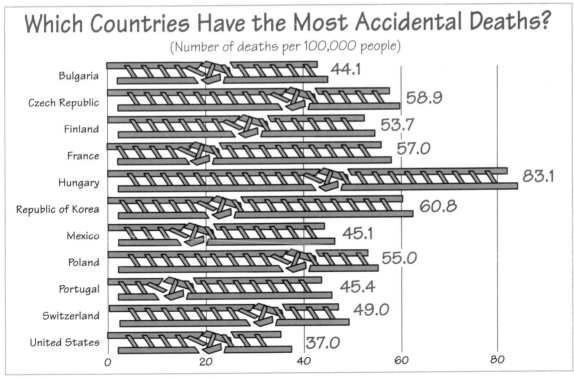

Which Countries Have the Most Accidental Deaths?

(Number of deaths per 100,000 people)

Country	Deaths
Bulgaria	44.1
Czech Republic	58.9
Finland	53.7
France	57.0
Hungary	83.1
Republic of Korea	60.8
Mexico	45.1
Poland	55.0
Portugal	45.4
Switzerland	49.0
United States	37.0

SOURCE: Based on data from World Health Organization

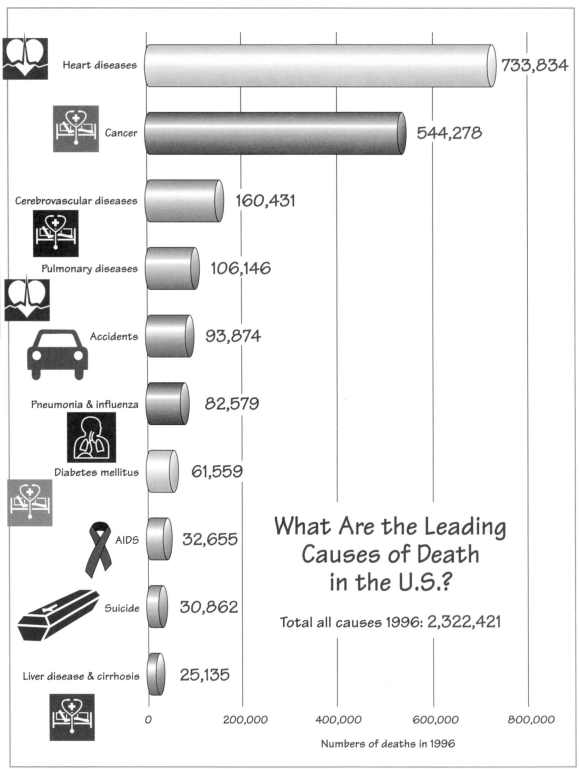

Heart diseases 733,834

Cancer 544,278

Cerebrovascular diseases 160,431

Pulmonary diseases 106,146

Accidents 93,874

Pneumonia & influenza 82,579

Diabetes mellitus 61,559

AIDS 32,655

Suicide 30,862

Liver disease & cirrhosis 25,135

What Are the Leading Causes of Death in the U.S.?

Total all causes 1996: 2,322,421

0   200,000   400,000   600,000   800,000

Numbers of deaths in 1996

Health

SOURCE: Based on data from National Center for Health Statistics, U.S. Dept. of Health and Human Services, 1997

Which Nations Have the Highest Death Rates?

(Projected number of deaths per 1,000 persons)

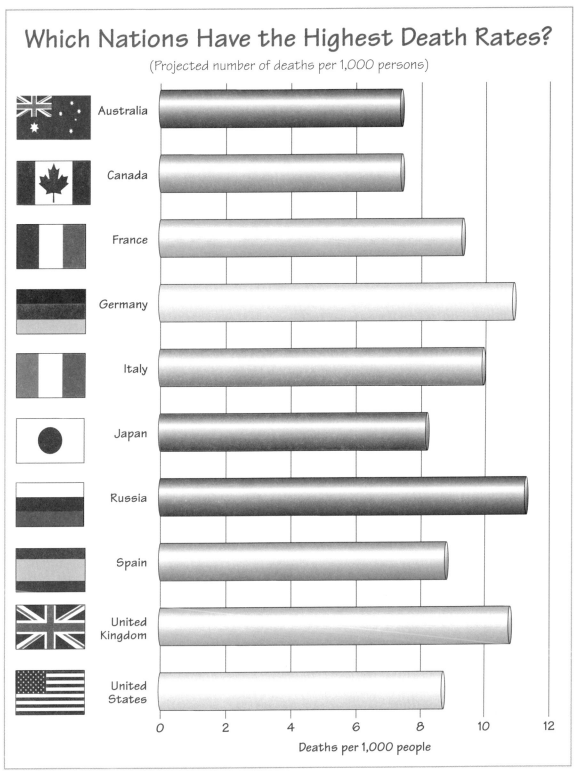

Deaths per 1,000 people

Health

SOURCE: Based on data from U.S. Bureau of the Census, International Data Base

Health

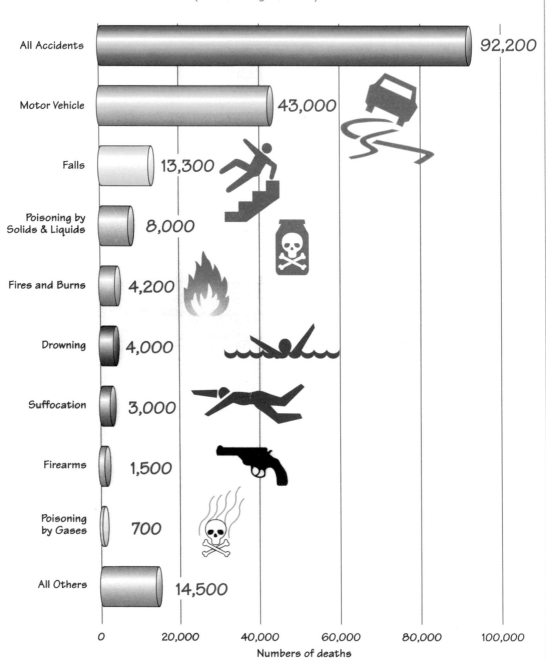

What Are the Most Common Types of Accidental Deaths in the U.S.?

(Total, all ages, 1995)

Category	Number
All Accidents	92,200
Motor Vehicle	43,000
Falls	13,300
Poisoning by Solids & Liquids	8,000
Fires and Burns	4,200
Drowning	4,000
Suffocation	3,000
Firearms	1,500
Poisoning by Gases	700
All Others	14,500

Numbers of deaths

0   20,000   40,000   60,000   80,000   100,000

SOURCE: Based on data from National Safety Council, 1995

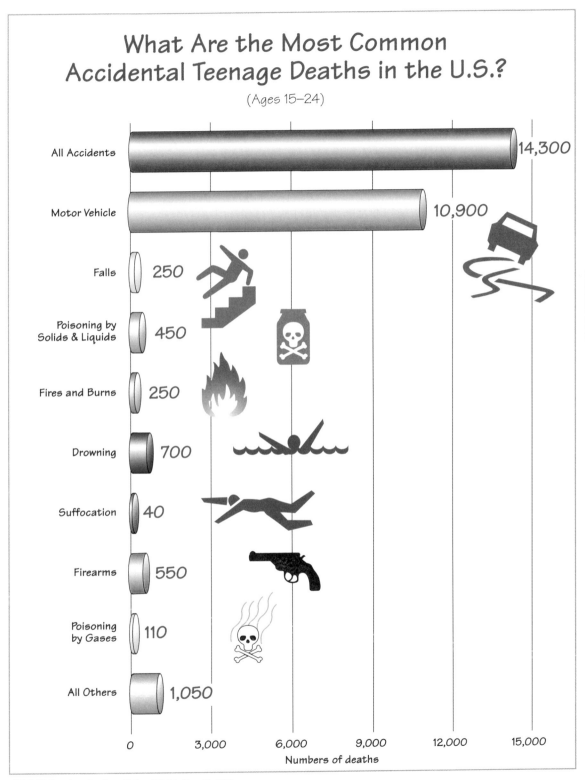

What Are the Most Common Accidental Teenage Deaths in the U.S.?

(Ages 15–24)

Category	Deaths
All Accidents	14,300
Motor Vehicle	10,900
Falls	250
Poisoning by Solids & Liquids	450
Fires and Burns	250
Drowning	700
Suffocation	40
Firearms	550
Poisoning by Gases	110
All Others	1,050

Numbers of deaths

SOURCE: Based on data from National Safety Council, 1995

Health

Health

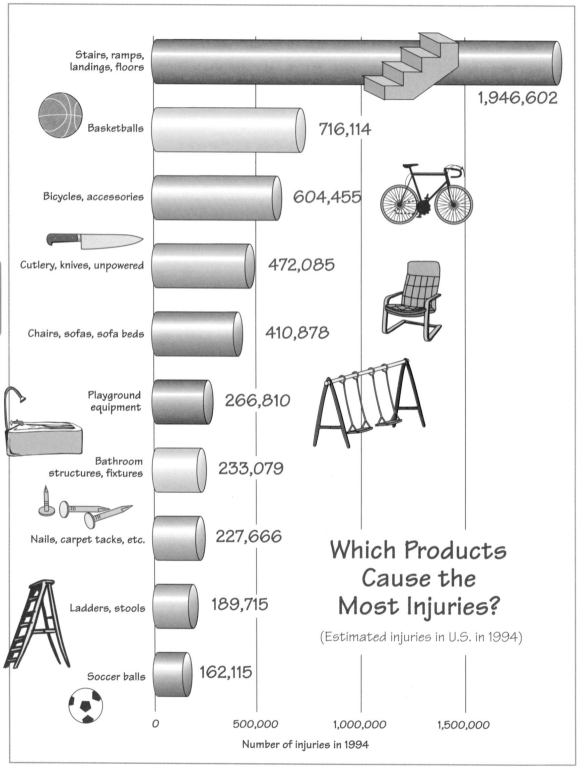

Stairs, ramps, landings, floors — 1,946,602

Basketballs — 716,114

Bicycles, accessories — 604,455

Cutlery, knives, unpowered — 472,085

Chairs, sofas, sofa beds — 410,878

Playground equipment — 266,810

Bathroom structures, fixtures — 233,079

Nails, carpet tacks, etc. — 227,666

Ladders, stools — 189,715

Soccer balls — 162,115

0   500,000   1,000,000   1,500,000

Number of injuries in 1994

Which Products Cause the Most Injuries?

(Estimated injuries in U.S. in 1994)

SOURCE: Based on data from Consumer Product Safety Commission, 1995

Estimated Number of People Living with AIDS, by Region, 1996

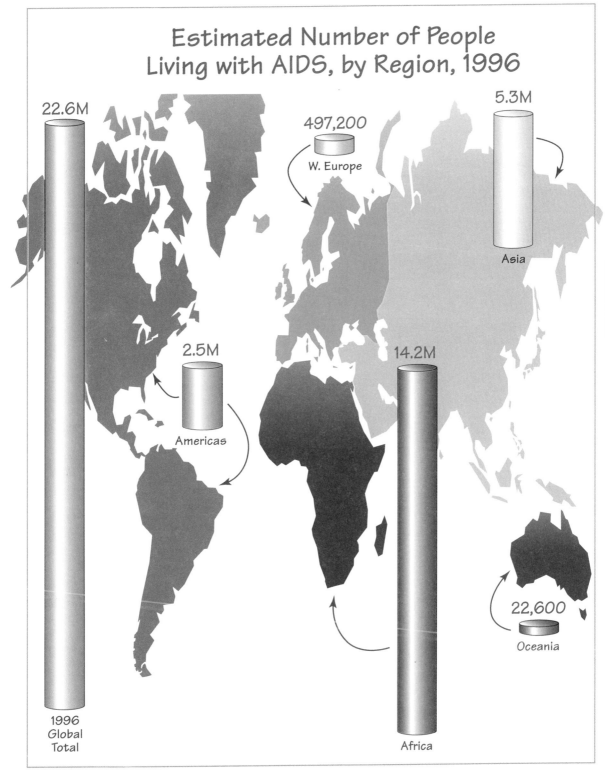

22.6M

1996 Global Total

497,200
W. Europe

5.3M
Asia

2.5M
Americas

14.2M

Africa

22,600
Oceania

Health

SOURCE: Based on data from World Health Organization, Global Programme on AIDS

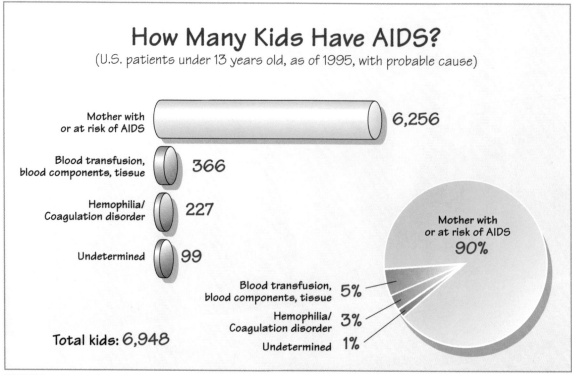

How Many Kids Have AIDS?

(U.S. patients under 13 years old, as of 1995, with probable cause)

Mother with or at risk of AIDS — 6,256

Blood transfusion, blood components, tissue — 366

Hemophilia/ Coagulation disorder — 227

Undetermined — 99

Total kids: 6,948

Mother with or at risk of AIDS
90%

Blood transfusion, blood components, tissue — 5%

Hemophilia/ Coagulation disorder — 3%

Undetermined — 1%

SOURCE: Based on data from U.S. Dept. of Health and Human Services, 1996

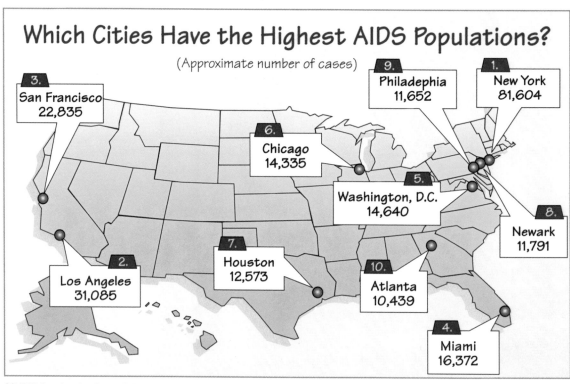

Which Cities Have the Highest AIDS Populations?

(Approximate number of cases)

3. San Francisco 22,835

9. Philadephia 11,652

1. New York 81,604

6. Chicago 14,335

5. Washington, D.C. 14,640

8. Newark 11,791

7. Houston 12,573

2. Los Angeles 31,085

10. Atlanta 10,439

4. Miami 16,372

SOURCE: Based on data from U.S. Dept. of Health and Human Services

Health

Estimated Cumulative HIV/AIDS Cases by Region, Mid-1996

(With percentage of adults living with HIV)

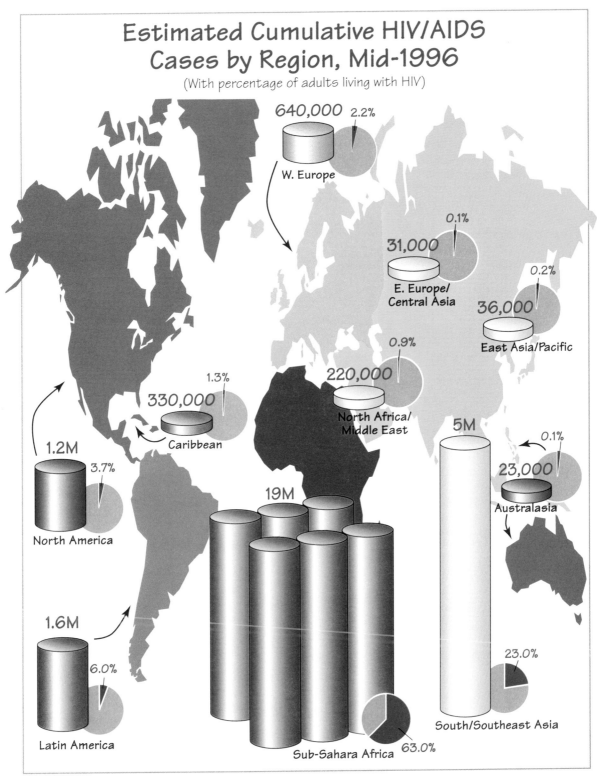

640,000 2.2%
W. Europe

31,000 0.1%
E. Europe/ Central Asia

36,000 0.2%
East Asia/Pacific

220,000 0.9%
North Africa/ Middle East

330,000 1.3%
Caribbean

1.2M 3.7%
North America

5M
23,000 0.1%
Australasia

19M
Sub-Sahara Africa 63.0%

1.6M 6.0%
Latin America

23.0%
South/Southeast Asia

SOURCE: Based on data from UNAIDS Program, United Nations

Health

Recreation

Kids have lots of free time—and lots of cool and exciting ways to fill it! Sports, games, dancing, amusement parks, movies and TV, hanging out with friends, talking on the phone—these are just a few of the things that kids do to relax and have fun.

Some recreational activities are more fun when done as part of a group, and kids are super joiners. About 5.3 million boys belong to the Boy Scouts of America. Almost 3.4 million girls are members of Girl Scouts of the U.S.A. Sports teams, school bands, 4-H clubs, and religious groups are other organizations that attract millions of young people each year.

Taking trips with the family are also popular recreations. In fact, vacations are the best-loved activities of 52% of kids ages 7 to 12! Some vacations include long-distance trips to see famous places such as national parks, historic monuments, and Disney World. Other vacations are highlighted by shorter family activities, such as outings to local beaches or afternoons spent learning how to fish.

Kidbits Tidbits

- A survey of teens in 26 countries found that 93% enjoyed watching TV but only 76% enjoyed playing sports.
- Bowling is among the most popular recreational activities. About 80 million Americans age 5 and older bowl each year.
- Americans spend more than $14 billion a year on boating.
- Almost $6 billion was spent at U.S. amusement parks in 1994.

Some activities are more popular with girls than boys, and vice versa. Boys and girls participate in swimming, bowling, and tennis in about equal numbers. But fishing and billiards are much more popular with boys. Horseback riding and volleyball, however, are more popular with girls. Age and finances also play roles in determining people's recreational favorites. More kids than adults play soccer—but more adults than kids can pay the fees required to ski and play golf.

People of all ages can have fun—and get a lot of satisfaction—while helping others. Almost half of the kids in grades 6 through 12 are involved in some kind of volunteer service. For example, a Florida boy organized a program to deliver unused school cafeteria food to poor people. A Boy Scout troop grew vegetables for a homeless shelter. Many teens carry out conservation projects, teach younger kids to read, or assist the elderly and people with disabilities. Teens say that one of the main reasons they lend a helping hand to others is because they feel compassion for people in need.

Of course, not all recreation is for a noble cause. Some of the most popular pastimes in America include going to the movies and watching TV and videos. In fact, about 60% of the U.S. population says they exercise and go to the movies with much of their free time. For kids ages 7–12, movies and TV are ranked behind vacations, outdoor play, and listening to music as favorites.

Recreation

Kidbits Tidbits

- Symphony orchestra concerts draw over 24 million attendees a year.
- Almost 50% of kids in grades 6 through 12 are involved in some kind of volunteer service.
- Teens who are asked to volunteer are much more likely to do so than teens who aren't asked.
- Each year, Americans donate about 20 billion hours of their time to help each other and their communities.

Recreation

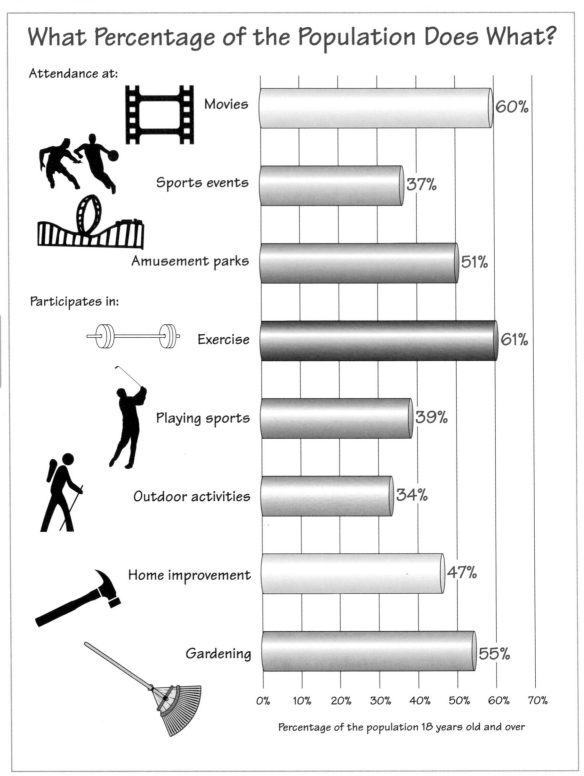

What Percentage of the Population Does What?

Attendance at:

Movies — 60%

Sports events — 37%

Amusement parks — 51%

Participates in:

Exercise — 61%

Playing sports — 39%

Outdoor activities — 34%

Home improvement — 47%

Gardening — 55%

0% 10% 20% 30% 40% 50% 60% 70%

Percentage of the population 18 years old and over

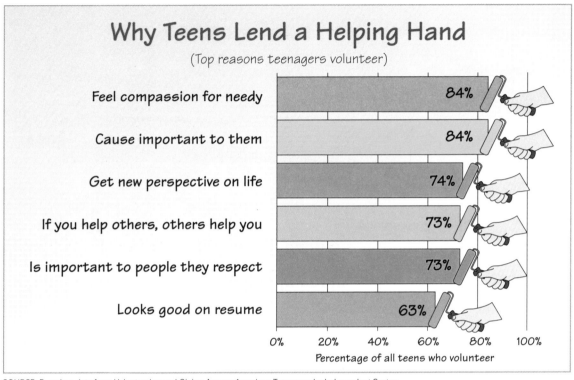

Why Teens Lend a Helping Hand

(Top reasons teenagers volunteer)

Feel compassion for needy	84%
Cause important to them	84%
Get new perspective on life	74%
If you help others, others help you	73%
Is important to people they respect	73%
Looks good on resume	63%

0% 20% 40% 60% 80% 100%

Percentage of all teens who volunteer

SOURCE: Based on data from Volunteering and Giving Among American Teenagers by Independent Sector

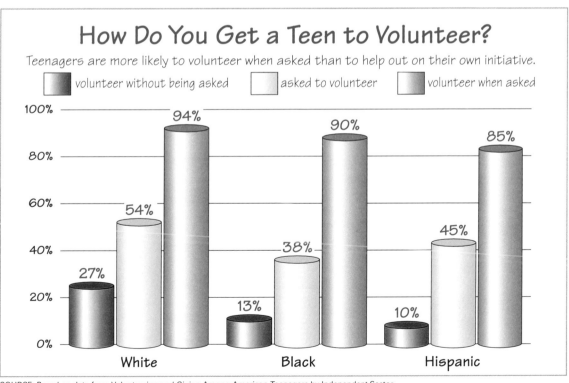

How Do You Get a Teen to Volunteer?

Teenagers are more likely to volunteer when asked than to help out on their own initiative.

■ volunteer without being asked   □ asked to volunteer   ▢ volunteer when asked

	White	Black	Hispanic
volunteer without being asked	27%	13%	10%
asked to volunteer	54%	38%	45%
volunteer when asked	94%	90%	85%

SOURCE: Based on data from Volunteering and Giving Among American Teenagers by Independent Sector

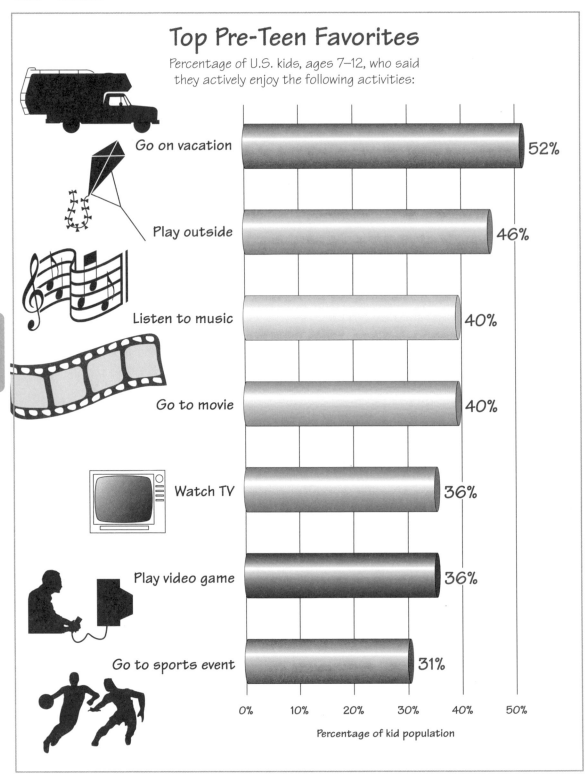

Top Pre-Teen Favorites

Percentage of U.S. kids, ages 7–12, who said
they actively enjoy the following activities:

Recreation

Go on vacation — 52%

Play outside — 46%

Listen to music — 40%

Go to movie — 40%

Watch TV — 36%

Play video game — 36%

Go to sports event — 31%

0% 10% 20% 30% 40% 50%

Percentage of kid population

SOURCE: Based on data from A.B.C. Global Kids Study

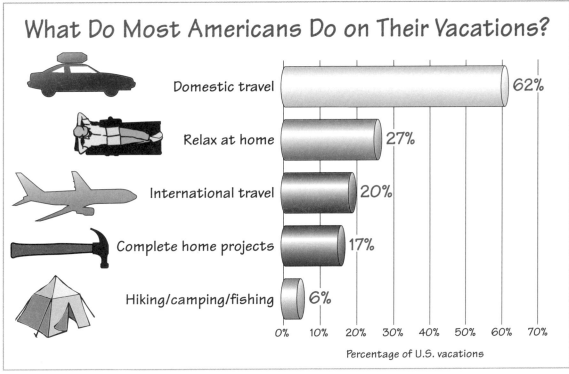

What Do Most Americans Do on Their Vacations?

Domestic travel — 62%

Relax at home — 27%

International travel — 20%

Complete home projects — 17%

Hiking/camping/fishing — 6%

Percentage of U.S. vacations

SOURCE: Based on data from Aragon Consulting Group

Recreation

Membership in the Boy Scouts and Girl Scouts

(In millions)

Members in millions

5.3M — Boy Scouts

3.4M — Girl Scouts

SOURCE: Based on data from Boy Scouts of America and Girl Scouts of the United States of America, 1994

Recreation

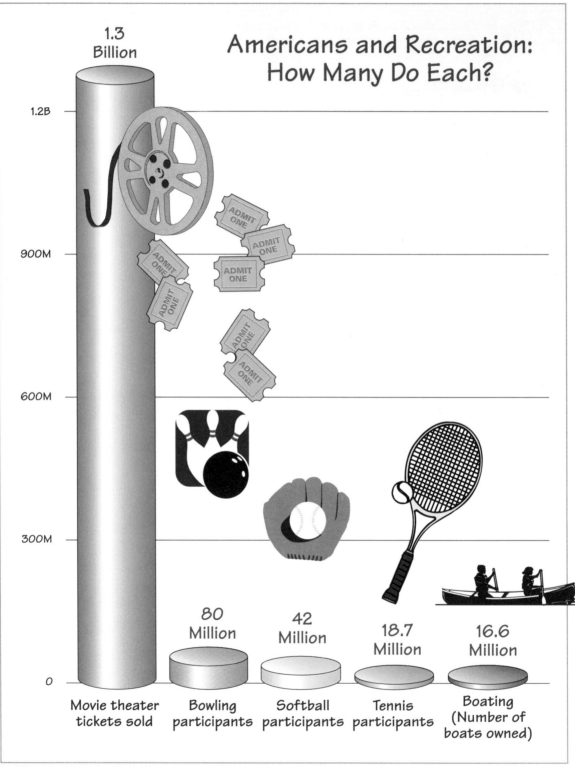

Americans and Recreation: How Many Do Each?

1.3 Billion

1.2B

900M

600M

300M

0

80 Million

42 Million

18.7 Million

16.6 Million

Movie theater tickets sold

Bowling participants

Softball participants

Tennis participants

Boating (Number of boats owned)

SOURCES: Based on data from Motion Picture Association of America, Inc.; National Bowling Council; Amateur Softball Association; Tennis Industry Association; National Marine Manufacturers Association

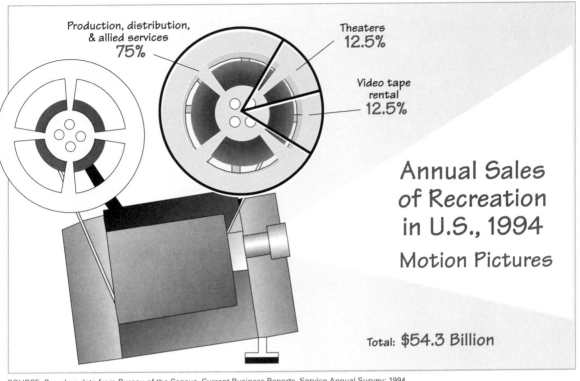

Production, distribution,
& allied services
75%

Theaters
12.5%

Video tape
rental
12.5%

Annual Sales of Recreation in U.S., 1994

Motion Pictures

Total: **$54.3 Billion**

SOURCE: Based on data from Bureau of the Census, Current Business Reports, Service Annual Survey: 1994

Recreation

Annual Sales of Recreation in U.S., 1994
Amusement & Recreation Services
Total: **$69.2 Billion**

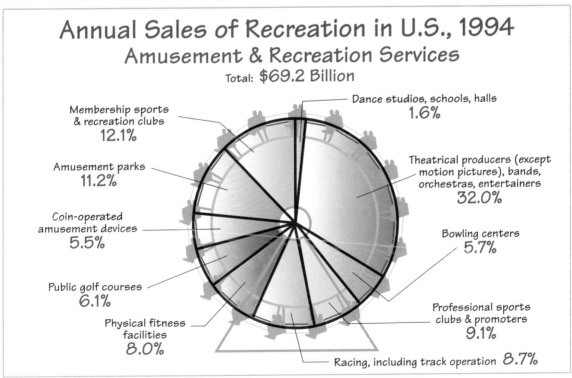

Dance studios, schools, halls
1.6%

Membership sports
& recreation clubs
12.1%

Amusement parks
11.2%

Theatrical producers (except
motion pictures), bands,
orchestras, entertainers
32.0%

Coin-operated
amusement devices
5.5%

Bowling centers
5.7%

Public golf courses
6.1%

Professional sports
clubs & promoters
9.1%

Physical fitness
facilities
8.0%

Racing, including track operation **8.7%**

SOURCE: Based on data from Bureau of the Census, Current Business Reports, Service Annual Survey: 1994

Recreation

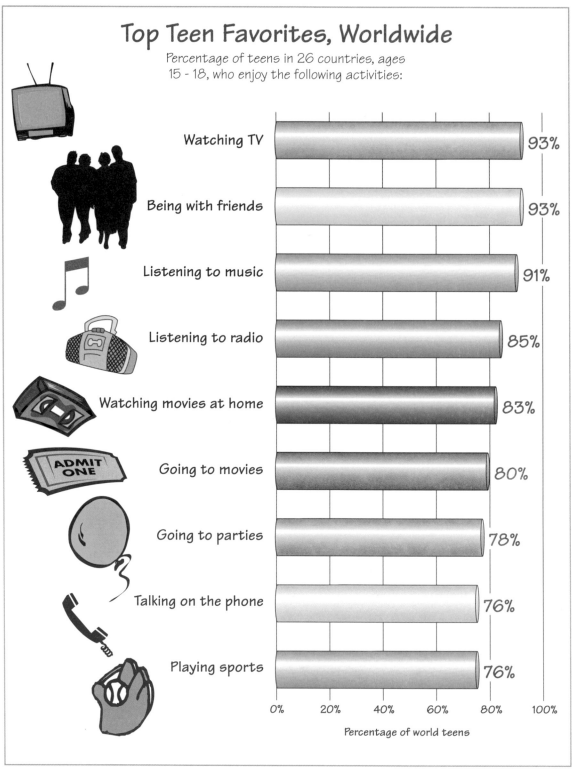

Top Teen Favorites, Worldwide

Percentage of teens in 26 countries, ages
15 - 18, who enjoy the following activities:

Activity	Percentage
Watching TV	93%
Being with friends	93%
Listening to music	91%
Listening to radio	85%
Watching movies at home	83%
Going to movies	80%
Going to parties	78%
Talking on the phone	76%
Playing sports	76%

0%   20%   40%   60%   80%   100%

Percentage of world teens

SOURCE: Based on data from New World Teen Study, The BrainWaves Group

Bike Paths to the Future

Between 1991 and 1997 more than $1 billion in highway taxes was spent on bike paths and walkways in America.
(In millions)

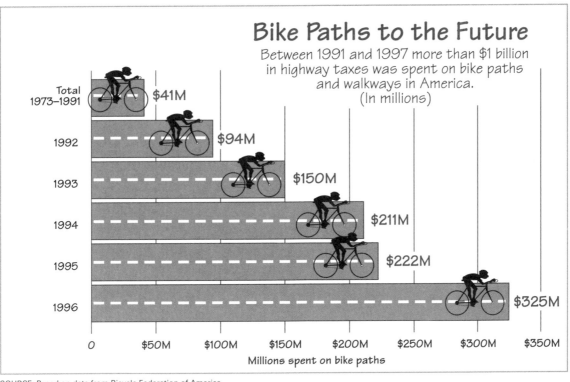

Total 1973–1991 — $41M
1992 — $94M
1993 — $150M
1994 — $211M
1995 — $222M
1996 — $325M

Millions spent on bike paths

SOURCE: Based on data from Bicycle Federation of America

Recreation

Reel Fun

About 18% of Americans older than 16—35.2 million people—fished in 1996, averaging 17.7 days of fishing per person. Most common types of fishing by fishers:

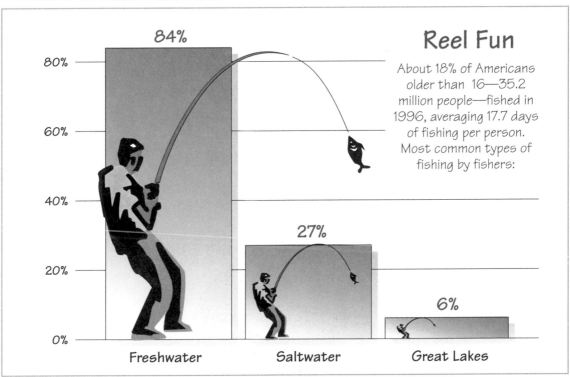

Freshwater 84%
Saltwater 27%
Great Lakes 6%

SOURCE: Based on data from Fishing, Hunting and Wildlife-Associated Recreation

Music

Music lovers today have lots of cool opportunities to hear their favorite groups on CDs, videos, television, and radio; in concert halls; and at live music festivals—even on the Internet! These days, it's not unusual for a CD to sell millions of copies in a matter of weeks, or for a concert to attract upwards of 100,000 fans!

Rock is by far the most popular type of music among young people, but many other kinds of music also enjoy wide appeal. Country, rap, pop, hip-hop, rhythm-and-blues, folk, gospel, jazz, and even classical all have solid followings. Some of American kids' favorite musicians are in their own age group. They're teenagers such as country singer LeAnn Rimes, blues singer Jonny Lang, and the pop phenom group Hanson, for example.

Americans spent a whopping $12.5 billion on recorded music in 1996. Out of that, American teens are the biggest customers: people ages 15 to 19 accounted for 17.2% of total sales; kids age 10 to 14 added another 7.9%. CDs are the most popular recorded music format, with 68.4% of 1996 sales. Cassettes were second with 19.3%.

Kidbits Tidbits

● In 1996, kids 15–19 accounted for 17.2% of all recorded music sales; kids 10–14 added another 7.9%.

● In 1996, rock was the most popular type of music sold, accounting for 32.6% of all sales. Country was next, with 14.7%.

● In the 1960s, about 45 new albums were released each week. By the late 1990s, an average of 710 CDs were released weekly.

● In 1996, Atlantic was the #1 music label, with 8% of the market.

Young people's favorites constantly change. What's "hot" with kids today won't be "cool" with kids tomorrow. But, while some musicians are one-hit wonders, others keep going for years and years. For example, Elvis Presley records are still selling strong more than 20 years after his death. As of the end of 1997, the best-selling albums of all time in the U.S. were Michael Jackson's *Thriller* (25 million copies) and *Their Greatest Hits* from the Eagles (24 million). And, though the Rolling Stones have been around for over 30 years, they managed to pull off the top grossing tour of 1997; their "Bridges to Babylon" tour took in $89.3 million.

There are more than 576 million radios in the U.S., including 367 million in homes and 142 million in cars. Each weekday, 95% of Americans over age 12 listen to radio for an average of 3 hours. There are over 12,000 radio stations, with country music stations the most common (2,525).

Enjoying music isn't always a couch potato activity. Millions of kids sing and play instruments. And when music has a good beat, everyone wants to jump up and dance. Dance crazes come and go. The '70s was disco. The 80's was slam-dancing. The mid-1990s was macarena time. Any guesses which dances kids will be doing 10 years from now and what kind of music will be #1 on the charts?

Kidbits Tidbits

● About half of all music albums are bought in record stores; about one-third are bought in discount stores such as Wal-Mart and K-Mart.

● Elvis Presley's records have sold more than 1 billion copies, making him the most successful solo recording artist ever.

● The best-selling single of all time is Elton John's *Candle in the Wind*, re-released when Princess Diana died.

● The top pop album in early 1998 was *Titanic*, featuring the soundtrack from the mega-hit film of the same name.

● Radios are everywhere: nearly every car in America has one and 98% of American homes own at least one.

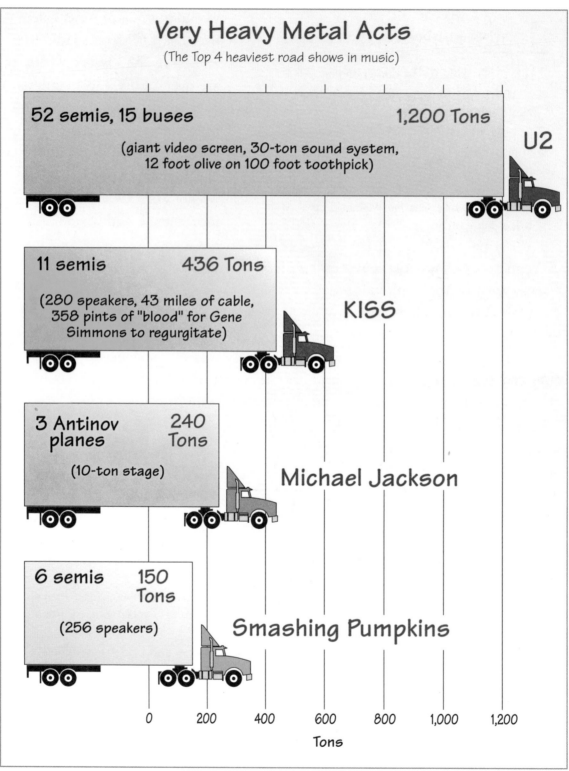

Very Heavy Metal Acts

(The Top 4 heaviest road shows in music)

52 semis, 15 buses   **1,200 Tons**

(giant video screen, 30-ton sound system,
12 foot olive on 100 foot toothpick)

U2

11 semis   **436 Tons**

(280 speakers, 43 miles of cable,
358 pints of "blood" for Gene
Simmons to regurgitate)

KISS

3 Antinov planes   **240 Tons**

(10-ton stage)

Michael Jackson

6 semis   **150 Tons**

(256 speakers)

Smashing Pumpkins

0   200   400   600   800   1,000   1,200

Tons

Music

SOURCE: Based on data from *LIVE!*

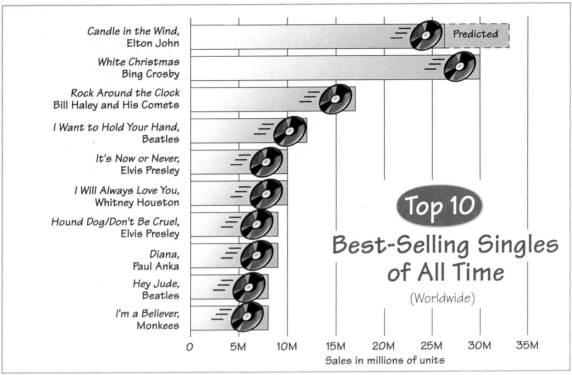

Top 10

Best-Selling Singles of All Time

(Worldwide)

Candle in the Wind, Elton John — Predicted
White Christmas, Bing Crosby
Rock Around the Clock, Bill Haley and His Comets
I Want to Hold Your Hand, Beatles
It's Now or Never, Elvis Presley
I Will Always Love You, Whitney Houston
Hound Dog/Don't Be Cruel, Elvis Presley
Diana, Paul Anka
Hey Jude, Beatles
I'm a Believer, Monkees

0   5M   10M   15M   20M   25M   30M   35M
Sales in millions of units

Source: Based on information given in *The Top 10 of Everything 1997*

Music

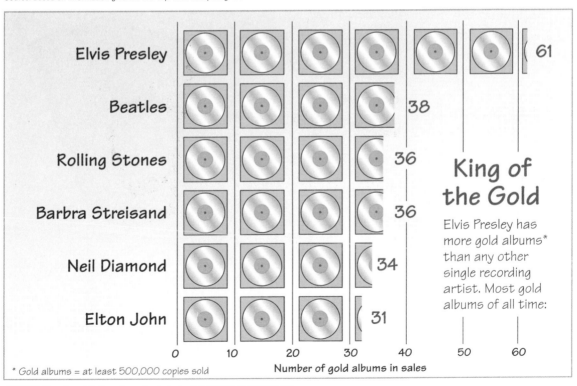

Elvis Presley — 61
Beatles — 38
Rolling Stones — 36
Barbra Streisand — 36
Neil Diamond — 34
Elton John — 31

King of the Gold

Elvis Presley has more gold albums* than any other single recording artist. Most gold albums of all time:

0   10   20   30   40   50   60
Number of gold albums in sales

* Gold albums = at least 500,000 copies sold

SOURCE: Based on data from Recording Industry Association of America, Inc.

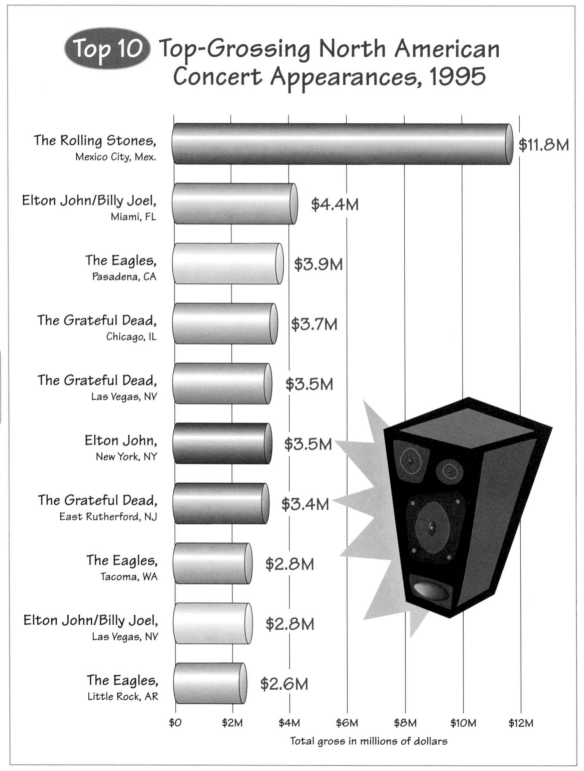

Top 10 Top-Grossing North American Concert Appearances, 1995

Artist	Total gross
The Rolling Stones, Mexico City, Mex.	$11.8M
Elton John/Billy Joel, Miami, FL	$4.4M
The Eagles, Pasadena, CA	$3.9M
The Grateful Dead, Chicago, IL	$3.7M
The Grateful Dead, Las Vegas, NV	$3.5M
Elton John, New York, NY	$3.5M
The Grateful Dead, East Rutherford, NJ	$3.4M
The Eagles, Tacoma, WA	$2.8M
Elton John/Billy Joel, Las Vegas, NV	$2.8M
The Eagles, Little Rock, AR	$2.6M

Total gross in millions of dollars

Music

SOURCE: Based on data from Pollstar, Fresno, CA

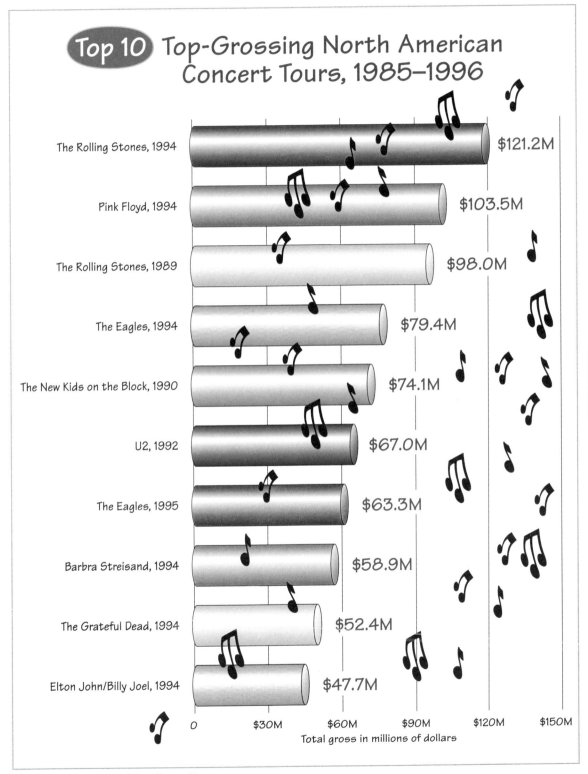

Top 10 Top-Grossing North American Concert Tours, 1985–1996

The Rolling Stones, 1994	$121.2M
Pink Floyd, 1994	$103.5M
The Rolling Stones, 1989	$98.0M
The Eagles, 1994	$79.4M
The New Kids on the Block, 1990	$74.1M
U2, 1992	$67.0M
The Eagles, 1995	$63.3M
Barbra Streisand, 1994	$58.9M
The Grateful Dead, 1994	$52.4M
Elton John/Billy Joel, 1994	$47.7M

0 $30M $60M $90M $120M $150M

Total gross in millions of dollars

Music

SOURCE: Based on data from Pollstar, Fresno, CA

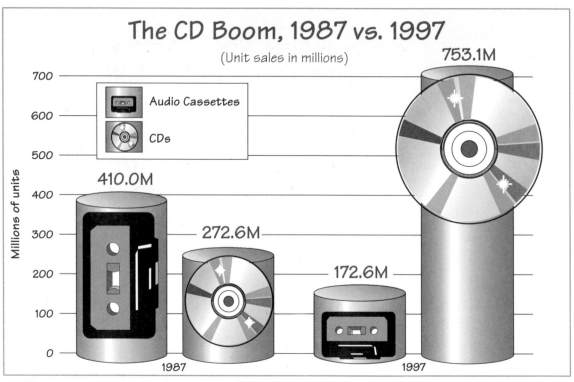

The CD Boom, 1987 vs. 1997

(Unit sales in millions)

753.1M

410.0M

272.6M

172.6M

Millions of units (y-axis: 0, 100, 200, 300, 400, 500, 600, 700)

- Audio Cassettes
- CDs

1987   1997

SOURCE: Based on data from Recording Industry Association of America, 1998

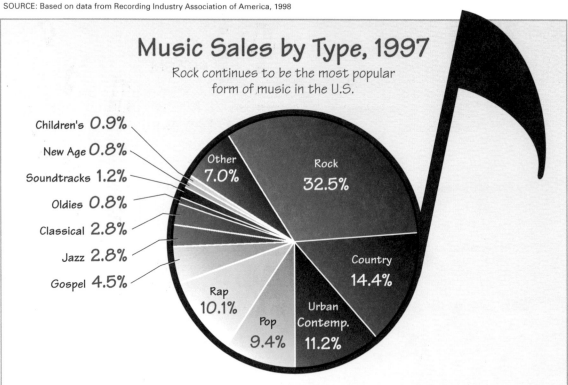

Music Sales by Type, 1997

Rock continues to be the most popular
form of music in the U.S.

Children's 0.9%
New Age 0.8%
Soundtracks 1.2%
Oldies 0.8%
Classical 2.8%
Jazz 2.8%
Gospel 4.5%

Other 7.0%
Rock 32.5%
Country 14.4%
Urban Contemp. 11.2%
Pop 9.4%
Rap 10.1%

SOURCE: Based on data from Recording Industry Association of America, 1998

Music

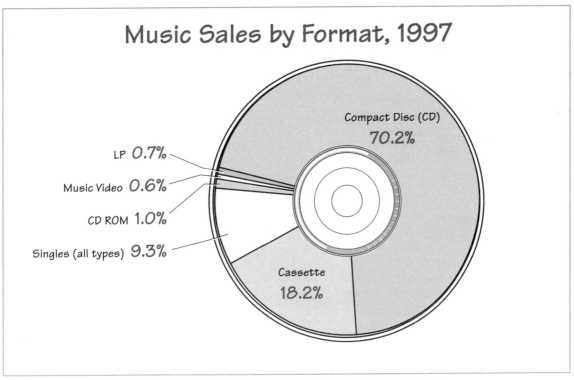

Music Sales by Format, 1997

LP **0.7%**

Music Video **0.6%**

CD ROM **1.0%**

Singles (all types) **9.3%**

Compact Disc (CD)
70.2%

Cassette
18.2%

SOURCE: Based on data from Recording Industry Association of America, 1998

Music

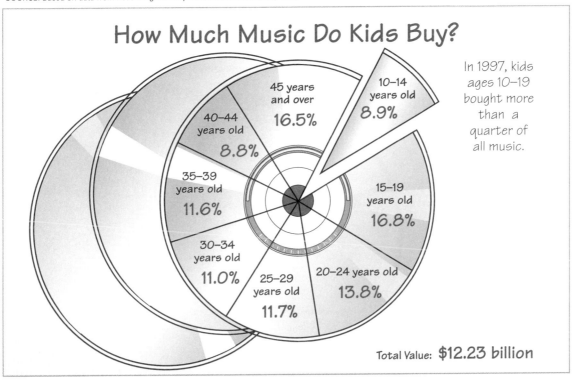

How Much Music Do Kids Buy?

45 years
and over
16.5%

40–44
years old
8.8%

35–39
years old
11.6%

30–34
years old
11.0%

25–29
years old
11.7%

20–24 years old
13.8%

15–19
years old
16.8%

10–14
years old
8.9%

In 1997, kids
ages 10–19
bought more
than a
quarter of
all music.

Total Value: **$12.23 billion**

SOURCE: Based on data from Recording Industry Association of America, 1998

Music

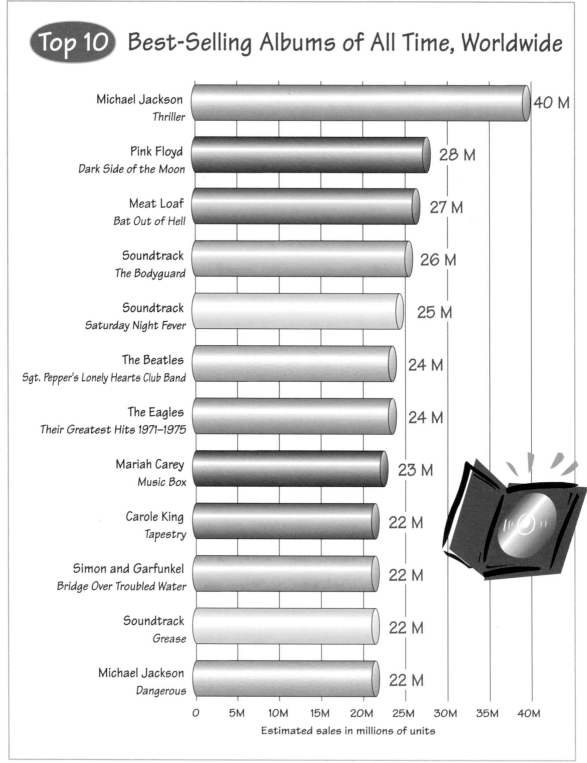

Top 10 Best-Selling Albums of All Time, Worldwide

Michael Jackson
Thriller — 40 M

Pink Floyd
Dark Side of the Moon — 28 M

Meat Loaf
Bat Out of Hell — 27 M

Soundtrack
The Bodyguard — 26 M

Soundtrack
Saturday Night Fever — 25 M

The Beatles
Sgt. Pepper's Lonely Hearts Club Band — 24 M

The Eagles
Their Greatest Hits 1971–1975 — 24 M

Mariah Carey
Music Box — 23 M

Carole King
Tapestry — 22 M

Simon and Garfunkel
Bridge Over Troubled Water — 22 M

Soundtrack
Grease — 22 M

Michael Jackson
Dangerous — 22 M

0   5M   10M   15M   20M   25M   30M   35M   40M

Estimated sales in millions of units

Source: Based on information given in *The Top 10 of Everything 1997*

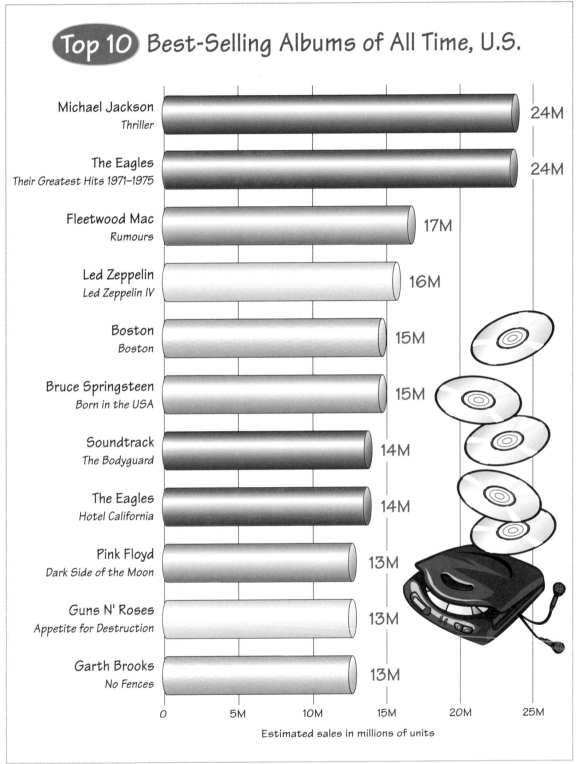

Top 10 Best-Selling Albums of All Time, U.S.

Michael Jackson
Thriller — 24M

The Eagles
Their Greatest Hits 1971–1975 — 24M

Fleetwood Mac
Rumours — 17M

Led Zeppelin
Led Zeppelin IV — 16M

Boston
Boston — 15M

Bruce Springsteen
Born in the USA — 15M

Soundtrack
The Bodyguard — 14M

The Eagles
Hotel California — 14M

Pink Floyd
Dark Side of the Moon — 13M

Guns N' Roses
Appetite for Destruction — 13M

Garth Brooks
No Fences — 13M

0   5M   10M   15M   20M   25M

Estimated sales in millions of units

Music

Source: Based on information given in *The Top 10 of Everything 1997*

Music

Top 10 Best-Selling Country Albums of All Time in the U.S.

	Artist	Title	Year
1	Garth Brooks	*No Fences*	1990
2	Garth Brooks	*Ropin' the Wind*	1991
3	Billy Ray Cyrus	*Some Gave All*	1992
4	Garth Brooks	*In Pieces*	1993
5	Garth Brooks	*Garth Brooks*	1990
6	Garth Brooks	*The Hits*	1995
7	Garth Brooks	*The Chase*	1992
8	Patsy Cline	*Greatest Hits*	1987
9	Brooks & Dunn	*Brand New Man*	1991
10	Alabama	*Feels So Right*	1981

Source: Based on information given in *The Top 10 of Everything 1997*

Top 5 Most Popular Kinds of U.S. Radio Stations

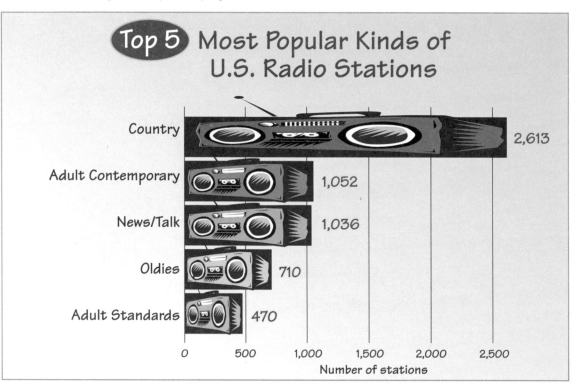

Kind	Number of stations
Country	2,613
Adult Contemporary	1,052
News/Talk	1,036
Oldies	710
Adult Standards	470

Number of stations

SOURCE: Based on data from Interep Research

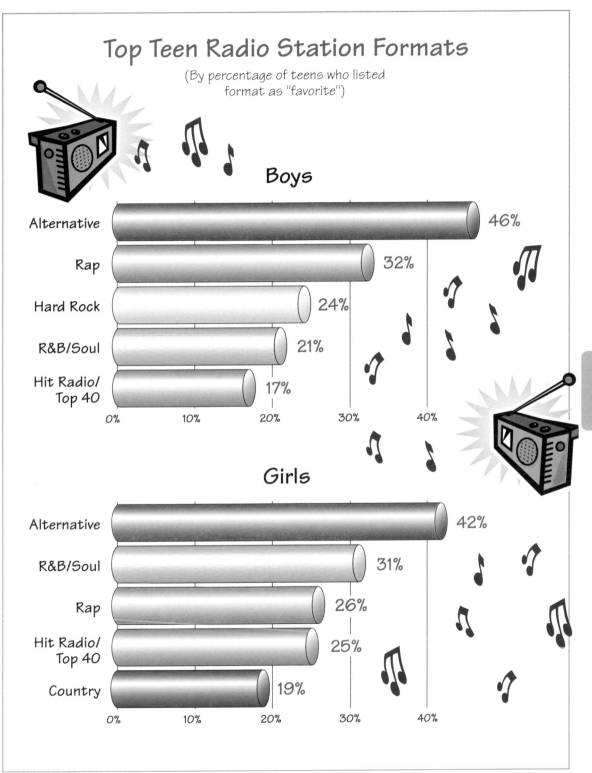

Top Teen Radio Station Formats

(By percentage of teens who listed
format as "favorite")

Boys

Alternative	46%
Rap	32%
Hard Rock	24%
R&B/Soul	21%
Hit Radio/ Top 40	17%

0%   10%   20%   30%   40%

Girls

Alternative	42%
R&B/Soul	31%
Rap	26%
Hit Radio/ Top 40	25%
Country	19%

0%   10%   20%   30%   40%

Music

SOURCE: Based on data from Teenage Research Unlimited, Inc.

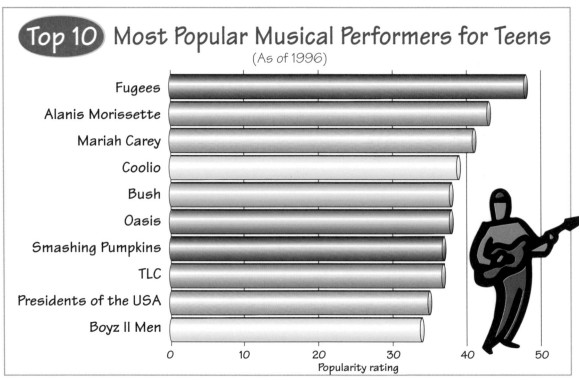

Top 10 Most Popular Musical Performers for Teens

(As of 1996)

- Fugees
- Alanis Morissette
- Mariah Carey
- Coolio
- Bush
- Oasis
- Smashing Pumpkins
- TLC
- Presidents of the USA
- Boyz II Men

0   10   20   30   40   50

Popularity rating

SOURCE: Based on data from Teenage Research Unlimited, Inc.

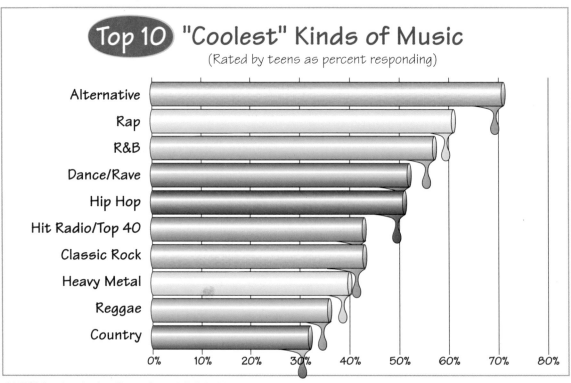

Top 10 "Coolest" Kinds of Music

(Rated by teens as percent responding)

- Alternative
- Rap
- R&B
- Dance/Rave
- Hip Hop
- Hit Radio/Top 40
- Classic Rock
- Heavy Metal
- Reggae
- Country

0%   10%   20%   30%   40%   50%   60%   70%   80%

SOURCE: Based on data from Teenage Research Unlimited, Inc.

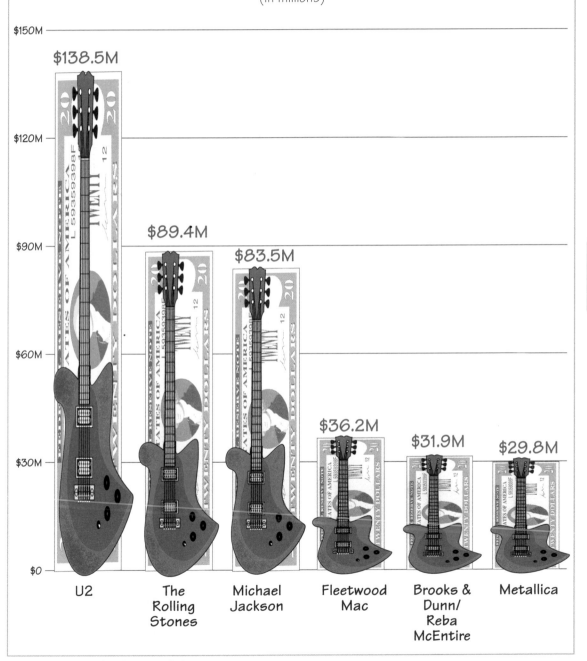

Top Worldwide Tour Moneymakers, 1997

Top-name music groups collectively brought in more than $1 billion in revenues from touring in 1997.

(In millions)

SOURCE: Based on data from Amusement Business

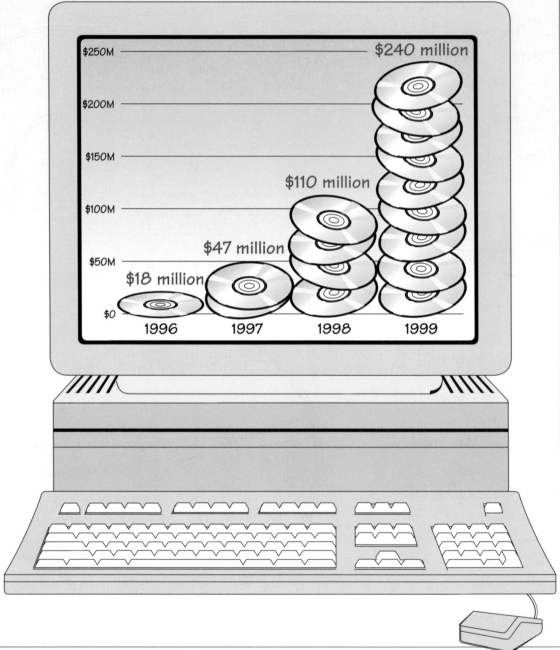

Notes on the Net

Sales of music through on-line channels is expected to explode before the year 2000. Projected growth:
(In millions of revenue dollars)

$240 million

$110 million

$47 million

$18 million

SOURCE: Based on data from Jupiter Communications

Music

Music

Top-Selling Albums, 1996

(In millions of units sold)

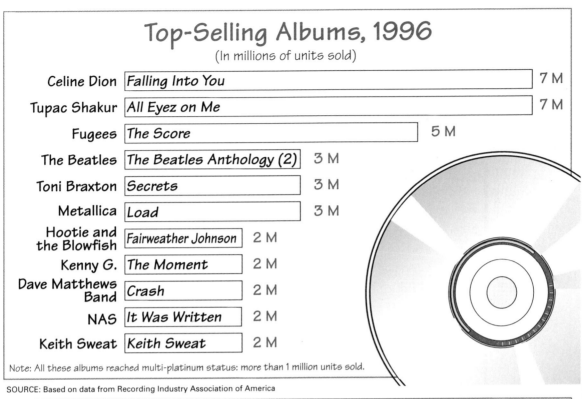

Celine Dion	Falling Into You	7 M
Tupac Shakur	All Eyez on Me	7 M
Fugees	The Score	5 M
The Beatles	The Beatles Anthology (2)	3 M
Toni Braxton	Secrets	3 M
Metallica	Load	3 M
Hootie and the Blowfish	Fairweather Johnson	2 M
Kenny G.	The Moment	2 M
Dave Matthews Band	Crash	2 M
NAS	It Was Written	2 M
Keith Sweat	Keith Sweat	2 M

Note: All these albums reached multi-platinum status: more than 1 million units sold.

SOURCE: Based on data from Recording Industry Association of America

Where Music Is Bought

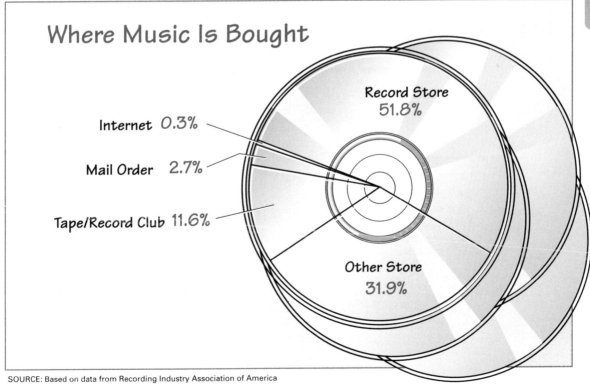

Record Store 51.8%

Internet 0.3%

Mail Order 2.7%

Tape/Record Club 11.6%

Other Store 31.9%

SOURCE: Based on data from Recording Industry Association of America

Music

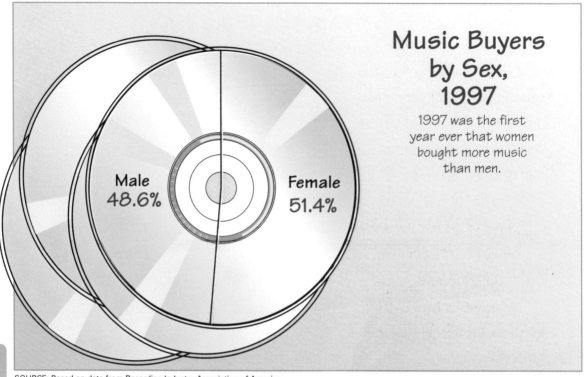

Music Buyers by Sex, 1997

1997 was the first year ever that women bought more music than men.

Male 48.6%

Female 51.4%

SOURCE: Based on data from Recording Industry Association of America

Total Dollar Value of U.S. Music Sales, 1988–97

(In billions of dollars)

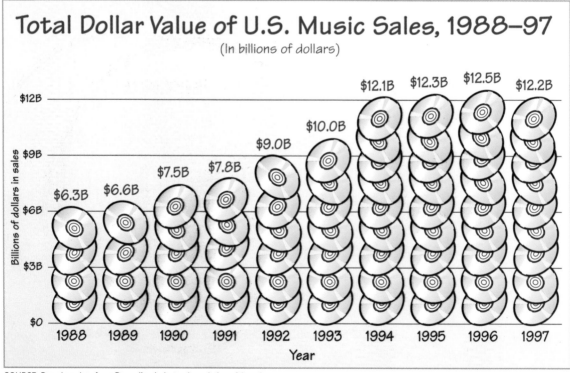

Billions of dollars in sales

$12B
$9B
$6B
$3B
$0

$6.3B $6.6B $7.5B $7.8B $9.0B $10.0B $12.1B $12.3B $12.5B $12.2B

1988 1989 1990 1991 1992 1993 1994 1995 1996 1997

Year

SOURCE: Based on data from Recording Industry Association of America

Selected MTV Video Music Awards, 1987-97
Best Video

Year	Artist	Video
1997	Jamiroquai	Virtual Insanity
1996	Smashing Pumpkins	Tonight, Tonight
1995	TLC	Waterfalls
1994	Aerosmith	Cryin'
1993	Pearl Jam	Jeremy
1992	Van Halen	Right Now
1991	R.E.M.	Losing My Religion
1990	Sinead O'Connor	Nothing Compares to You
1989	Neil Young	This Note's For You
1988	INXS	Need You Tonight/Mediate
1987	Peter Gabriel	Sledgehammer

SOURCE: Based on data from Press Department, MTV Networks

Selected MTV Video Music Awards, 1987-97
Best Male Video

Year	Artist	Video
1997	Beck	Devil's Haircut
1996	Beck	Where It's At
1995	Tom Petty and the Heartbreakers	You Don't Know How it Feels
1994	Tom Petty and the Heartbreakers	Mary Jane's Last Dance
1993	Lenny Kravitz	Are You Gonna Go My Way
1992	Eric Clapton	Tears in Heaven
1991	Chris Isaak	Wicked Game
1990	Don Henley	End of the Innocence
1989	Elvis Costello	Veronica
1988	Prince	U Got the Look
1987	Peter Gabriel	Sledgehammer

SOURCE: Based on data from Press Department, MTV Networks

Selected MTV Video Music Awards, 1987-97
Best Female Video

Year	Artist	Video
1997	Jewel	You Were Meant For Me
1996	Alanis Morissette	Ironic
1995	Madonna	Take a Bow
1994	Janet Jackson	If
1993	k.d. lang	Constant Craving
1992	Annie Lennox	Why
1991	Janet Jackson	Love Will Never Do Without You
1990	Sinead O'Connor	Nothing Compares to You
1989	Paula Abdul	Straight Up
1988	Suzanne Vega	Luka
1987	Madonna	Papa Don't Preach

SOURCE: Based on data from Press Department, MTV Networks

Selected MTV Video Music Awards, 1987-97
Best Group Video

Year	Artist	Video
1997	No Doubt	Don't Speak
1996	Foo Fighters	Big Me
1995	TLC	Waterfalls
1994	Aerosmith	Cryin'
1993	Pearl Jam	Jeremy
1992	U2	Even Better Than the Real Thing
1991	R.E.M.	Losing My Religion
1990	B-52s	Love Shack
1989	Living Color	Cult of Personality
1988	INXS	Need You Tonight/Mediate
1987	Talking Heads	Wild Wild Life

SOURCE: Based on data from Press Department, MTV Networks

Selected MTV Video Music Awards, 1987-97
Best New Artist in a Video

Year	Artist	Video
1997	Fiona Apple	Sleep to Dream
1996	Alanis Morissette	Ironic
1995	Hootie & the Blowfish	Hold My Hand
1994	Counting Crows	Mr. Jones
1993	Stone Temple Pilots	Plush
1992	Nirvana	Smells Like Teen Spirit
1991	Jesus Jones	Right Here, Right Now
1990	Michael Penn	No Myth
1989	Living Color	Cult of Personality
1988	Guns N' Roses	Welcome to the Jungle
1987	Crowded House	Don't Dream It's Over

SOURCE: Based on data from Press Department, MTV Networks

Music

Selected Grammy Winners, 1988-98
Record of the Year

Year	Artist	Record
1998	Shawn Colvin	Sunny Came Home
1997	Eric Clapton	Change the World
1996	Seal	Kiss From a Rose
1995	Sheryl Crow	All I Wanna Do
1994	Whitney Houston	I Will Always Love You
1993	Eric Clapton	Tears in Heaven
1992	Natalie Cole	Unforgettable
1991	Phil Collins	Another Day in Paradise
1990	Bette Midler	Wind Beneath My Wings
1989	Bobby McFerrin	Don't Worry, Be Happy
1988	Paul Simon	Graceland

SOURCE: Based on data from National Academy of Recording Arts and Sciences

Music

Selected Grammy Winners, 1988-98
Album of the Year

Year	Artist	Album
1998	Bob Dylan	Time Out of Mind
1997	Celine Dion	Falling Into You
1996	Alanis Morissette	Jagged Little Pill
1995	Tony Bennett	MTV Unplugged
1994	Whitney Houston	The Bodyguard
1993	Eric Clapton	MTV Unplugged
1992	Natalie Cole	Unforgettable
1991	Quincy Jones	Back on the Block
1990	Bonnie Raitt	Nick of Time
1989	George Michael	Faith
1988	U2	The Joshua Tree

SOURCE: Based on data from National Academy of Recording Arts and Sciences

Selected Grammy Winners, 1988-98
Song of the Year

Year	Artist	Song
1998	Shawn Colvin	Sunny Came Home
1997	Wayne Kirkpatrick & Tommy Sims	Change the World
1996	Seal	Kiss From a Rose
1995	Bruce Springsteen	Streets of Philadelphia
1994	Alan Menken & Tim Rice	A Whole New World (Aladdin's Theme)
1993	Eric Clapton	Tears in Heaven
1992	Irving Gordon	Unforgettable
1991	Julie Gold	From a Distance
1990	Bette Midler	Wind Beneath My Wings
1989	Bobby McFerrin	Don't Worry, Be Happy
1988	Linda Ronstadt & James Ingram	Somewhere Out There

SOURCE: Based on data from National Academy of Recording Arts and Sciences

Selected Grammy Winners, 1988-98
Best Male Vocal Performance

Year	Artist	Performance
1998	Elton John	Candle in the Wind 1997
1997	Eric Clapton	Change the World
1996	Seal	Kiss From a Rose
1995	Elton John	Can You Feel the Love Tonight
1994	Sting	If I Ever Lose My Faith in You
1993	Eric Clapton	Tears in Heaven
1992	Michael Bolton	When a Man Loves a Woman
1991	Roy Orbison	Oh, Pretty Woman
1990	Michael Bolton	How Am I Supposed to Live Without You
1989	Bobby McFerrin	Don't Worry, Be Happy
1988	Sting	Bring on the Night

SOURCE: Based on data from National Academy of Recording Arts and Sciences

Selected Grammy Winners, 1988-98
Best Female Vocal Performance

Year	Artist	Performance
1998	Sarah McLachlan	Building a Mystery
1997	Toni Braxton	Unbreak My Heart
1996	Annie Lennox	No More "I Love Yous"
1995	Sheryl Crow	All I Wanna Do
1994	Whitney Houston	I Will Always Love You
1993	k.d. lang	Constant Craving
1992	Bonnie Raitt	Something to Talk About
1991	Mariah Carey	Vision of Love
1990	Bonnie Raitt	Nick of Time
1989	Tracy Chapman	Fast Car
1988	Whitney Houston	I Wanna Dance With Somebody (Who Loves Me)

SOURCE: Based on data from National Academy of Recording Arts and Sciences

Television

Almost every U.S. home has at least one color television set. Most have two or more sets. And these sets are busy! On average, a home has at least one TV on for more than 7 hours every day. The typical American watches about 4 hours of television daily. On average, adults watch more TV than children do.

Most viewing time is spent watching shows on the major networks, such as ABC, CBS, FOX, and NBC. Cable networks, such as ESPN and CNN, haven't been around as long, but they have been growing in popularity. By 1997, a total of 66% of U.S. homes with television sets subscribed to basic cable services. Of those, the top pay channel—by far—is HBO. The next big thing in television is high-definition television, or HDTV. This technology brings wide-screen, super-sharp pictures into the average home, complete with six-channel "surround sound."

Kids enjoy all kinds of programs, including comedies, cartoons, movies, and animal shows. Sports—from football games to ice-skating competitions—are among the most popular shows. If a show includes young people, so much the better. Nickelodeon's

Kidbits Tidbits

- 98% of U.S. homes have at least one color TV set.
- In 1996, about 78.8 million U.S. homes had at least one VCR.
- Children ages 2 to 11 watch about 3 hours of television a day. Those ages 12 to 17 watch almost as much.
- In early 1998, "E.R." was the #1 show among whites, but ranked #18 with blacks. "Between Brothers" was the most popular show among blacks, and #107 among whites.

series "The Secret Life of Alex Mack" became a hit because of its 16-year-old star, Larisa Oleynik. And Rosie O'Donnell's show drew lots of young viewers when Justin Miller—who published his first cookbook in 1997 at age 7—was on the air whipping up a batch of cookies.

Television use is monitored by the A.C. Nielsen Company. If a show has a Nielsen rating of 12, it was watched by 12% of all television owners. During the 1996-97 season, America's top-rated show was "E.R." It had a rating of 21.2. It was followed by "Seinfeld" at 20.5 and "Suddenly Susan" at 17.0.

Most TV programs are paid for by companies that buy advertising time. The bigger the audience a program gets, the

more companies are willing to pay to advertise their products during its commercial breaks. For example, it cost an average of $1.3 million for a 30-second ad during the 1998 Super Bowl, an event that drew as many as 140 million viewers. Why do companies pay so much? Can you think of another way to get the attention of 140 million people all at once for 30 seconds?

In addition to TVs, the great majority of U.S. homes have at least one VCR. Most people use their VCRs to watch rental videos. But Americans also bought a total of 392 million blank cassettes in 1996—to record TV shows, family parties, vacations, high school games, and so on.

Kidbits Tidbits

- Basic cable systems had more than 64 million subscribers in 1997.
- The pay-cable service with the most subscribers in 1996 was Home Box Office. The Disney Channel was second.
- In 1980, the average monthly cable bill was $7.69. In 1995, it was $23.07.
- HDTV uses digital signals, just like a computer. Conventional TVs use analog waves for broadcasting.
- Advertisers paid $1.3 million for half-minute ads during the 1998 Super Bowl—that's $43,333 a second!

Television

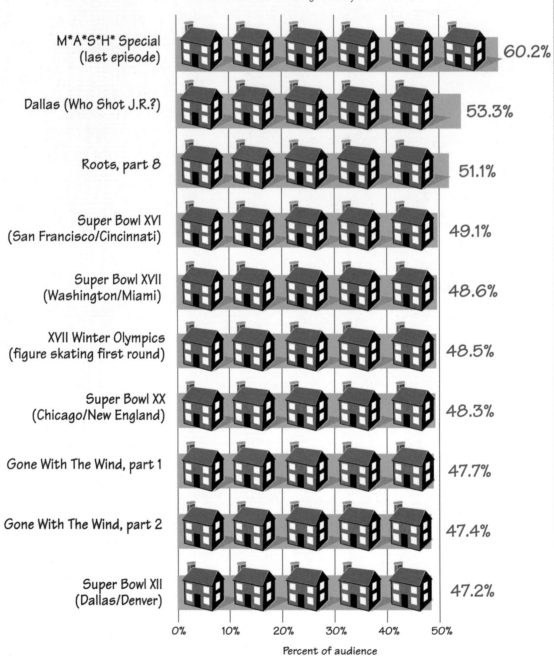

Top 10 Highest TV Ratings in History

(By percentage of audience—all TV-owning households as of July 1996)

Program	Percent of audience
M*A*S*H* Special (last episode)	60.2%
Dallas (Who Shot J.R.?)	53.3%
Roots, part 8	51.1%
Super Bowl XVI (San Francisco/Cincinnati)	49.1%
Super Bowl XVII (Washington/Miami)	48.6%
XVII Winter Olympics (figure skating first round)	48.5%
Super Bowl XX (Chicago/New England)	48.3%
Gone With The Wind, part 1	47.7%
Gone With The Wind, part 2	47.4%
Super Bowl XII (Dallas/Denver)	47.2%

0%   10%   20%   30%   40%   50%

Percent of audience

SOURCE: Based on data from Nielsen Media Research

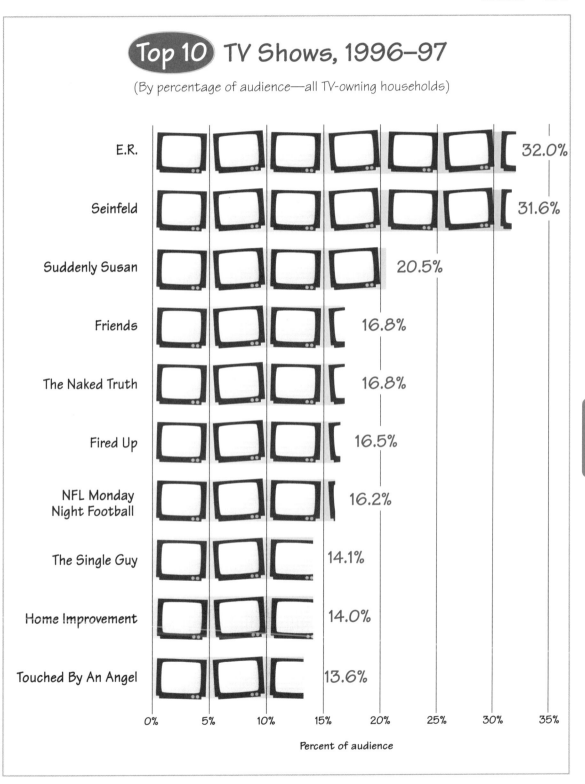

Top 10 TV Shows, 1996–97

(By percentage of audience—all TV-owning households)

Show	Percent
E.R.	32.0%
Seinfeld	31.6%
Suddenly Susan	20.5%
Friends	16.8%
The Naked Truth	16.8%
Fired Up	16.5%
NFL Monday Night Football	16.2%
The Single Guy	14.1%
Home Improvement	14.0%
Touched By An Angel	13.6%

0% 5% 10% 15% 20% 25% 30% 35%

Percent of audience

Television

SOURCE: Based on data from Nielsen Media Research

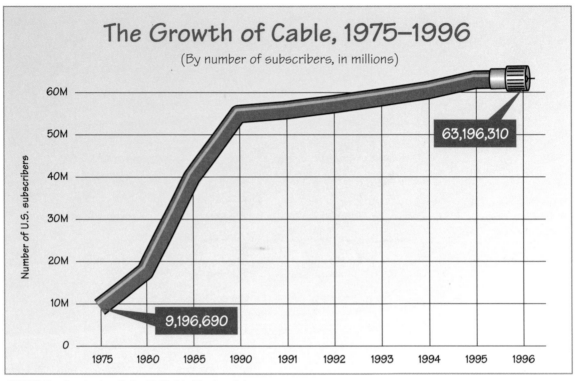

The Growth of Cable, 1975–1996
(By number of subscribers, in millions)

63,196,310

9,196,690

SOURCE: Based on data from National Cable Television Association

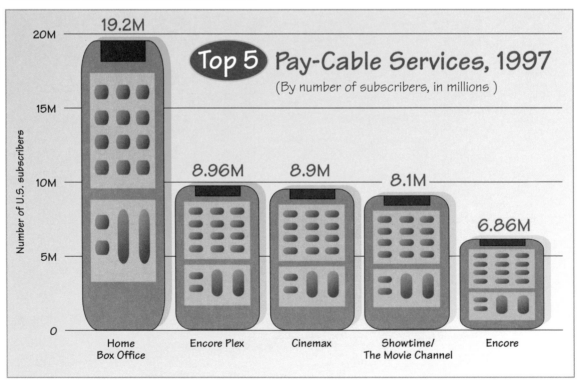

Top 5 Pay-Cable Services, 1997
(By number of subscribers, in millions)

19.2M — Home Box Office

8.96M — Encore Plex

8.9M — Cinemax

8.1M — Showtime/ The Movie Channel

6.86M — Encore

SOURCE: Based on data from National Cable Television Association

Television

Top 10 Cable TV Networks, 1995

Network	Number of subscribers (In millions)
1. ESPN	67.9
2. Cable News Network (CNN)	67.8
3. TBS	67.6
4. USA Network	67.2
5. The Discovery Channel	67.0
6. Turner Network Television (TNT)	66.6
7. C-SPAN	66.1
8. MTV: Music Network	65.9
9. Arts and Entertainment Network (A&E)	65.0
10. The Nashville Network (TNN)	64.8

SOURCE: Based on data from National Cable Television Association

Average Kids and Teens TV Viewing Time

(Per week)

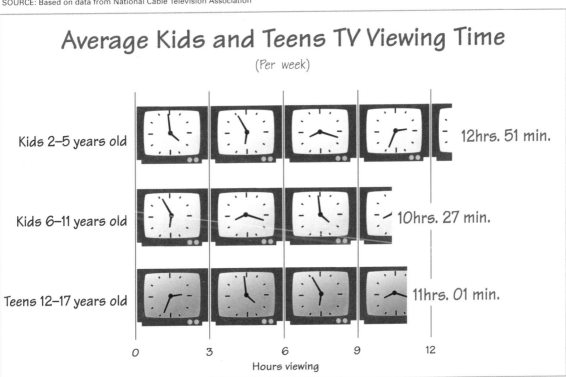

Kids 2–5 years old — 12hrs. 51 min.

Kids 6–11 years old — 10hrs. 27 min.

Teens 12–17 years old — 11hrs. 01 min.

Hours viewing

0   3   6   9   12

SOURCE: Based on data from Nielsen Media Research

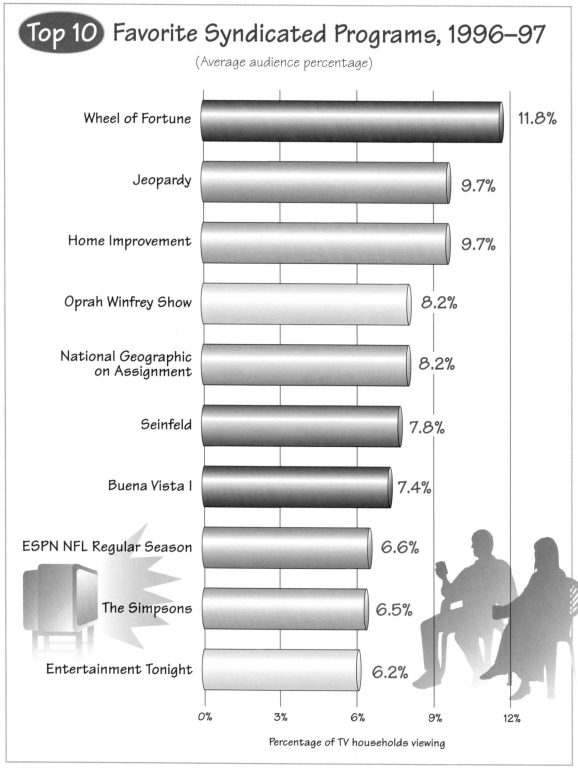

Top 10 Favorite Syndicated Programs, 1996–97

(Average audience percentage)

Program	Percentage
Wheel of Fortune	11.8%
Jeopardy	9.7%
Home Improvement	9.7%
Oprah Winfrey Show	8.2%
National Geographic on Assignment	8.2%
Seinfeld	7.8%
Buena Vista I	7.4%
ESPN NFL Regular Season	6.6%
The Simpsons	6.5%
Entertainment Tonight	6.2%

0%   3%   6%   9%   12%

Percentage of TV households viewing

Television

SOURCE: Based on data from Nielsen Media Research

Getting Wired: U.S. Households With Cable TV

(Percentage of homes with TVs getting cable 1977–1995)

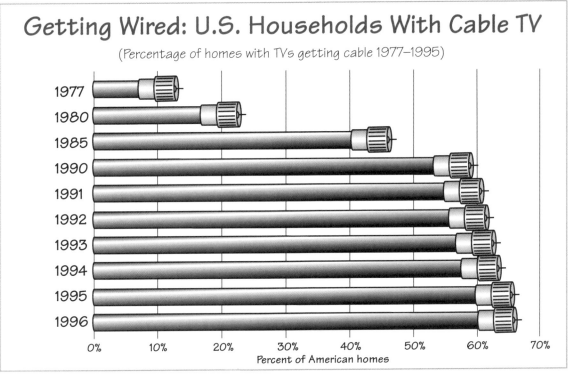

Percent of American homes

1977, 1980, 1985, 1990, 1991, 1992, 1993, 1994, 1995, 1996

0% 10% 20% 30% 40% 50% 60% 70%

SOURCE: Based on data from Nielsen Media Research

Top 10 Most Popular Cartoon Charactors for 6–11-Year-Olds

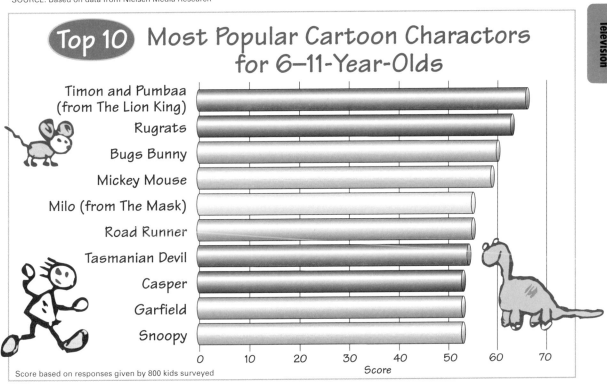

Timon and Pumbaa (from The Lion King)
Rugrats
Bugs Bunny
Mickey Mouse
Milo (from The Mask)
Road Runner
Tasmanian Devil
Casper
Garfield
Snoopy

0 10 20 30 40 50 60 70

Score

Score based on responses given by 800 kids surveyed

SOURCE: Based on data from Marketing Evaluations/TVQ

Television

Top 5 Most-Watched U.S. Daytime Soap Operas

Program	Number of Households viewing	Percentage of Households viewing
The Young and the Restless	8,084,000	8.6%
All My Children	6,204,000	6.6%
General Hospital	5,828,000	6.2%
The Bold and the Beautiful	5,730,000	6.1%
As the World Turns	5,452,000	5.8%

SOURCE: Based on data from Nielsen Media Research

Television

Top 5 Most Watched U.S. Sports Events of All Time

Program	Number of Households viewing	Percentage of Households viewing
Super Bowl XVI San Francisco vs. Cincinnati	40,020,000	49.1%
Super Bowl XVII Washington vs. Miami	40,500,000	48.6%
XVII Winter Olympics	45,690,000	48.5%
Super Bowl XX Chicago vs. New England	41,490,000	48.3%
Super Bowl XII Dallas vs. Denver	34,410,000	47.2%

SOURCE: Based on data from Nielsen Media Research

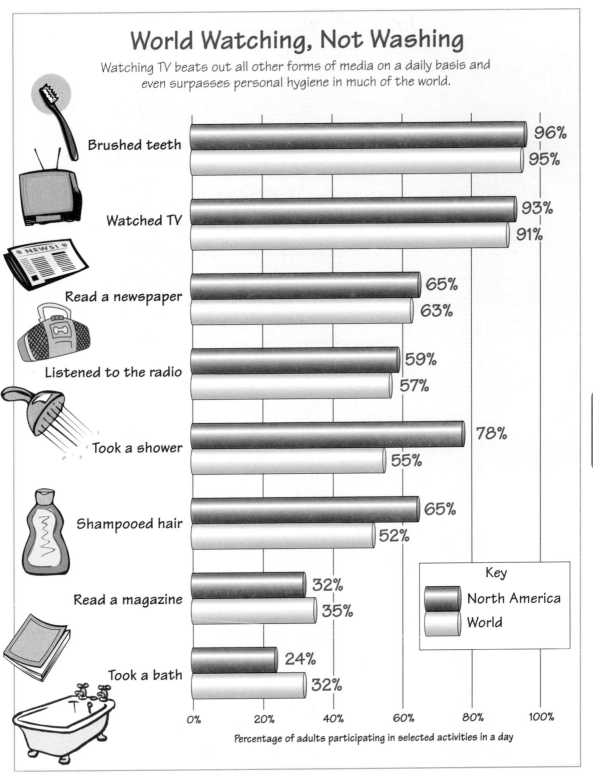

World Watching, Not Washing

Watching TV beats out all other forms of media on a daily basis and even surpasses personal hygiene in much of the world.

Activity	North America	World
Brushed teeth	96%	95%
Watched TV	93%	91%
Read a newspaper	65%	63%
Listened to the radio	59%	57%
Took a shower	78%	55%
Shampooed hair	65%	52%
Read a magazine	32%	35%
Took a bath	24%	32%

Key
North America
World

Percentage of adults participating in selected activities in a day

Television

SOURCE: Based on data from Roper Starch Worldwide

Television

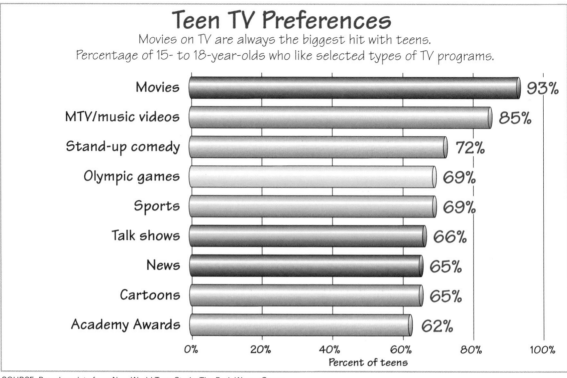

Teen TV Preferences

Movies on TV are always the biggest hit with teens.
Percentage of 15- to 18-year-olds who like selected types of TV programs.

Program	Percent
Movies	93%
MTV/music videos	85%
Stand-up comedy	72%
Olympic games	69%
Sports	69%
Talk shows	66%
News	65%
Cartoons	65%
Academy Awards	62%

Percent of teens

SOURCE: Based on data from New World Teen Study, The BrainWaves Group

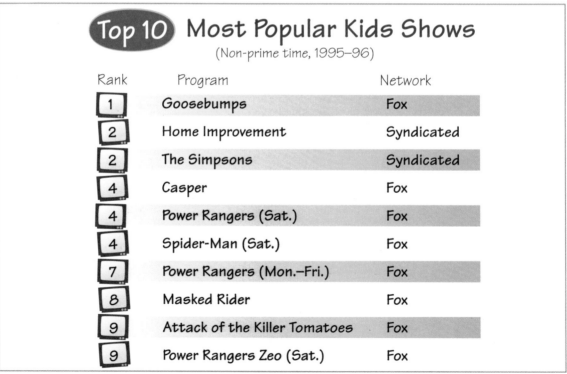

Top 10 Most Popular Kids Shows

(Non-prime time, 1995–96)

Rank	Program	Network
1	Goosebumps	Fox
2	Home Improvement	Syndicated
2	The Simpsons	Syndicated
4	Casper	Fox
4	Power Rangers (Sat.)	Fox
4	Spider-Man (Sat.)	Fox
7	Power Rangers (Mon.–Fri.)	Fox
8	Masked Rider	Fox
9	Attack of the Killer Tomatoes	Fox
9	Power Rangers Zeo (Sat.)	Fox

SOURCE: Based on data from Nielsen Media Research

Top 10 Favorite Programs for Younger Viewers

(All hours, 1995–96)

Rank	Program	Network
1	Aliens in the Family	ABC
2	Boy Meets World	ABC
3	Step by Step	ABC
4	Muppets Tonight	ABC
5	Family Matters	ABC
6	Hangin' With Mr. Cooper	ABC
7	America's Funniest Home Videos 2	ABC
8	Home Improvement	ABC
9	Lois & Clark	ABC
10	The Simpsons	Fox

SOURCE: Based on data from Nielsen Media Research

Who Watches the Most Sports?

(Percentage of broadcast markets)

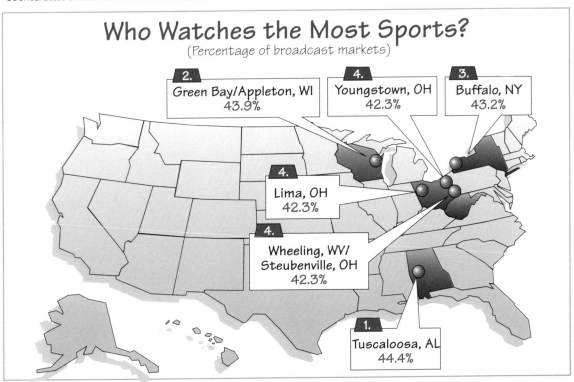

2.
Green Bay/Appleton, WI
43.9%

4.
Youngstown, OH
42.3%

3.
Buffalo, NY
43.2%

4.
Lima, OH
42.3%

4.
Wheeling, WV/
Steubenville, OH
42.3%

1.
Tuscaloosa, AL
44.4%

SOURCE: Based on data from Polk

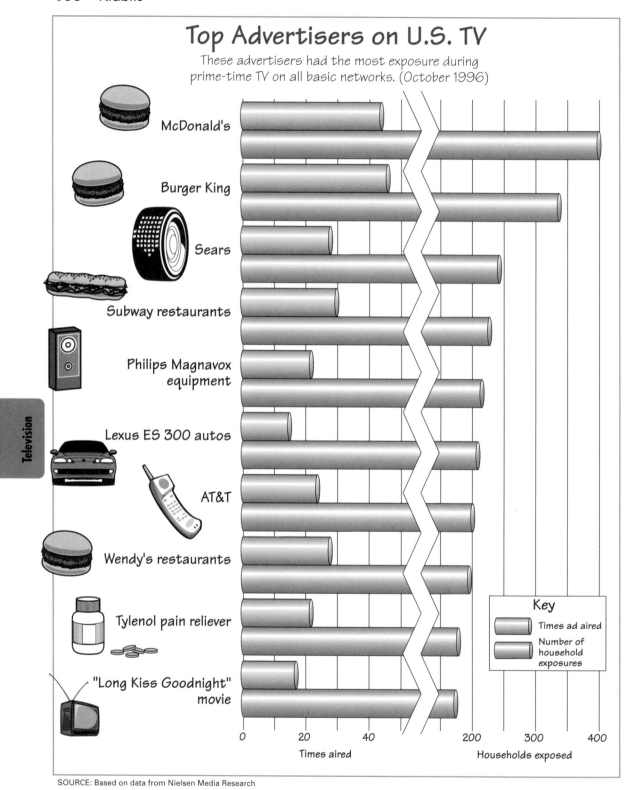

Top Advertisers on U.S. TV

These advertisers had the most exposure during prime-time TV on all basic networks. (October 1996)

McDonald's

Burger King

Sears

Subway restaurants

Philips Magnavox equipment

Lexus ES 300 autos

AT&T

Wendy's restaurants

Tylenol pain reliever

"Long Kiss Goodnight" movie

Times aired: 0, 20, 40

Households exposed: 200, 300, 400

Key
Times ad aired
Number of household exposures

Television

SOURCE: Based on data from Nielsen Media Research

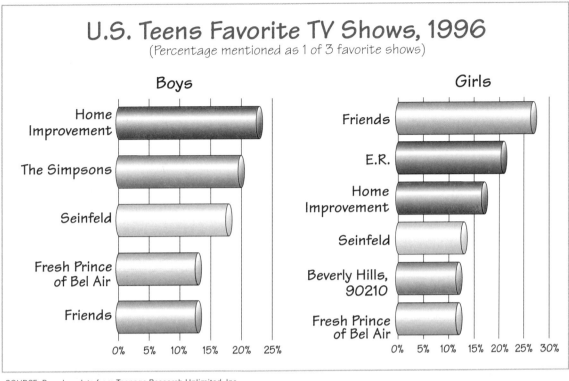

U.S. Teens Favorite TV Shows, 1996
(Percentage mentioned as 1 of 3 favorite shows)

Boys

- Home Improvement
- The Simpsons
- Seinfeld
- Fresh Prince of Bel Air
- Friends

0% 5% 10% 15% 20% 25%

Girls

- Friends
- E.R.
- Home Improvement
- Seinfeld
- Beverly Hills, 90210
- Fresh Prince of Bel Air

0% 5% 10% 15% 20% 25% 30%

SOURCE: Based on data from Teenage Research Unlimited, Inc.

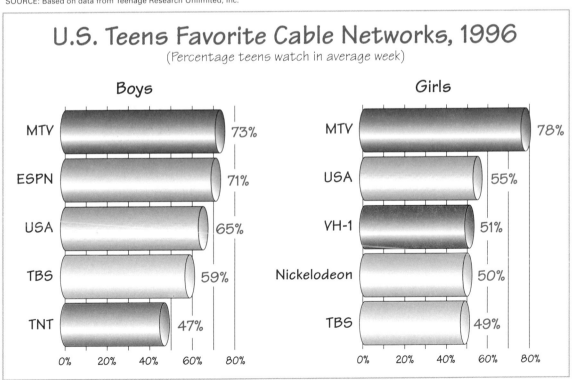

U.S. Teens Favorite Cable Networks, 1996
(Percentage teens watch in average week)

Boys

- MTV — 73%
- ESPN — 71%
- USA — 65%
- TBS — 59%
- TNT — 47%

0% 20% 40% 60% 80%

Girls

- MTV — 78%
- USA — 55%
- VH-1 — 51%
- Nickelodeon — 50%
- TBS — 49%

0% 20% 40% 60% 80%

SOURCE: Based on data from Teenage Research Unlimited, Inc.

Television

Television

Teens  Top 5 Least-Favorite TV Commercials

Mentos — Any Mentos commercial

McDonald's — Arch Deluxe commercial

Budweiser — Budweiser frog commercials

Rogaine — Any Rogaine commercial

Sprint — Any with Candice Bergen as the "Dime Lady"

Favorite Teen TV Commercials

75% of teens' favorite commercials are for food products.

Budweiser — Frog commercials

Pepsi — Goldfish plays dead for Pepsi

Milk — Man gets called by radio station ("Aaron Burr")

M&M's — With Red and Yellow M&M characters

McDonald's — Baby in swing cries when can't see McDonald's sign

Edy's Ice Cream — Baby boy gets up and starts dancing for Edy's Ice Cream

Nike — Lil' Penny

Polaroid — Dog takes picture of cat getting into garbage can

Television

SOURCE: Based on data from Teenage Research Unlimited, Inc.

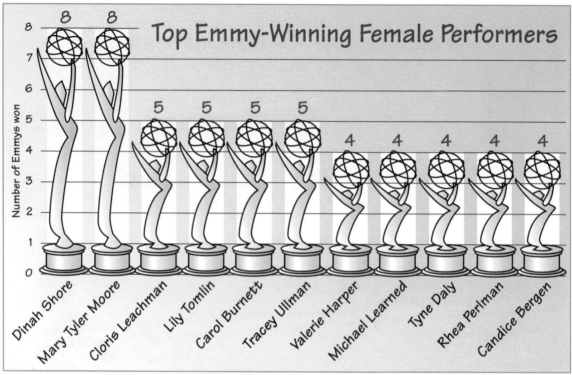

Top Emmy-Winning Female Performers

Number of Emmys won

8 — Dinah Shore
8 — Mary Tyler Moore
5 — Cloris Leachman
5 — Lily Tomlin
5 — Carol Burnett
5 — Tracey Ullman
4 — Valerie Harper
4 — Michael Learned
4 — Tyne Daly
4 — Rhea Perlman
4 — Candice Bergen

SOURCE: Based on data from Academy of Television Arts and Sciences

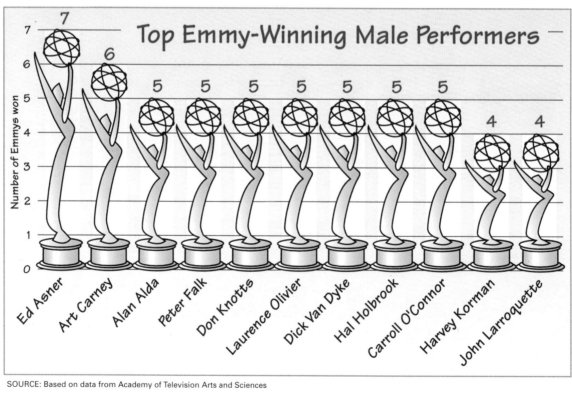

Top Emmy-Winning Male Performers

Number of Emmys won

7 — Ed Asner
6 — Art Carney
5 — Alan Alda
5 — Peter Falk
5 — Don Knotts
5 — Laurence Olivier
5 — Dick Van Dyke
5 — Hal Holbrook
5 — Carroll O'Connor
4 — Harvey Korman
4 — John Larroquette

SOURCE: Based on data from Academy of Television Arts and Sciences

Television

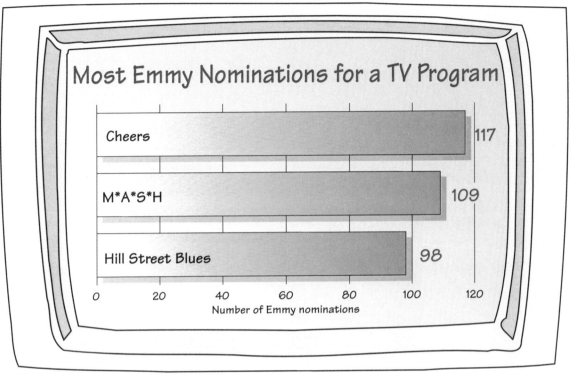

Most Emmy Nominations for a TV Program

Cheers — 117
M*A*S*H — 109
Hill Street Blues — 98

Number of Emmy nominations

SOURCE: Based on data from Academy of Television Arts and Sciences

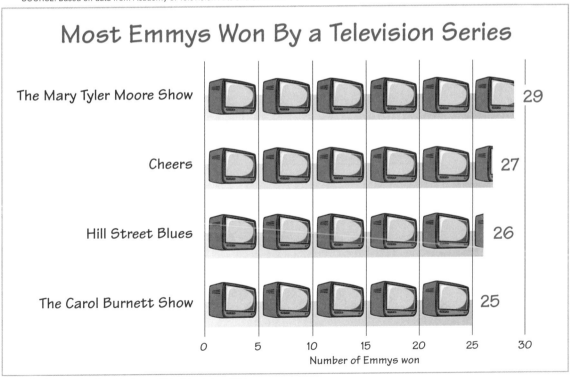

Most Emmys Won By a Television Series

The Mary Tyler Moore Show — 29
Cheers — 27
Hill Street Blues — 26
The Carol Burnett Show — 25

Number of Emmys won

Television

SOURCE: Based on data from Academy of Television Arts and Sciences

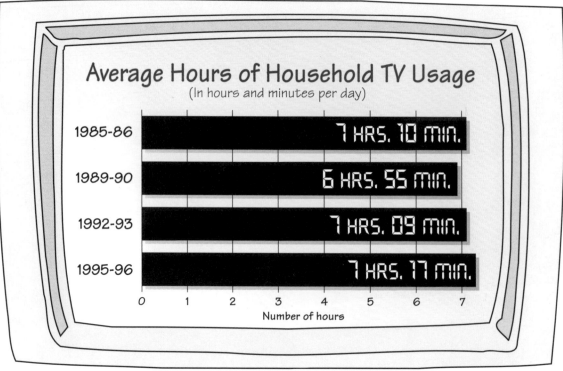

Average Hours of Household TV Usage
(In hours and minutes per day)

1985-86	7 HRS. 10 MIN.
1989-90	6 HRS. 55 MIN.
1992-93	7 HRS. 09 MIN.
1995-96	7 HRS. 17 MIN.

Number of hours

SOURCE: Based on data from Nielsen Media Research

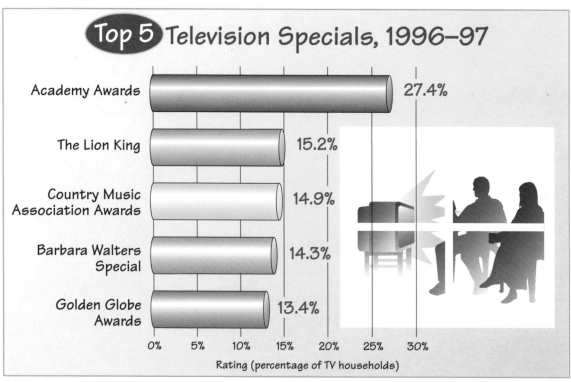

Top 5 Television Specials, 1996–97

Academy Awards	27.4%
The Lion King	15.2%
Country Music Association Awards	14.9%
Barbara Walters Special	14.3%
Golden Globe Awards	13.4%

Rating (percentage of TV households)

SOURCE: Based on data from Nielsen Media Research

Who Watches What?

(Average audience)

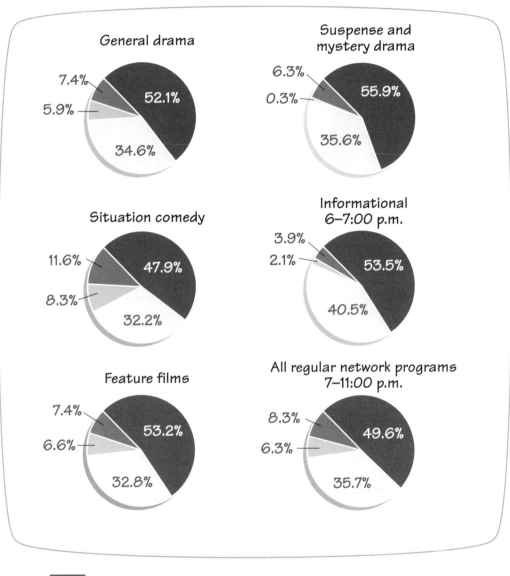

General drama

7.4%
5.9%
52.1%
34.6%

Suspense and mystery drama

6.3%
0.3%
55.9%
35.6%

Situation comedy

11.6%
8.3%
47.9%
32.2%

Informational 6–7:00 p.m.

3.9%
2.1%
53.5%
40.5%

Feature films

7.4%
6.6%
53.2%
32.8%

All regular network programs 7–11:00 p.m.

8.3%
6.3%
49.6%
35.7%

Women (18 and over)
Men (18 and over)
Teens (12-17)
Children (2-11)

Television

SOURCE: Based on data from Nielsen Media Research

U.S. Television Ownership, 1997

(By household)

Color TV sets
82,350,000
85%

One set
25,220,000
27%

2 or more sets
71,780,000
73%

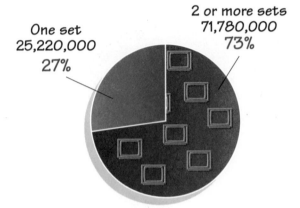

Total TV households
97,000,000
97.3%

SOURCE: Based on data from Nielsen Media Research

Television

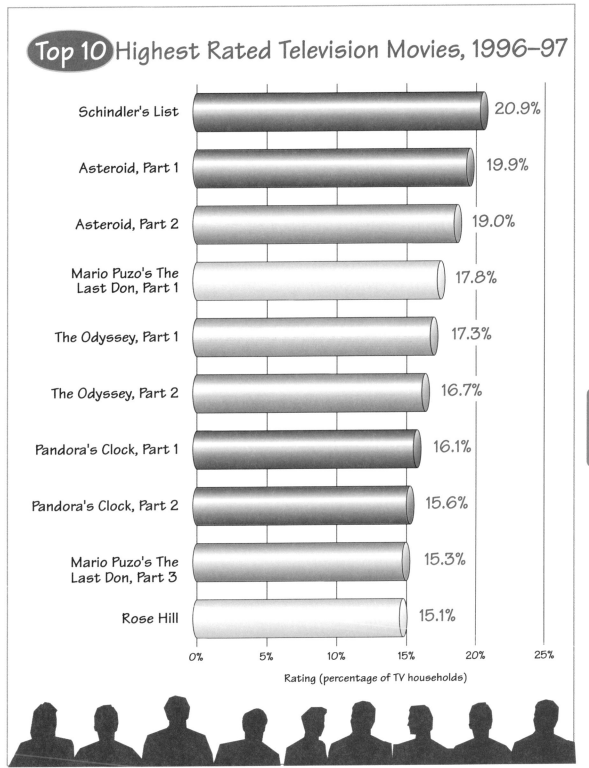

Top 10 Highest Rated Television Movies, 1996–97

Movie	Rating
Schindler's List	20.9%
Asteroid, Part 1	19.9%
Asteroid, Part 2	19.0%
Mario Puzo's The Last Don, Part 1	17.8%
The Odyssey, Part 1	17.3%
The Odyssey, Part 2	16.7%
Pandora's Clock, Part 1	16.1%
Pandora's Clock, Part 2	15.6%
Mario Puzo's The Last Don, Part 3	15.3%
Rose Hill	15.1%

Rating (percentage of TV households)

Television

SOURCE: Based on data from Nielsen Media Research

Emmy Winners, 1987–1997
Lead Actress in a Comedy Series

Year	Actress	Character	Program
1997	Helen Hunt	Jamie Buchman	Mad About You
1996	Helen Hunt	Jamie Buchman	Mad About You
1995	Candice Bergen	Murphy Brown	Murphy Brown
1994	Candice Bergen	Murphy Brown	Murphy Brown
1993	Roseanne	Roseanne Arnold	Roseanne
1992	Candice Bergen	Murphy Brown	Murphy Brown
1991	Kirstie Alley	Rebecca Howe	Cheers
1990	Candice Bergen	Murphy Brown	Murphy Brown
1989	Candice Bergen	Murphy Brown	Murphy Brown
1988	Beatrice Arthur	Dorothy	The Golden Girls
1987	Rue McClanahan	Blanche	The Golden Girls

SOURCE: Based on data from Academy of Television Arts and Sciences

Television

Emmy Winners, 1987–1997
Lead Actor in a Comedy Series

Year	Actor	Character	Program
1997	John Lithgow	Dick Solomon	3rd Rock From the Sun
1996	John Lithgow	Dick Solomon	3rd Rock From the Sun
1995	Kelsey Grammer	Dr. Frasier Crane	Frasier
1994	Kelsey Grammer	Dr. Frasier Crane	Frasier
1993	Ted Danson	Sam Malone	Cheers
1992	Craig T. Nelson	Hayden Fox	Coach
1991	Burt Reynolds	Wood Newton	Evening Shade
1990	Ted Danson	Sam Malone	Cheers
1989	Richard Mulligan	Harry Weston	Empty Nest
1988	Michael J. Fox	Alex Keaton	Family Ties
1987	Michael J. Fox	Alex Keaton	Family Ties

SOURCE: Based on data from Academy of Television Arts and Sciences

Emmy Winners, 1987–1997
Lead Actress in a Drama Series

Year	Actress	Character	Program
1997	Gillian Anderson	Agent Dana Scully	The X-Files
1996	Kathy Baker	Jill Brock	Picket Fences
1995	Kathy Baker	Jill Brock	Picket Fences
1994	Sela Ward	Teddy Reed	Sisters
1993	Kathy Baker	Jill Brock	Picket Fences
1992	Dana Delany	Colleen McMurphy	China Beach
1991	Patricia Wettig	Nancy Weston	Thirtysomething
1990	Patricia Wettig	Nancy Weston	Thirtysomething
1989	Dana Delany	Colleen McMurphy	China Beach
1988	Tyne Daly	Mary Beth Lacey	Cagney & Lacey
1987	Sharon Gless	Christine Cagney	Cagney & Lacey

SOURCE: Based on data from Academy of Television Arts and Sciences

Emmy Winners, 1987–1997
Lead Actor in a Drama Series

Year	Actor	Character	Program
1997	Dennis Franz	Detective Andy Sipowicz	NYPD Blue
1996	Dennis Franz	Detective Andy Sipowicz	NYPD Blue
1995	Mandy Patinkin	Dr. Jeffrey Geiger	Chicago Hope
1994	Dennis Franz	Detective Andy Sipowicz	NYPD Blue
1993	Tom Skerritt	Jimmy Brock	Picket Fences
1992	Christopher Lloyd	Alistair Dimple	Avonlea
1991	James Earl Jones	Gabriel Bird	Gabriel's Fire
1990	Peter Falk	Lieutenant Columbo	Columbo
1989	Carroll O'Connor	Chief Bill Gillespie	In The Heat of the Night
1988	Richard Kiley	Joe Gardner	A Year in the Life
1987	Bruce Willis	David Addison	Moonlighting

SOURCE: Based on data from Academy of Television Arts and Sciences

Television

Emmy Winners, 1987–1997
Best Comedy Series

Year	Program
1997	Frasier
1996	Frasier
1995	Frasier
1994	Frasier
1993	Seinfeld
1992	Murphy Brown
1991	Cheers
1990	Murphy Brown
1989	Cheers
1988	The Wonder Years
1987	The Golden Girls

SOURCE: Based on data from Academy of Television Arts and Sciences

Television

Emmy Winners, 1987–1997
Best Drama Series

Year	Program
1997	Law & Order
1996	E.R.
1995	NYPD Blue
1994	Picket Fences
1993	Picket Fences
1992	Northern Exposure
1991	L.A. Law
1990	L.A. Law
1989	L.A. Law
1988	Thirtysomething
1987	L.A. Law

SOURCE: Based on data from Academy of Television Arts and Sciences

Emmy Winners, 1987–1997
Supporting Actor in a Comedy Series

Year	Actor	Character	Program
1997	Michael Richards	Kramer	Seinfeld
1996	Rip Torn	Arthur	The Larry Sanders Show
1995	David Hyde Pierce	Dr. Niles Crane	Frasier
1994	Michael Richards	Kramer	Seinfeld
1993	Michael Richards	Kramer	Seinfeld
1992	Michael Jeter	Herman Stiles	Evening Shade
1991	Jonathon Winters	Gunny Davies	Davis Rules
1990	Jay Thomas	Jerry Gold	Murphy Brown
1989	Woody Harrelson	Woody Boyd	Cheers
1988	John Larroquette	Dan Fielding	Night Court
1987	John Larroquette	Dan Fielding	Night Court

SOURCE: Based on data from Academy of Television Arts and Sciences

Emmy Winners, 1987–1997
Supporting Actress in a Comedy Series

Year	Actress	Character	Program
1997	Kristen Johnston	Sally Solomon	3rd Rock From the Sun
1996	Julia Louis-Dreyfus	Elaine Benes	Seinfeld
1995	Christine Baranski	Maryann Thorpe	Cybill
1994	Laurie Metcalf	Jackie Harris	Roseanne
1993	Laurie Metcalf	Jackie Harris	Roseanne
1992	Laurie Metcalf	Jackie Harris	Roseanne
1991	Bebe Neuwirth	Dr. Lillith Sternin-Crane	Cheers
1990	Bebe Neuwirth	Dr. Lillith Sternin-Crane	Cheers
1989	Rhea Perlman	Carla Tortelli Lebec	Cheers
1988	Estelle Getty	Sophia	The Golden Girls
1987	Jackee Harry	Sandra	227

SOURCE: Based on data from Academy of Television Arts and Sciences

Television

Movies and Videos

About 400 new films are released in the United States each year. Some disappear quickly. Others remain popular for years and years—not only in cinemas and on video, but in the spin-offs and merchandise they create: toys and games, clothing, and recordings of their musical scores.

Americans spend about $6 billion a year on movie tickets, with an average admission charge of $4.42. As 1998 began, the film that held the U.S. record for making the most money at the box office was *Star Wars*, a 1977 movie that had sold $460 million worth of tickets. Worldwide, the record was held by the 1993 film *Jurassic Park*, which had pulled in a total of $913 million. But on March 1, 1998, the 1997 film *Titanic* became the first film to surpass $1 billion worldwide. It also became the first movie to tie the all-time record for Oscar nominations, with 14 total. On Oscar night in March 1998, it also became the first movie to tie the all-time record for Oscar wins: the film tied the 1959 epic *Ben-Hur* with 11 awards.

Kidbits Tidbits

- The movie industry had $5.9 billion in box office receipts in 1996.
- In 1997, *Titanic* became the most expensive movie ever made. It cost $200 million.
- The average cost of making a movie surged to $39.8 million by 1996. In addition, spending on advertising and publicity averaged $19.8 million per movie.
- *Ben-Hur*, a 1959 movie, held the Oscar record of 11 Academy Awards for 39 years, until *Titanic* tied in 1998.

Teenagers make up a hefty portion of the movie audience, in part because they have more leisure time than older people. In a recent study, 48% of 12- to 17-year-olds said they see a movie at least once a month, as compared with only 26% of people age 18 and older. Also, unlike adults, teenagers will see a movie over and over again if they like it. To some degree, boys and girls have different theatrical tastes—young males like action films while young women prefer romantic tales. But just about every teenager loves a spooky horror movie, or a film with dazzling computer-generated special effects, such as stalking dinosaurs and cataclysmic natural disasters.

In addition to viewing movies in cinemas, kids watch lots of movies at home. More than 81% of U.S. homes have VCRs—a higher percentage than in any other country in the world. Most of these homes rent at least one movie a month.

Of all the categories of movies being rented, action films and comedies are the favorites. In 1996, rental income from action films was about $631 million, with comedies close behind at $611.5 million.

Films are given a rating by the Motion Picture Association of America. The rating is a reflection of a movie's violence and sexual content. The majority of the films released each year receive an "R" rating, which means that people under age 17 can be admitted only if accompanied by a parent or adult guardian. Other ratings include G (general audience), PG (parental guidance advised), PG-13 (may not be suitable for preteens), and NC-17 (persons under age 17 not admitted).

Kidbits Tidbits

- The top kid's video in early 1998 was Walt Disney's *Sleeping Beauty*.
- The top-selling video of all time is *The Lion King*. The #1 rental video of all time is *Top Gun*.
- Movies often reinforce misleading images of society. For example, one survey of top-grossing films of the 1990s found that 80% of the male leads smoked.

Movies and Videos

How Many Videos Are Rented Each Month?

On average, 63% of all U.S. adults rent at least one movie per month. Here's how the renters break down:

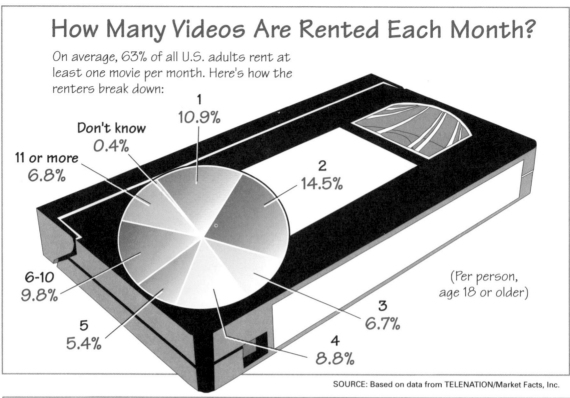

Don't know
0.4%

1
10.9%

11 or more
6.8%

2
14.5%

6-10
9.8%

5
5.4%

3
6.7%

4
8.8%

(Per person, age 18 or older)

SOURCE: Based on data from TELENATION/Market Facts, Inc.

Top 10 Top-Selling Videos of All Time
(Worldwide)

1   The Lion King
2   Aladdin
3   Beauty and the Beast
4   Snow White and the Seven Dwarfs
5   Forrest Gump
6   101 Dalmations
7   Jurassic Park
8   The Little Mermaid
9   Pinocchio
10 E.T.: The Extra-Terrestrial

SOURCE: Based on data from Alexander & Associates

Top 10 Top-Renting Videos of All Time

(In U.S.)

1   Top Gun
2   Pretty Woman
3   Home Alone
4   Ghost
5   The Little Mermaid
6   Terminator II: Judgment Day
7   Cinderella
8   Beauty and the Beast
9   Dances with Wolves
10 Batman

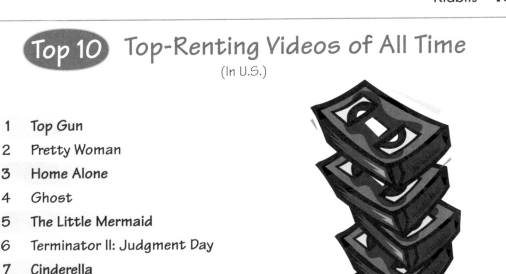

SOURCE: Based on data from Alexander & Associates

U.S. Box-Office Revenues, 1926–95

Box Office Receipts (In billions)

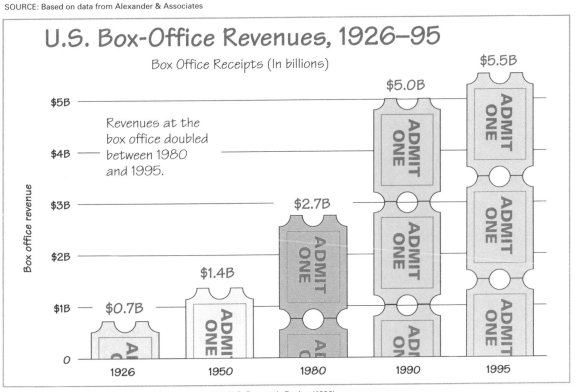

Revenues at the box office doubled between 1980 and 1995.

$5.5B
$5.0B
$2.7B
$1.4B
$0.7B

Box office revenue

$5B
$4B
$3B
$2B
$1B
0

1926   1950   1980   1990   1995

Movies and Videos

SOURCE: Based on data from U.S. Dept. of Commerce; 1995 *U.S. Economic Review* (1996)

Movie Advertising

The movie industry spends about $1.7 billion a year on advertising. How the money is spent:

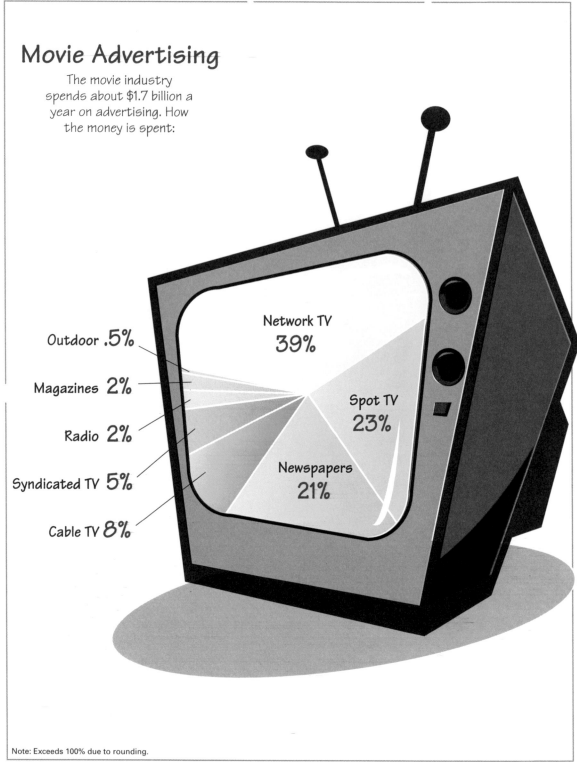

Outdoor .5%

Magazines 2%

Radio 2%

Syndicated TV 5%

Cable TV 8%

Network TV 39%

Spot TV 23%

Newspapers 21%

Movies and Videos

Note: Exceeds 100% due to rounding.

SOURCE: Based on data from Competitive Media Reporting

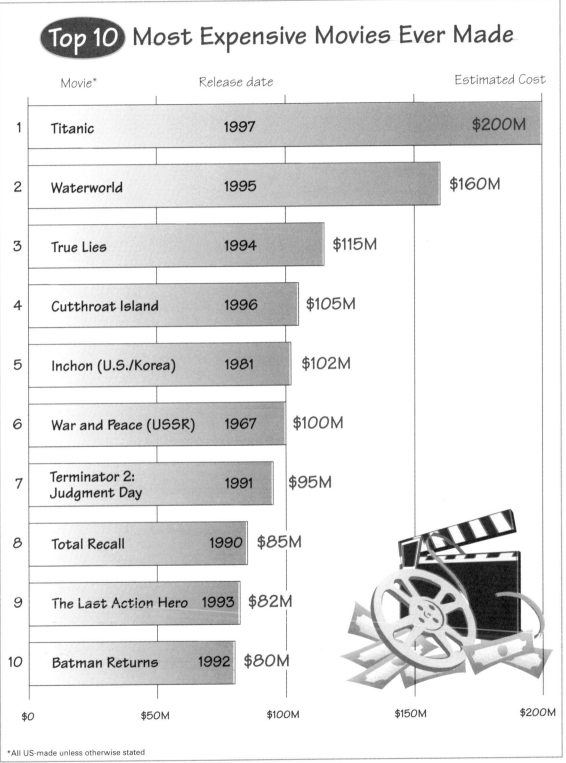

Top 10 Most Expensive Movies Ever Made

	Movie*	Release date	Estimated Cost
1	Titanic	1997	$200M
2	Waterworld	1995	$160M
3	True Lies	1994	$115M
4	Cutthroat Island	1996	$105M
5	Inchon (U.S./Korea)	1981	$102M
6	War and Peace (USSR)	1967	$100M
7	Terminator 2: Judgment Day	1991	$95M
8	Total Recall	1990	$85M
9	The Last Action Hero	1993	$82M
10	Batman Returns	1992	$80M

$0 $50M $100M $150M $200M

Movies and Videos

*All US-made unless otherwise stated

SOURCE: Based partially on information given in *The Top 10 of Everything 1997*

Top 10 Highest-Grossing Movies in the U.S.

(In box-office revenues, not adjusted for inflation)

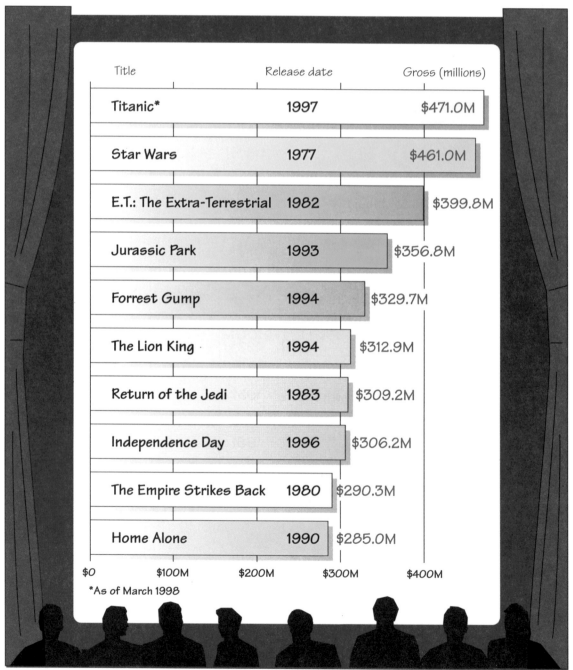

Title	Release date	Gross (millions)
Titanic*	1997	$471.0M
Star Wars	1977	$461.0M
E.T.: The Extra-Terrestrial	1982	$399.8M
Jurassic Park	1993	$356.8M
Forrest Gump	1994	$329.7M
The Lion King	1994	$312.9M
Return of the Jedi	1983	$309.2M
Independence Day	1996	$306.2M
The Empire Strikes Back	1980	$290.3M
Home Alone	1990	$285.0M

*As of March 1998

Movies and Videos

SOURCE: Based partially on data from Exhibitor Relations Co. Inc.

Top 10 Highest-Grossing Movies in the U.S.

(In box-office revenues, adjusted for inflation)

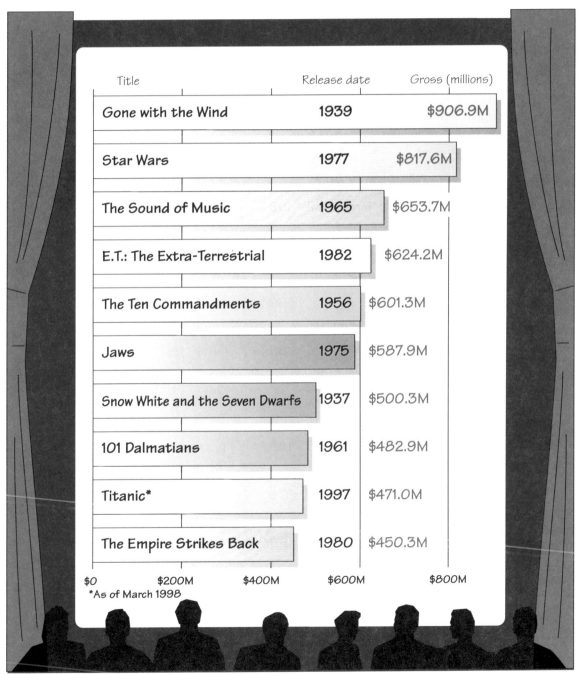

Title	Release date	Gross (millions)
Gone with the Wind	1939	$906.9M
Star Wars	1977	$817.6M
The Sound of Music	1965	$653.7M
E.T.: The Extra-Terrestrial	1982	$624.2M
The Ten Commandments	1956	$601.3M
Jaws	1975	$587.9M
Snow White and the Seven Dwarfs	1937	$500.3M
101 Dalmatians	1961	$482.9M
Titanic*	1997	$471.0M
The Empire Strikes Back	1980	$450.3M

$0 $200M $400M $600M $800M

*As of March 1998

Movies and Videos

SOURCE: Based partially on data from Exhibitor Relations Co. Inc.

Top Oscar Winners

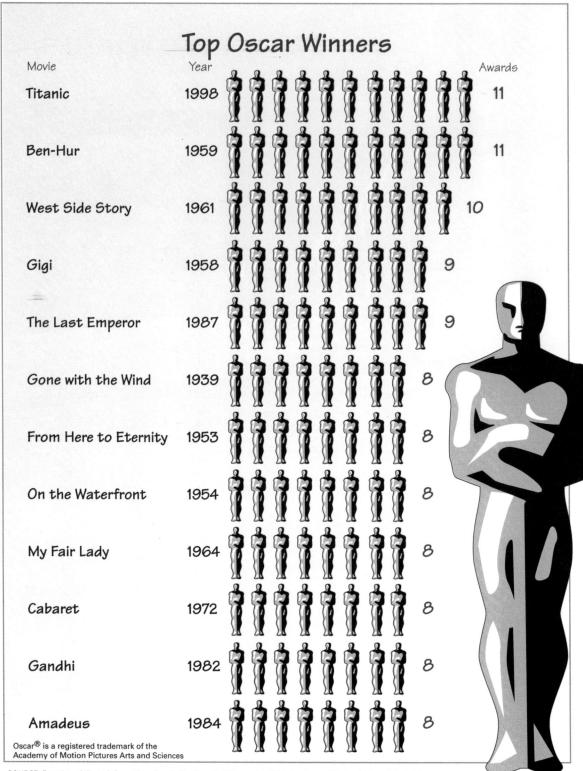

Movie	Year	Awards
Titanic	1998	11
Ben-Hur	1959	11
West Side Story	1961	10
Gigi	1958	9
The Last Emperor	1987	9
Gone with the Wind	1939	8
From Here to Eternity	1953	8
On the Waterfront	1954	8
My Fair Lady	1964	8
Cabaret	1972	8
Gandhi	1982	8
Amadeus	1984	8

Movies and Videos

Oscar® is a registered trademark of the
Academy of Motion Pictures Arts and Sciences

SOURCE: Based partially on information given in *The Top 10 of Everything 1997; Academy of Motion Picture Arts & Sciences*

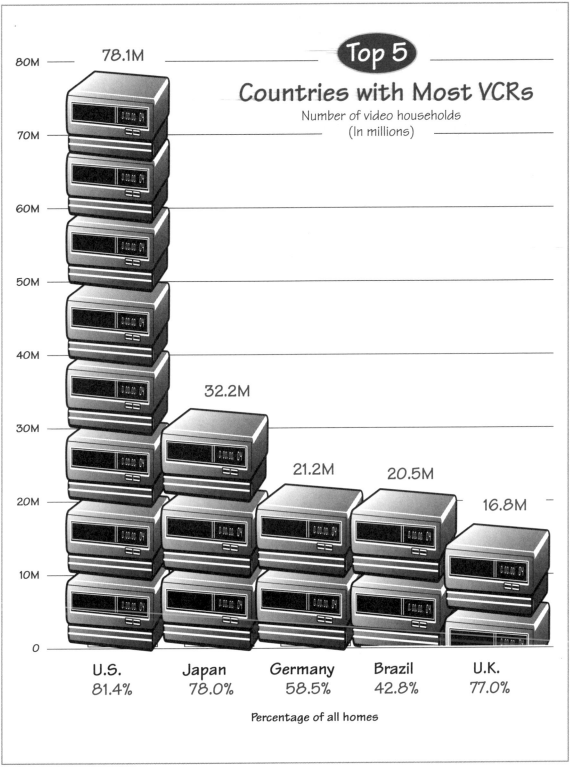

Top 5

Countries with Most VCRs

Number of video households
(In millions)

80M — 78.1M

70M

60M

50M

40M

32.2M

30M

21.2M   20.5M

20M   16.8M

10M

0

| U.S. | Japan | Germany | Brazil | U.K. |
| 81.4% | 78.0% | 58.5% | 42.8% | 77.0% |

Percentage of all homes

Movies and Videos

SOURCE: Based on information given in *The Top 10 of Everything 1997*

Million Dollar Movie Days

Steven Spielberg's *The Lost World*, sequel to *Jurassic Park*, did a record $90.1 million at the box office in its first 5 days. It is the fastest movie to gross $100 million:

The Lost World (1997) — 5 Days

Independence Day (1996) — 7 Days

Jurassic Park (1993) — 9 Days

Batman (1989) — 10 Days

Batman Forever (1995) — 10 Days

Days to reach $100 million

SOURCE: Based on data from Exhibitor Relations

The Rating Game

Movies and Videos

About 60% of all movies get an "R" rating. How the ratings broke down for the 713 movies of 1996:

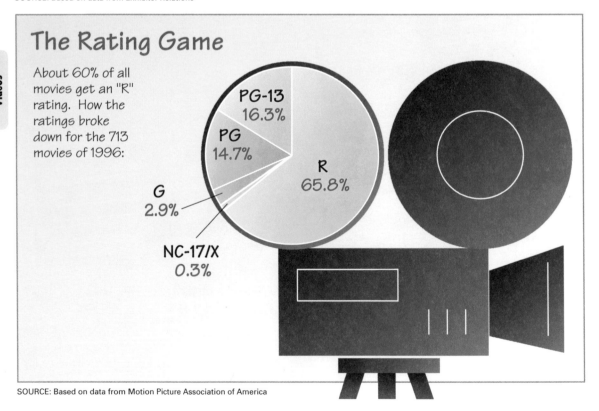

PG-13
16.3%

PG
14.7%

G
2.9%

NC-17/X
0.3%

R
65.8%

SOURCE: Based on data from Motion Picture Association of America

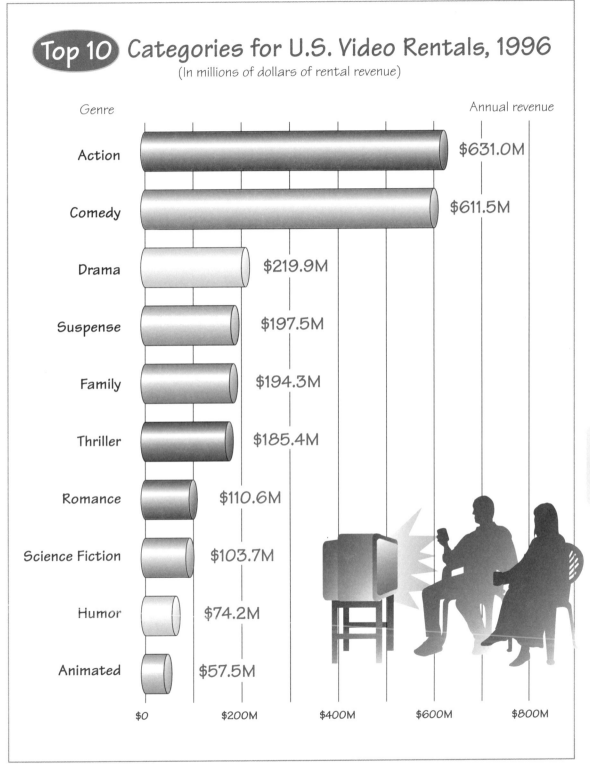

Top 10 Categories for U.S. Video Rentals, 1996

(In millions of dollars of rental revenue)

Genre

Annual revenue

Action	$631.0M
Comedy	$611.5M
Drama	$219.9M
Suspense	$197.5M
Family	$194.3M
Thriller	$185.4M
Romance	$110.6M
Science Fiction	$103.7M
Humor	$74.2M
Animated	$57.5M

$0 $200M $400M $600M $800M

Movies and Videos

SOURCE: Based on data from *Video Store Magazine*

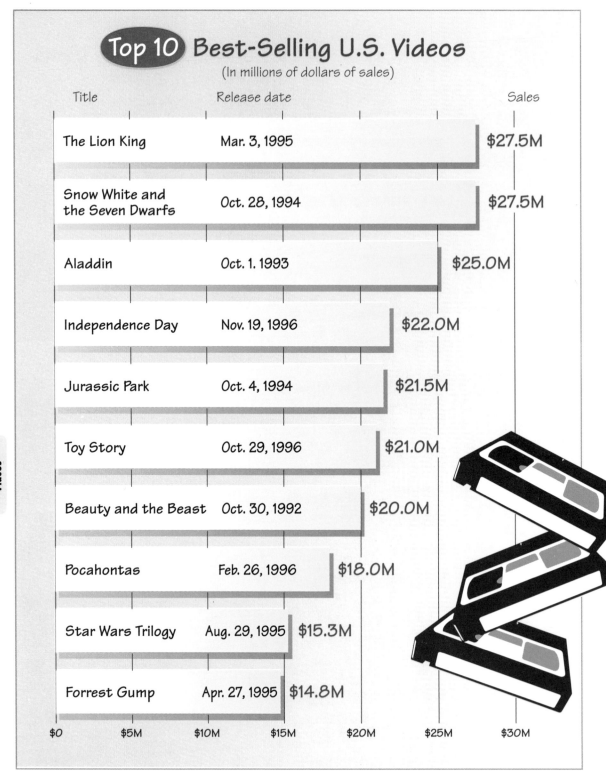

Top 10 Best-Selling U.S. Videos

(In millions of dollars of sales)

Title	Release date	Sales
The Lion King	Mar. 3, 1995	$27.5M
Snow White and the Seven Dwarfs	Oct. 28, 1994	$27.5M
Aladdin	Oct. 1. 1993	$25.0M
Independence Day	Nov. 19, 1996	$22.0M
Jurassic Park	Oct. 4, 1994	$21.5M
Toy Story	Oct. 29, 1996	$21.0M
Beauty and the Beast	Oct. 30, 1992	$20.0M
Pocahontas	Feb. 26, 1996	$18.0M
Star Wars Trilogy	Aug. 29, 1995	$15.3M
Forrest Gump	Apr. 27, 1995	$14.8M

$0 $5M $10M $15M $20M $25M $30M

Movies and Videos

SOURCE: Based on data from *Video Store Magazine*

Top 10 Video Rentals in U.S., 1996

(In millions of dollars of revenue)

Film	Release date	Revenue ($)*
Twister	Oct. 1	$41.9M
Independence Day	Nov. 22	$41.0M
Broken Arrow	July 2	$39.9M
Ace Ventura: When Nature Calls	Mar. 12	$36.1M
Toy Story	Oct. 29	$34.5M
Eraser	Oct. 29	$34.5M
Babe	Mar. 18	$32.7M
Braveheart	Mar. 12	$32.7M
Dangerous Minds	Feb. 12	$32.0M
A Time to Kill	Dec. 31	$30.4M

$0 $10M $20M $30M $40M

Movies and Videos

* Spent by U.S. consumers renting the title during its first four months of release

SOURCE: Based on data from *Video Store Magazine*

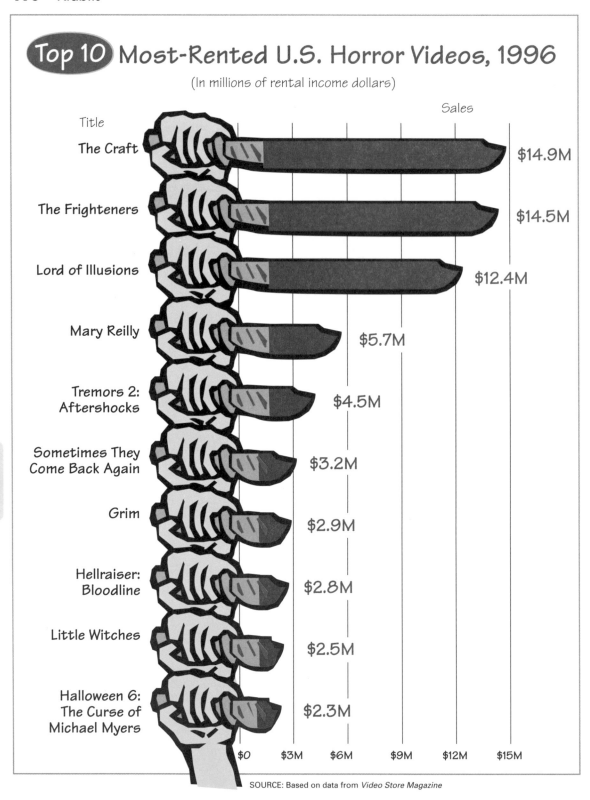

Top 10 Most-Rented U.S. Horror Videos, 1996

(In millions of rental income dollars)

Sales

Title

Title	
The Craft	$14.9M
The Frighteners	$14.5M
Lord of Illusions	$12.4M
Mary Reilly	$5.7M
Tremors 2: Aftershocks	$4.5M
Sometimes They Come Back Again	$3.2M
Grim	$2.9M
Hellraiser: Bloodline	$2.8M
Little Witches	$2.5M
Halloween 6: The Curse of Michael Myers	$2.3M

$0 $3M $6M $9M $12M $15M

Movies and Videos

SOURCE: Based on data from *Video Store Magazine*

Top 10 Most-Rented Sci-Fi Videos, 1996

(In rental income dollars)

Title   Sales

Independence Day — $41.0M

12 Monkeys — $18.4M

The Island of Dr. Moreau — $17.6M

Strange Days — $9.7M

The Arrival — $5.5M

Lawnmower Man 2: Jobe's War — $3.9M

Nemesis 3 — $2.8M

It Came From Outer Space — $500,000

Forbidden Zone: Alien Abduction — $470,000

The Silencers — $450,000

$0 $10M $20M $30M $40M

Movies and Videos

SOURCE: Based on data from *Video Store Magazine*

Golden Globe Awards for "Best Performance by an Actor in a Motion Picture—Drama," 1988–1998

Year	Actor	Film
1998	Peter Fonda	Ulee's Gold
1997	Geoffrey Rush	Shine
1996	Nicolas Cage	Leaving Las Vegas
1995	Tom Hanks	Forrest Gump
1994	Tom Hanks	Philadelphia
1993	Al Pacino	Scent of a Woman
1992	Nick Nolte	The Prince of Tides
1991	Jeremy Irons	Reversal of Fortune
1990	Tom Cruise	Born on the Fourth of July
1989	Dustin Hoffman	Rain Man
1988	Michael Douglas	Wall Street

SOURCE: Based on data from Motion Picture Association of America

Golden Globe Awards For "Best Performance by an Actress in a Motion Picture—Drama," 1988–1998

Year	Actress	Film
1998	Judi Dench	Mrs. Brown
1997	Brenda Blethyn	Secrets and Lies
1996	Sharon Stone	Casino
1995	Jessica Lange	Blue Sky
1994	Holly Hunter	The Piano
1993	Emma Thompson	Howard's End
1992	Jodie Foster	The Silence of the Lambs
1991	Kathy Bates	Misery
1990	Michelle Pfeiffer	The Fabulous Baker Boys
1989	Jodie Foster* Shirley MacLaine*	The Accused* Madame Sousatzka* *Prize shared
1988	Shirley Kirkland	Anna

SOURCE: Based on data from Motion Picture Association of America

Golden Globe Awards for "Best Performance by an Actor in a Motion Picture—Musical or Comedy," 1988–1998

Year	Actor and Film
1998	Jack Nicholson in *As Good As It Gets*
1997	Tom Cruise in *Jerry Maguire*
1996	John Travolta in *Get Shorty*
1995	Hugh Grant in *Four Weddings and a Funeral*
1994	Robin Williams in *Mrs. Doubtfire*
1993	Tim Robbins in *The Player*
1992	Robin Williams in *The Fisher King*
1991	Gerard Depardieu in *Green Card*
1990	Morgan Freeman in *Driving Miss Daisy*
1989	Tom Hanks in *Big*
1988	Robin Williams in *Good Morning, Vietnam*

SOURCE: Based on statistics from E! Online and the Academy of Motion Picture Arts and Sciences

Golden Globe Awards for "Best Performance by an Actress in a Motion Picture—Musical or Comedy," 1988–1998

Year	Actress and Film
1998	Helen Hunt in *As Good As It Gets*
1997	Madonna in *Evita*
1996	Nicole Kidman in *To Die For*
1995	Jamie Lee Curtis in *True Lies*
1994	Angela Bassett in *What's Love Got To Do With It?*
1993	Miranda Richardson in *Enchanted April*
1992	Bette Midler in *For the Boys*
1991	Julia Roberts in *Pretty Woman*
1990	Jessica Tandy in *Driving Miss Daisy*
1989	Melanie Griffith in *Working Girl*
1988	Cher in *Moonstruck*

Movies and Videos

SOURCE: Based on statistics from E! Online and the Academy of Motion Picture Arts and Sciences

Golden Globe Awards for "Best Motion Picture—Musical or Comedy," 1988–1998

Year	Film
1998	As Good As It Gets
1997	Evita
1996	Babe
1995	The Lion King
1994	Mrs. Doubtfire
1993	The Player
1992	Beauty and the Beast
1991	Green Card
1990	Driving Miss Daisy
1989	Working Girl
1988	Hope and Glory

SOURCE: Based on statistics from E! Online and the Academy of Motion Picture Arts and Sciences

The Top Oscar-Nominated Movies of All Time

Year	Film	Nominations
1997	Titanic	14
1950	All About Eve	14
1939	Gone with the Wind	13
1953	From Here to Eternity	13
1964	Mary Poppins	13
1966	Who's Afraid of Virginia Woolf?	13
1994	Forrest Gump	13

Oscar® is a registered trademark of the Academy of Motion Picture Arts and Sciences

SOURCE: Based on statistics from E! Online and the Academy of Motion Picture Arts and Sciences

Best Picture Oscars: 1988–1998

Year	Film
1998	Titanic
1997	The English Patient
1996	Braveheart
1995	Forrest Gump
1994	Schindler's List
1993	Unforgiven
1992	The Silence of the Lambs
1991	Dances with Wolves
1990	Driving Miss Daisy
1989	Rain Man
1988	The Last Emperor

SOURCE: Based on data from Motion Picture Association of America

Best Director Oscars: 1988–1998

Year	Director	Film
1998	James Cameron	Titanic
1997	Anthony Minghella	The English Patient
1996	Mel Gibson	Braveheart
1995	Robert Zemeckis	Forrest Gump
1994	Steven Spielberg	Schindler's List
1993	Clint Eastwood	Unforgiven
1992	Jonathan Demme	The Silence of the Lambs
1991	Kevin Costner	Dances with Wolves
1990	Oliver Stone	Born on the Fourth of July
1989	Barry Levinson	Rain Man
1988	Bernardo Bertolucci	The Last Emperor

Movies and Videos

SOURCE: Based on data from Motion Picture Association of America

Best Actress Oscars: 1988–1998

Year	Actress
1998	Helen Hunt (*As Good As It Gets*)
1997	Frances McDormand (*Fargo*)
1996	Susan Sarandon (*Dead Man Walking*)
1995	Jessica Lange (*Blue Sky*)
1994	Holly Hunter (*The Piano*)
1993	Emma Thompson (*Howard's End*)
1992	Jodie Foster (*The Silence of the Lambs*)
1991	Kathy Bates (*Misery*)
1990	Jessica Tandy (*Driving Miss Daisy*)
1989	Jodie Foster (*The Accused*)
1988	Cher (*Moonstruck*)

SOURCE: Based on data from Motion Picture Association of America

Best Actor Oscars: 1988–1998

Year	Actor
1998	Jack Nicholson (*As Good As It Gets*)
1997	Geoffrey Rush (*Shine*)
1996	Nicolas Cage (*Leaving Las Vegas*)
1995	Tom Hanks (*Forrest Gump*)
1994	Tom Hanks (*Philadelphia*)
1993	Al Pacino (*Scent of a Woman*)
1992	Anthony Hopkins (*The Silence of the Lambs*)
1991	Jeremy Irons (*Reversal of Fortune*)
1990	Daniel Day-Lewis (*My Left Foot*)
1989	Dustin Hoffman (*Rain Man*)
1988	Michael Douglas (*Wall Street*)

SOURCE: Based on data from Motion Picture Association of America

Movies and Videos

Best Supporting Actress Oscars: 1988–1998

Year	Actress
1998	Kim Basinger (*L.A. Confidential*)
1997	Juliette Binoche (*The English Patient*)
1996	Mira Sorvino (*Mighty Aphrodite*)
1995	Dianne Wiest (*Bullets Over Broadway*)
1994	Anna Paquin (*The Piano*)
1993	Marisa Tomei (*My Cousin Vinny*)
1992	Mercedes Ruehl (*The Fisher King*)
1991	Whoopi Goldberg (*Ghost*)
1990	Brenda Fricker (*My Left Foot*)
1989	Geena Davis (*The Accidental Tourist*)
1988	Olympia Dukakis (*Moonstruck*)

SOURCE: Based on data from Motion Picture Association of America

Best Supporting Actor Oscars: 1988–1998

Movies and Videos

Year	Actor
1998	Robin Williams (*Good Will Hunting*)
1997	Cuba Gooding Jr. (*Jerry Maguire*)
1996	Kevin Spacey (*The Usual Suspects*)
1995	Martin Landau (*Ed Wood*)
1994	Tommy Lee Jones (*The Fugitive*)
1993	Gene Hackman (*Unforgiven*)
1992	Jack Palance (*City Slickers*)
1991	Joe Pesci (*Goodfellas*)
1990	Denzel Washington (*Glory*)
1989	Kevin Kline (*A Fish Called Wanda*)
1988	Sean Connery (*The Untouchables*)

SOURCE: Based on data from Motion Picture Association of America

Pro Sports

Even very young children love to follow professional sports. By the time they enter middle school and high school, millions of kids are fanatics! They root for their favorite team, collect trading cards that picture their favorite players, and wear sweatshirts and caps with team logos. Many dream of the day when they, too, might become pro players. Of course, very few children realize these dreams. Very few develop the skills needed to compete at a professional level. But for those who are successful, the payoff can be enormous.

Top professionals earn millions of dollars each year, not only in salaries but also from their endorsements of clothing, video games, cereals, and other products. Professionals are paid for their endorsements because companies know that they'll sell more merchandise—especially to young people—if it carries Michael Jordan's picture or Tiger Wood's name.

This wasn't always true. Professional sports have changed tremendously over the years. In 1959, members of the

Kidbits Tidbits

- In 1996, baseball star Ken Griffey Jr. earned $7 million—more than 172 times the median American household income.
- The top-paying position in football is quarterback; starters had average salaries of $2.4 million in 1996.
- In 1997, Michael Jordan earned an estimated $38 million by endorsing products. This was in addition to his salary, which was over $30 million for the 1996–97 season.

Professional Bowlers Association competed in three tournaments for prizes worth a total of $49,500; by 1997 they were competing in four seasonal tours for more than $8 million in prize money. When Babe Ruth played baseball, there were no night games, no domed ballparks, no coast-to-coast travel, no million-dollar salaries—and no black players in the major leagues. When Ray Harroun won the first Indianapolis 500 in 1911, he drove at an average speed of less than 75 mph; when Arie Luyendyk won in 1997, his average speed was 145.8 mph!

Today, the media—particularly TV—spends big bucks on sports. These dollars help pay for salaries. In return, the media has a large part in deciding everything from the starting times of games to playing dates.

Another big change has been the growth of women's professional sports. For example, the 1990s saw the beginning of the Women's National Basketball Association and other pro leagues. Much of the credit for this change belongs to the passage of a federal law in 1972. The law—called Title IX—outlaws discrimination in school sports on the basis of gender. The law meant that girls could have equal opportunities to develop as athletes. As a result, many girls have grown up to be strong, skilled professional athletes. Women's winnings and salaries, however, still do not equal those of men. For example, the #1 woman golfer in 1996 earned $1,002,000. The #1 male golfer earned $1,780,159.

Kidbits Tidbits

- In 1997, at the ripe old age of 21, Tiger Woods became the youngest golfer ever to win the Masters.
- The most valuable NFL franchise in 1996 was the Dallas Cowboys ($272 million). The most valuable NBA franchise was the New York Knicks ($205 million).
- The leading advertiser in the sports sector in 1995 was Anheuser-Busch ($143 million), followed by Chevrolet ($119 million) and Miller Brewing ($96 million).

Pro Sports

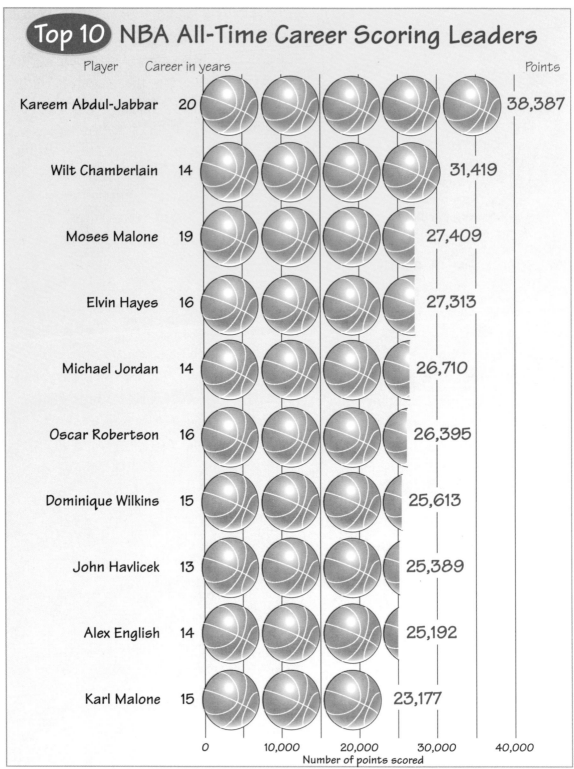

Top 10 NBA All-Time Career Scoring Leaders

Player	Career in years		Points
Kareem Abdul-Jabbar	20		38,387
Wilt Chamberlain	14		31,419
Moses Malone	19		27,409
Elvin Hayes	16		27,313
Michael Jordan	14		26,710
Oscar Robertson	16		26,395
Dominique Wilkins	15		25,613
John Havlicek	13		25,389
Alex English	14		25,192
Karl Malone	15		23,177

0   10,000   20,000   30,000   40,000

Number of points scored

SOURCE: Based on data from National Basketball Association

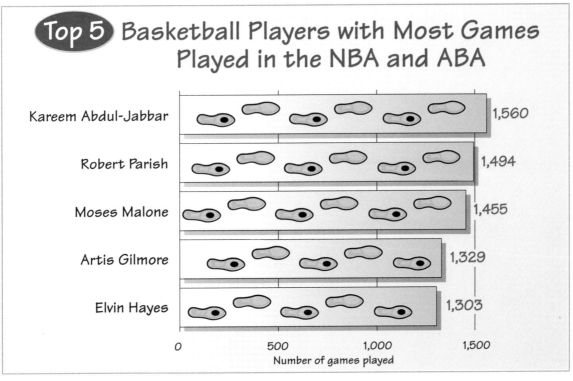

Top 5 Basketball Players with Most Games Played in the NBA and ABA

Player	Number of games played
Kareem Abdul-Jabbar	1,560
Robert Parish	1,494
Moses Malone	1,455
Artis Gilmore	1,329
Elvin Hayes	1,303

SOURCE: Based on information given in *The Top 10 of Everything 1997*

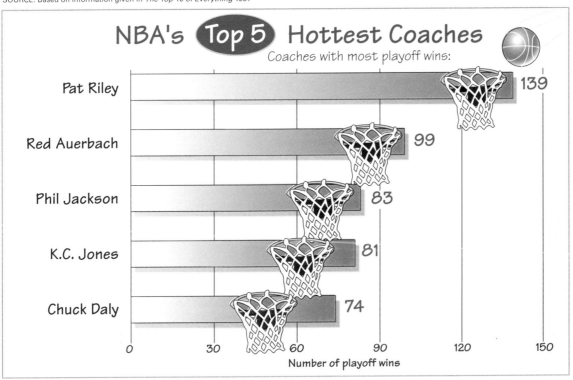

NBA's Top 5 Hottest Coaches

Coaches with most playoff wins:

Coach	Number of playoff wins
Pat Riley	139
Red Auerbach	99
Phil Jackson	83
K.C. Jones	81
Chuck Daly	74

SOURCE: Based on data from NBA

Pro Sports

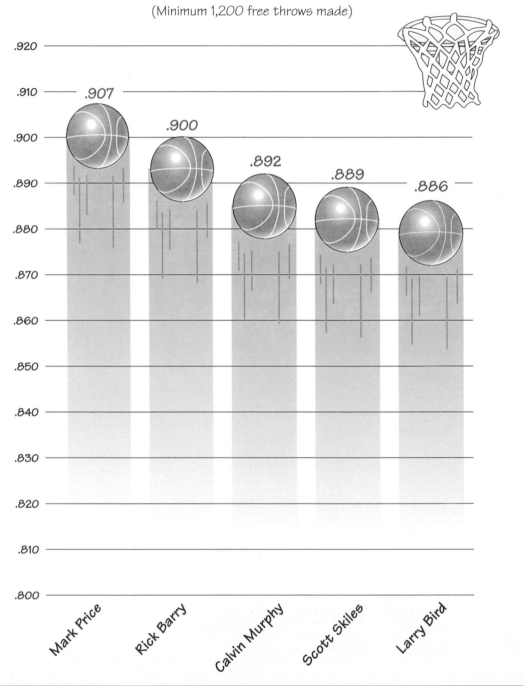

Top 5 Basketball Players, by Free Throw Percentages

(Minimum 1,200 free throws made)

.907 Mark Price
.900 Rick Barry
.892 Calvin Murphy
.889 Scott Skiles
.886 Larry Bird

Pro Sports

SOURCE: Based on statistics from the NBA

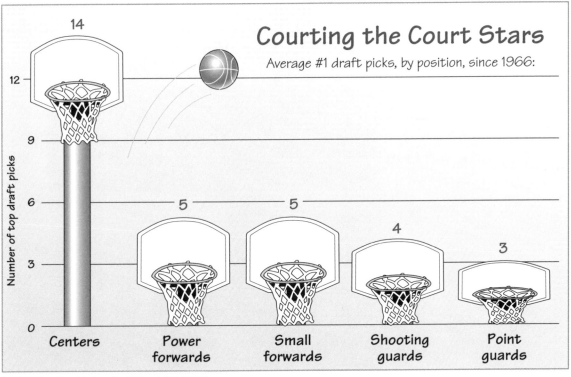

Courting the Court Stars

Average #1 draft picks, by position, since 1966:

Number of top draft picks

Centers	Power forwards	Small forwards	Shooting guards	Point guards
14	5	5	4	3

SOURCE: Based on data from the NBA and *USA TODAY*

Top Earners in the NBA, 1997

(In millions)

Michael Jordan Chicago Bulls	Horace Grant Orlando Magic	Reggie Miller Indiana Pacers
$30.14M	$14.86M	$11.25M

SOURCE: Based on data from *USA TODAY*

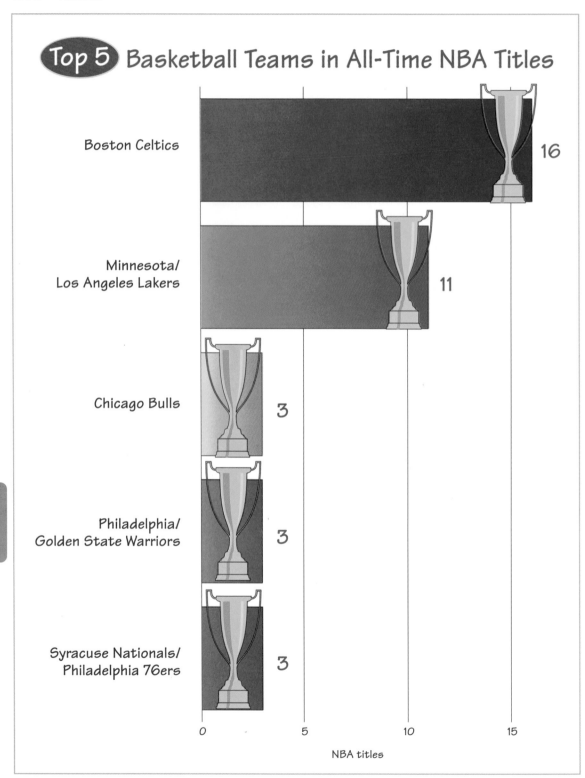

Top 5 Basketball Teams in All-Time NBA Titles

Boston Celtics — 16

Minnesota/ Los Angeles Lakers — 11

Chicago Bulls — 3

Philadelphia/ Golden State Warriors — 3

Syracuse Nationals/ Philadelphia 76ers — 3

0   5   10   15

NBA titles

Pro Sports

SOURCE: Based on information given in *The Top 10 of Everything 1997*

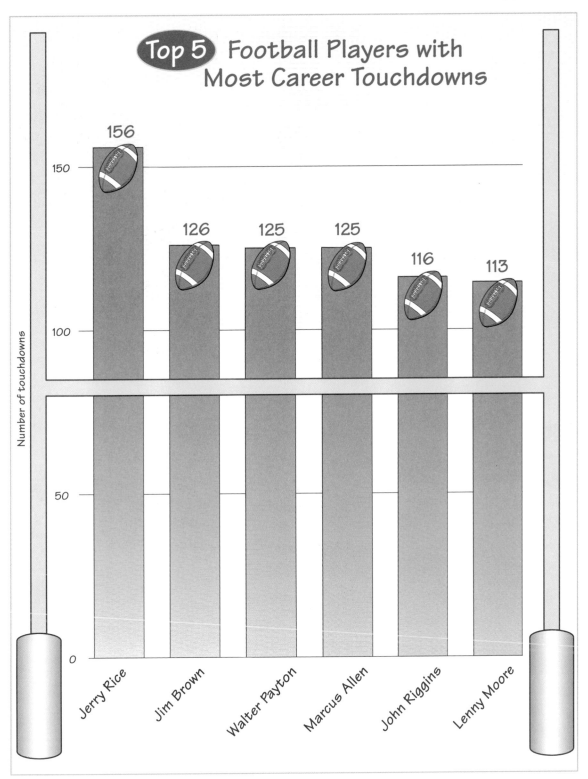

Top 5 Football Players with Most Career Touchdowns

Number of touchdowns

156
126
125
125
116
113

150

100

50

0

Jerry Rice
Jim Brown
Walter Payton
Marcus Allen
John Riggins
Lenny Moore

Pro Sports

SOURCE: Based on information given in *The Top 10 of Everything 1997*

NFL's Top 5 Single-Season Point-Scorers

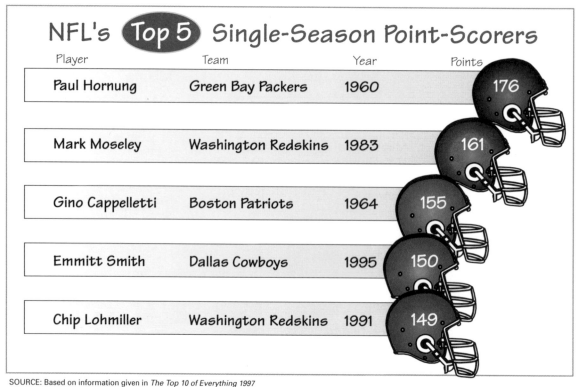

Player	Team	Year	Points
Paul Hornung	Green Bay Packers	1960	176
Mark Moseley	Washington Redskins	1983	161
Gino Cappelletti	Boston Patriots	1964	155
Emmitt Smith	Dallas Cowboys	1995	150
Chip Lohmiller	Washington Redskins	1991	149

SOURCE: Based on information given in *The Top 10 of Everything 1997*

Top 5 Most Successful Career Rushers in the NFL

(Total yards gained rushing)

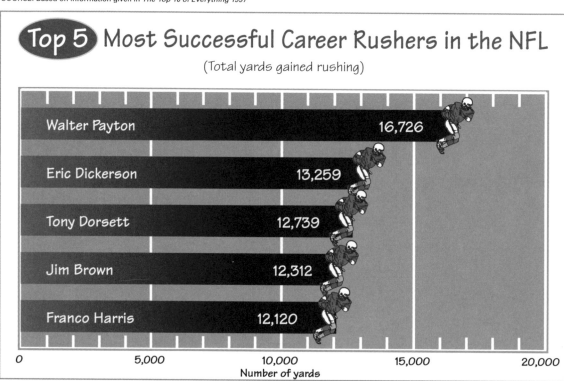

Player	Number of yards
Walter Payton	16,726
Eric Dickerson	13,259
Tony Dorsett	12,739
Jim Brown	12,312
Franco Harris	12,120

Number of yards: 0 — 5,000 — 10,000 — 15,000 — 20,000

Pro Sports

SOURCE: Based on information given in *The Top 10 of Everything 1997*

Top All-Time Passing Records in the NFL

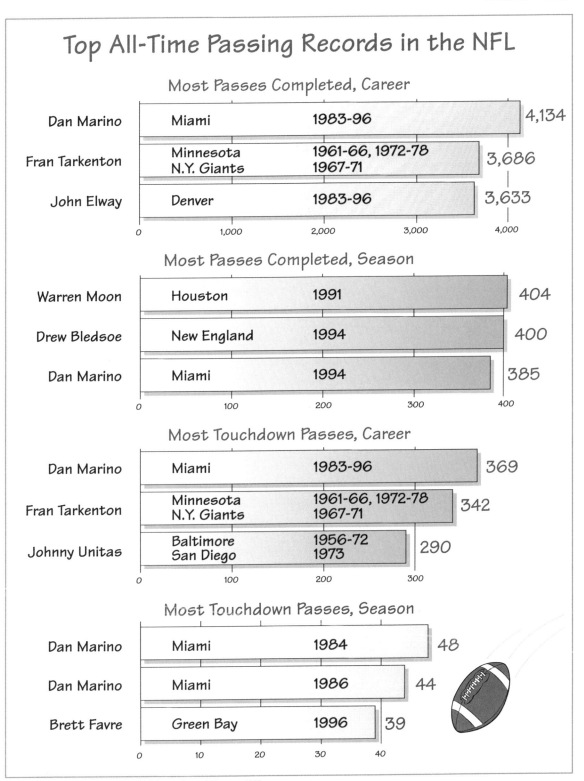

Most Passes Completed, Career

Dan Marino	Miami	1983-96	4,134
Fran Tarkenton	Minnesota / N.Y. Giants	1961-66, 1972-78 / 1967-71	3,686
John Elway	Denver	1983-96	3,633

(scale: 0, 1,000, 2,000, 3,000, 4,000)

Most Passes Completed, Season

Warren Moon	Houston	1991	404
Drew Bledsoe	New England	1994	400
Dan Marino	Miami	1994	385

(scale: 0, 100, 200, 300, 400)

Most Touchdown Passes, Career

Dan Marino	Miami	1983-96	369
Fran Tarkenton	Minnesota / N.Y. Giants	1961-66, 1972-78 / 1967-71	342
Johnny Unitas	Baltimore / San Diego	1956-72 / 1973	290

(scale: 0, 100, 200, 300)

Most Touchdown Passes, Season

Dan Marino	Miami	1984	48
Dan Marino	Miami	1986	44
Brett Favre	Green Bay	1996	39

(scale: 0, 10, 20, 30, 40)

Pro Sports

SOURCE: Based on data from *The Wall Street Journal Almanac 1998*

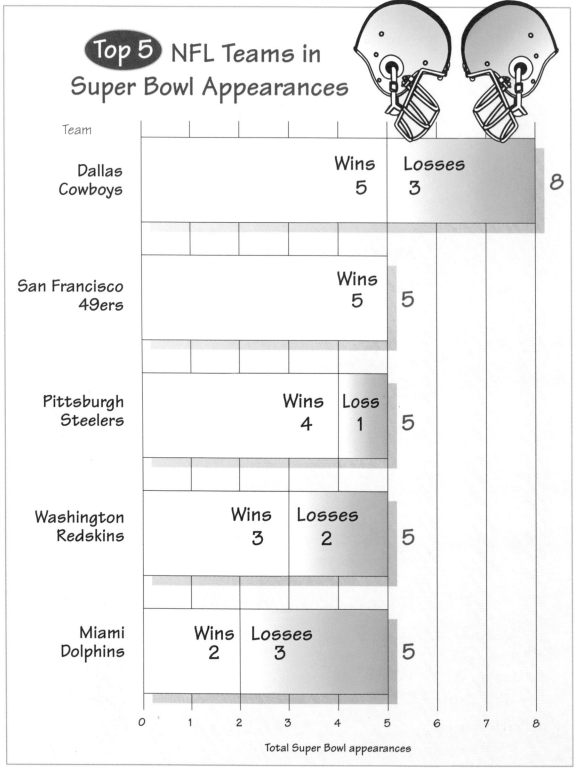

Top 5 NFL Teams in Super Bowl Appearances

Team

Dallas Cowboys	Wins 5 — Losses 3 — 8
San Francisco 49ers	Wins 5 — 5
Pittsburgh Steelers	Wins 4 — Loss 1 — 5
Washington Redskins	Wins 3 — Losses 2 — 5
Miami Dolphins	Wins 2 — Losses 3 — 5

0   1   2   3   4   5   6   7   8

Total Super Bowl appearances

Pro Sports

SOURCE: Based on data from National Football League

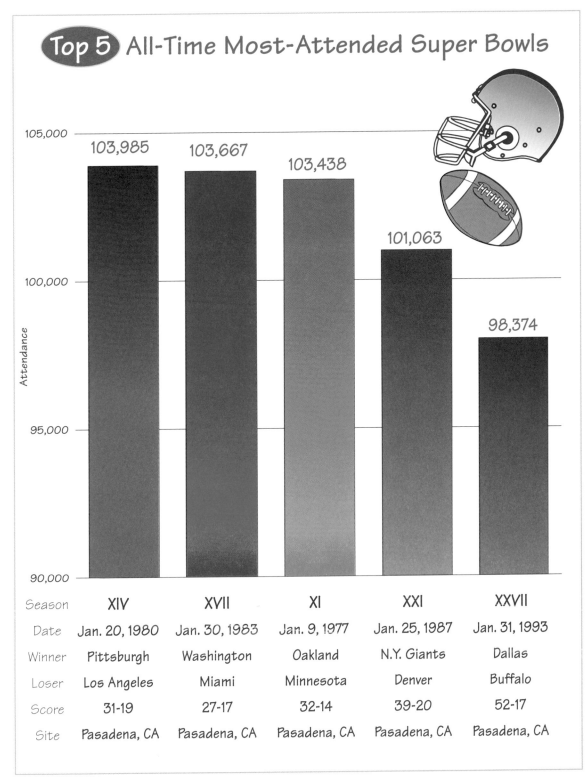

Top 5 All-Time Most-Attended Super Bowls

Attendance

	103,985	103,667	103,438	101,063	98,374

Season	XIV	XVII	XI	XXI	XXVII
Date	Jan. 20, 1980	Jan. 30, 1983	Jan. 9, 1977	Jan. 25, 1987	Jan. 31, 1993
Winner	Pittsburgh	Washington	Oakland	N.Y. Giants	Dallas
Loser	Los Angeles	Miami	Minnesota	Denver	Buffalo
Score	31-19	27-17	32-14	39-20	52-17
Site	Pasadena, CA	Pasadena, CA	Pasadena, CA	Pasadena, CA	Pasadena, CA

Pro Sports

SOURCE: Based on data from National Football League

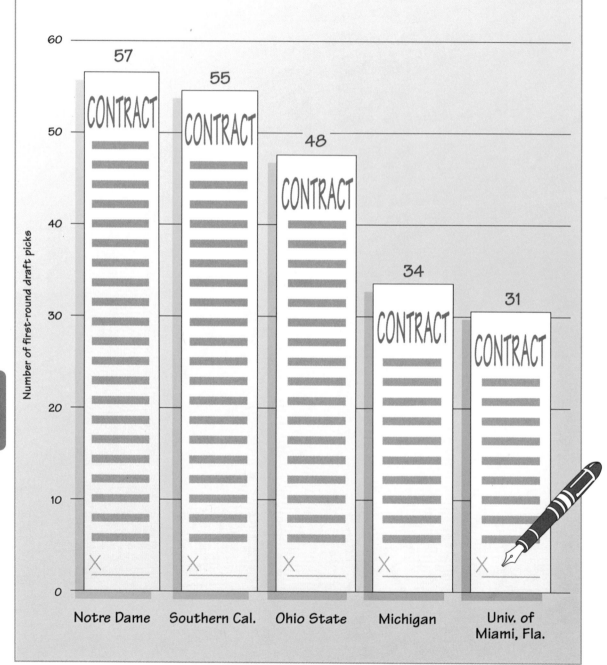

Top 5 Draft Suppliers to the NFL

Colleges and universities who have had the most
first-round draft players since 1936:

Number of first-round draft picks

| Notre Dame | Southern Cal. | Ohio State | Michigan | Univ. of Miami, Fla. |
| 57 | 55 | 48 | 34 | 31 |

Pro Sports

SOURCE: Based on data from NFL

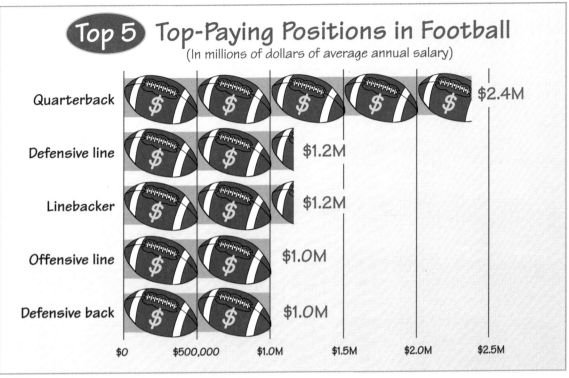

Top-Paying Positions in Football

Top 5

(In millions of dollars of average annual salary)

Quarterback — $2.4M

Defensive line — $1.2M

Linebacker — $1.2M

Offensive line — $1.0M

Defensive back — $1.0M

$0 $500,000 $1.0M $1.5M $2.0M $2.5M

SOURCE: Based on data from *USA Today* analysis of 1996 NFL salaries

Top Earners in NFL, 1996

(In millions)

$6M

$5.37M $5.33M $4.98M

$5M

$4M

$3M

$2M

$1M

$0

Troy Aikman
Dallas Cowboys

Dan Marino
Miami Dolphins

Steve Young
San Francisco 49ers

SOURCE: Based on data from *USA TODAY*

Pro Sports

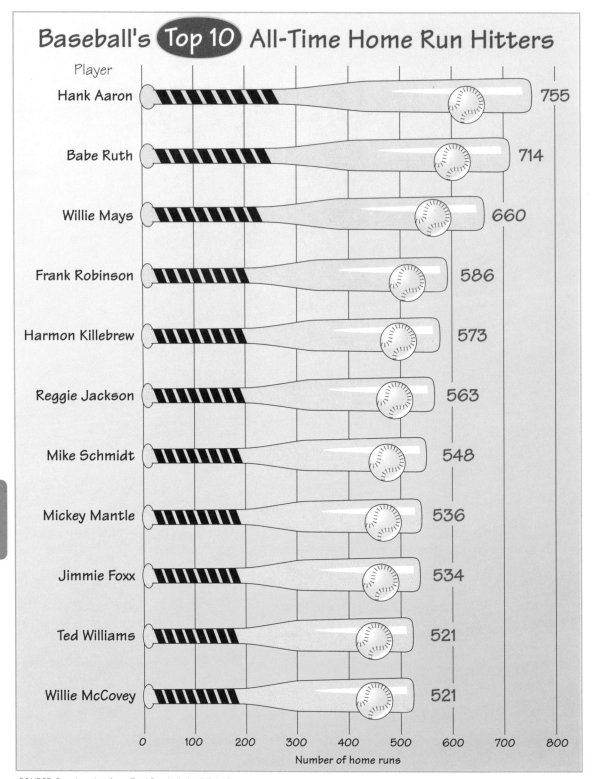

Baseball's (Top 10) All-Time Home Run Hitters

Player

Hank Aaron — 755

Babe Ruth — 714

Willie Mays — 660

Frank Robinson — 586

Harmon Killebrew — 573

Reggie Jackson — 563

Mike Schmidt — 548

Mickey Mantle — 536

Jimmie Foxx — 534

Ted Williams — 521

Willie McCovey — 521

0   100   200   300   400   500   600   700   800

Number of home runs

SOURCE: Based on data from *Total Baseball, the Official Encyclopedia of Major League Baseball*

Top Baseball Players with Highest Career Batting Averages

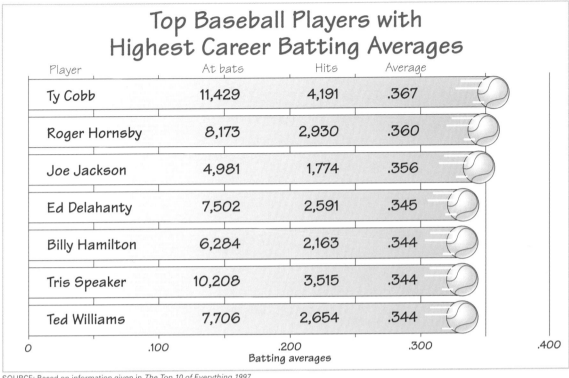

Player	At bats	Hits	Average
Ty Cobb	11,429	4,191	.367
Roger Hornsby	8,173	2,930	.360
Joe Jackson	4,981	1,774	.356
Ed Delahanty	7,502	2,591	.345
Billy Hamilton	6,284	2,163	.344
Tris Speaker	10,208	3,515	.344
Ted Williams	7,706	2,654	.344

Batting averages

SOURCE: Based on information given in *The Top 10 of Everything 1997*

Top 5 Baseball Players with Most Career Games

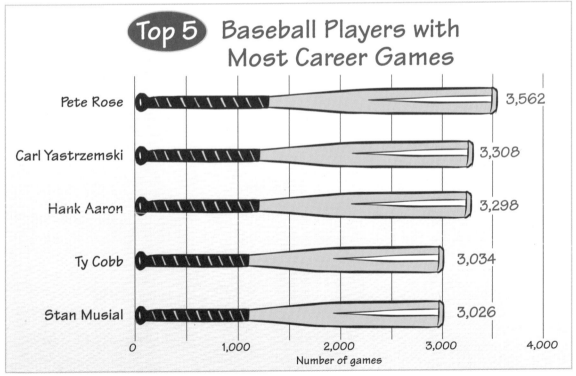

Player	Number of games
Pete Rose	3,562
Carl Yastrzemski	3,308
Hank Aaron	3,298
Ty Cobb	3,034
Stan Musial	3,026

Number of games

SOURCE: Based on information given in *The Top 10 of Everything 1997*

Pro Sports

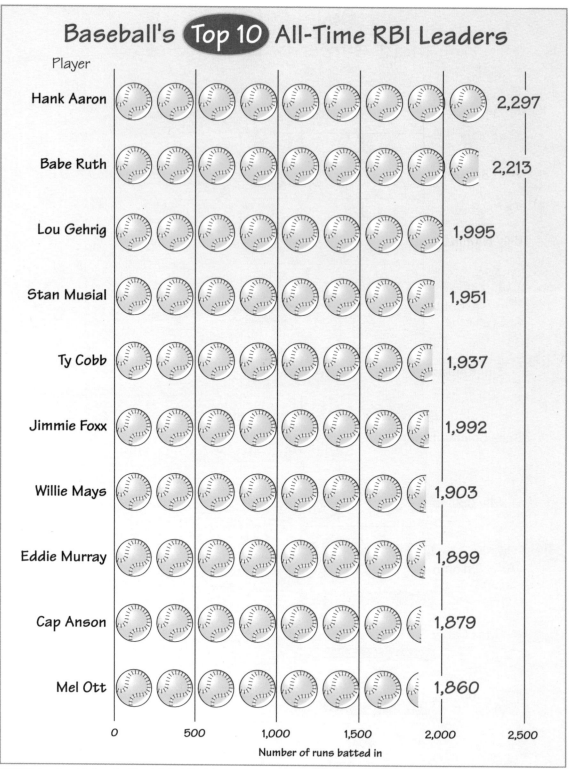

Baseball's (Top 10) All-Time RBI Leaders

Player

Player	RBI
Hank Aaron	2,297
Babe Ruth	2,213
Lou Gehrig	1,995
Stan Musial	1,951
Ty Cobb	1,937
Jimmie Foxx	1,992
Willie Mays	1,903
Eddie Murray	1,899
Cap Anson	1,879
Mel Ott	1,860

0   500   1,000   1,500   2,000   2,500

Number of runs batted in

SOURCE: Based on data from *Total Baseball, the Official Encyclopedia of Major League Baseball*

Pro Sports

Baseball's (Top 10) All-Time Base Stealers

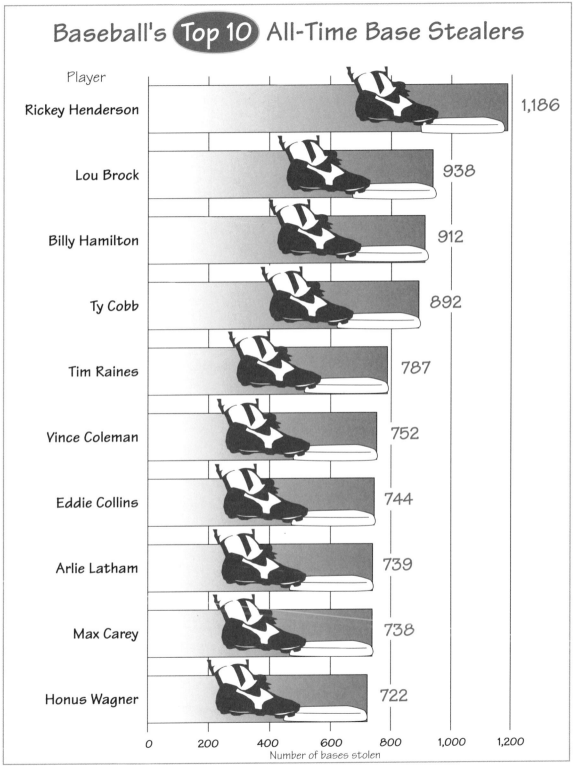

Player

Player	Number of bases stolen
Rickey Henderson	1,186
Lou Brock	938
Billy Hamilton	912
Ty Cobb	892
Tim Raines	787
Vince Coleman	752
Eddie Collins	744
Arlie Latham	739
Max Carey	738
Honus Wagner	722

0   200   400   600   800   1,000   1,200

Number of bases stolen

Pro Sports

SOURCE: Based on data from *Total Baseball, the Official Encyclopedia of Major League Baseball*

Pro Sports

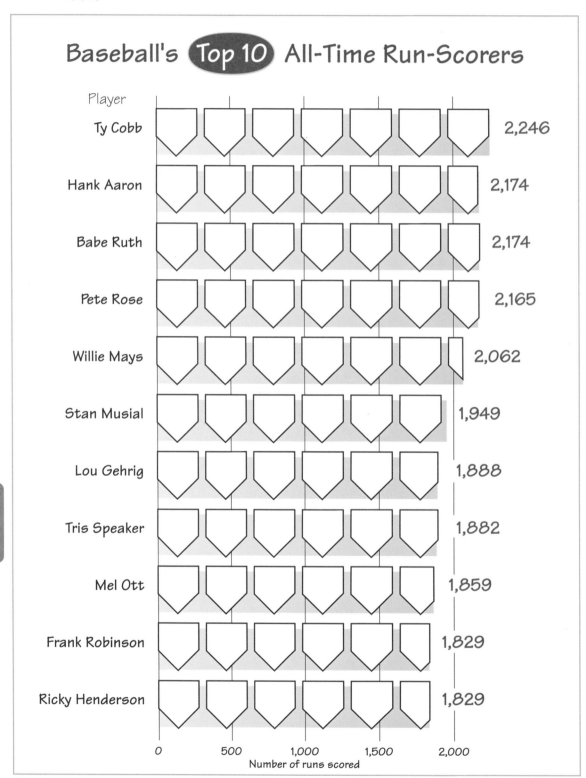

Baseball's Top 10 All-Time Run-Scorers

Player	Number of runs scored	
Ty Cobb		2,246
Hank Aaron		2,174
Babe Ruth		2,174
Pete Rose		2,165
Willie Mays		2,062
Stan Musial		1,949
Lou Gehrig		1,888
Tris Speaker		1,882
Mel Ott		1,859
Frank Robinson		1,829
Ricky Henderson		1,829

Number of runs scored: 0, 500, 1,000, 1,500, 2,000

SOURCE: Based on data from *Total Baseball, the Official Encyclopedia of Major League Baseball*

Top Earners in Major League Baseball, 1997
(In millions)

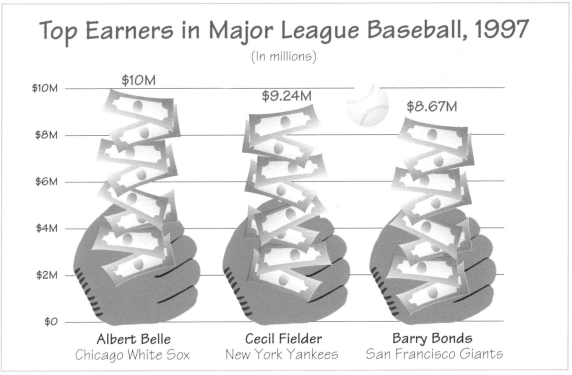

Albert Belle	**Cecil Fielder**	**Barry Bonds**
Chicago White Sox	New York Yankees	San Francisco Giants

SOURCE: Based on data from *USA TODAY*

Top 5 Oldest U.S. Baseball Stadiums
(Still in use)

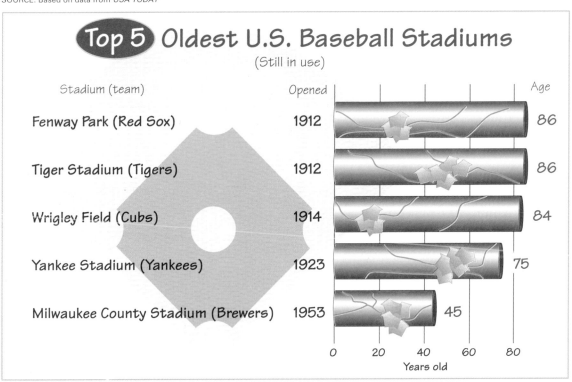

Stadium (team)	Opened	Age
Fenway Park (Red Sox)	1912	86
Tiger Stadium (Tigers)	1912	86
Wrigley Field (Cubs)	1914	84
Yankee Stadium (Yankees)	1923	75
Milwaukee County Stadium (Brewers)	1953	45

Years old

SOURCE: Based on data from *USA TODAY*

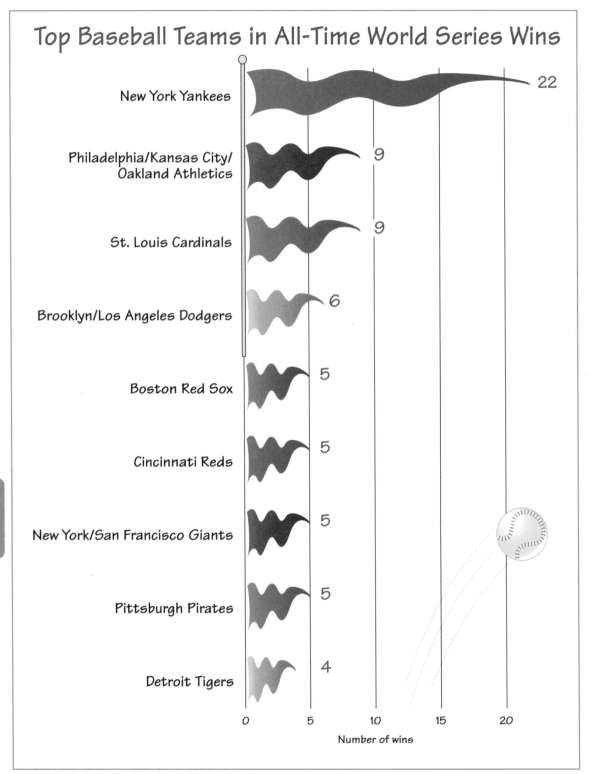

Top Baseball Teams in All-Time World Series Wins

New York Yankees — 22

Philadelphia/Kansas City/Oakland Athletics — 9

St. Louis Cardinals — 9

Brooklyn/Los Angeles Dodgers — 6

Boston Red Sox — 5

Cincinnati Reds — 5

New York/San Francisco Giants — 5

Pittsburgh Pirates — 5

Detroit Tigers — 4

0   5   10   15   20

Number of wins

Pro Sports

SOURCE: Based on information given in *The Top 10 of Everything 1997*

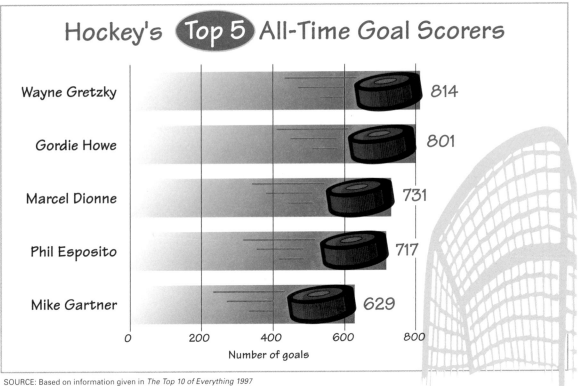

Hockey's Top 5 All-Time Goal Scorers

Player	Goals
Wayne Gretzky	814
Gordie Howe	801
Marcel Dionne	731
Phil Esposito	717
Mike Gartner	629

Number of goals

SOURCE: Based on information given in *The Top 10 of Everything 1997*

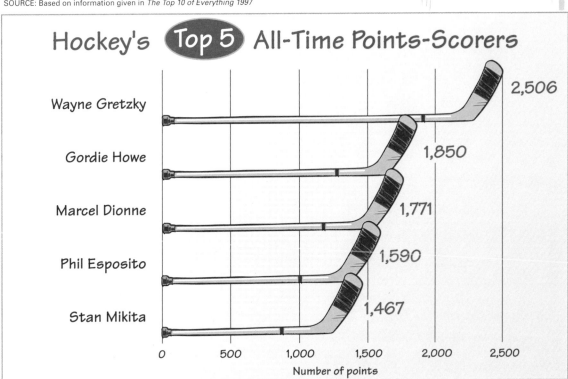

Hockey's Top 5 All-Time Points-Scorers

Player	Points
Wayne Gretzky	2,506
Gordie Howe	1,850
Marcel Dionne	1,771
Phil Esposito	1,590
Stan Mikita	1,467

Number of points

Pro Sports

SOURCE: Based on information given in *The Top 10 of Everything 1997*

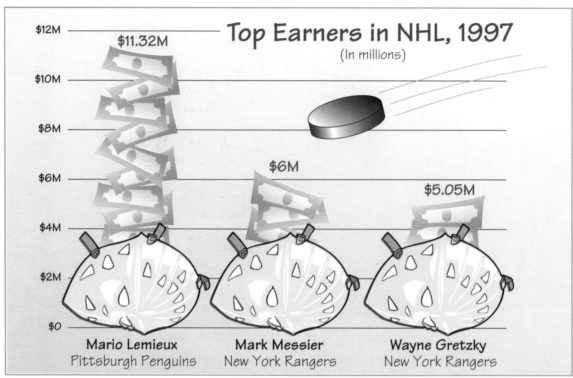

Top Earners in NHL, 1997
(In millions)

$12M
$11.32M
$10M
$8M
$6M — $6M
$6M
$5.05M
$4M
$2M
$0

Mario Lemieux
Pittsburgh Penguins

Mark Messier
New York Rangers

Wayne Gretzky
New York Rangers

SOURCE: Based on data from *USA TODAY*

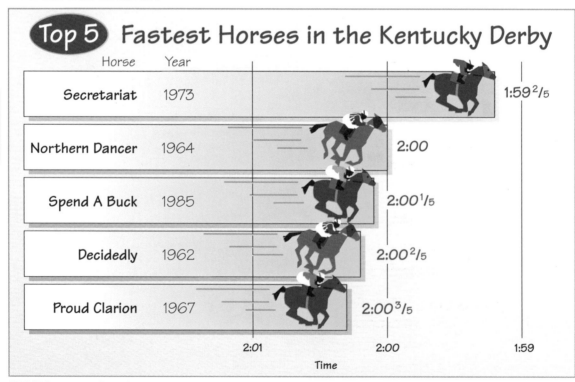

Top 5 Fastest Horses in the Kentucky Derby

Horse	Year	Time
Secretariat	1973	$1:59^2/_5$
Northern Dancer	1964	2:00
Spend A Buck	1985	$2:00^1/_5$
Decidedly	1962	$2:00^2/_5$
Proud Clarion	1967	$2:00^3/_5$

2:01   2:00   1:59

Time

SOURCE: Based on data from *USA TODAY*

Top 5 Fastest-Winning Speeds of the Indianapolis 500

Driver	Car	Year	mph
Arie Luyendyk (Netherlands)	Lola-Chevrolet	1990	185.984
Rick Mears (U.S.A.)	Chevrolet-Lumina	1991	176.457
Bobby Rahal (U.S.A.)	March-Cosworth	1986	170.722
Emerson Fittipaldi (Brazil)	Penske-Chevrolet	1989	167.581
Rick Mears (U.S.A.)	March-Cosworth	1984	163.612

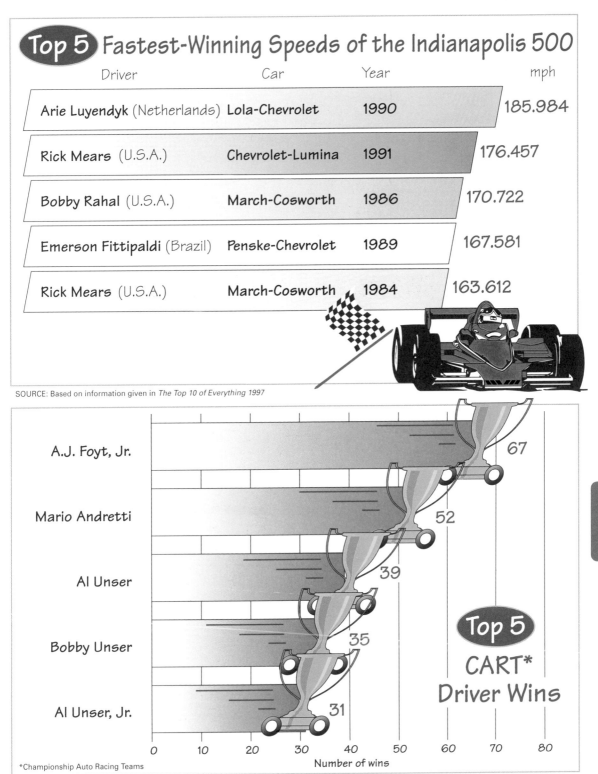

SOURCE: Based on information given in *The Top 10 of Everything 1997*

Pro Sports

Top 5 CART* Driver Wins

Driver	Number of wins
A.J. Foyt, Jr.	67
Mario Andretti	52
Al Unser	39
Bobby Unser	35
Al Unser, Jr.	31

*Championship Auto Racing Teams

SOURCE: Based on information given in *The Top 10 of Everything 1997*

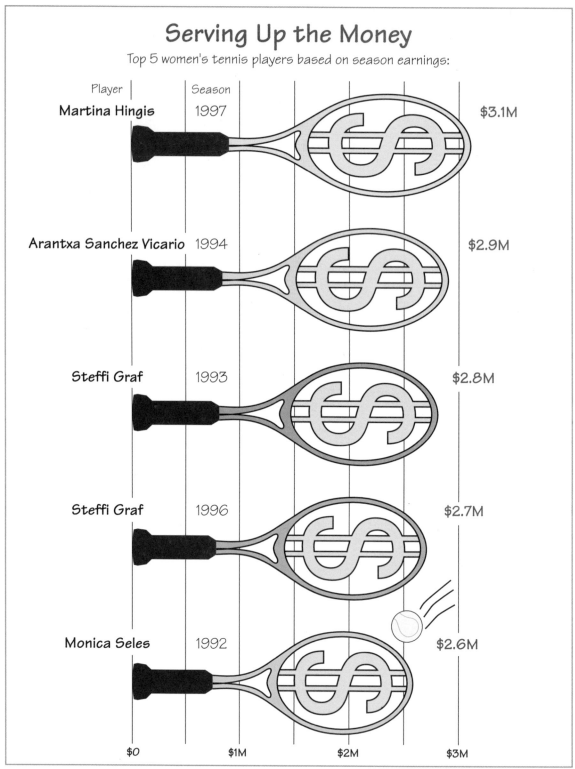

Serving Up the Money

Top 5 women's tennis players based on season earnings:

Player	Season	Earnings
Martina Hingis	1997	$3.1M
Arantxa Sanchez Vicario	1994	$2.9M
Steffi Graf	1993	$2.8M
Steffi Graf	1996	$2.7M
Monica Seles	1992	$2.6M

$0 $1M $2M $3M

SOURCE: Based on data from WTA Tour

Top Wimbledon Champions—Men

Player	# of titles	Years earned
William Renshaw	7	1880-89
Bjorn Borg	5	1975-81
H. Laurie Doherty	5	1897-1906
Reginald F. Doherty	4	1897-1905
Rod Laver	4	1959-71
Pete Sampras	4	1990-97
Tony Wilding	4	1906-14

SOURCE: Based on data from United States Tennis Association

Top Wimbledon Champions—Women

Player	# of titles	Years earned
Martina Navratilova	9	1974-95
Helen Wills Moody	8	1923-38
Steffi Graf	7	1987-96
Billie Jean King	6	1961-81
Suzanne Lenglen	6	1919-26

SOURCE: Based on data from United States Tennis Association

Pro Sports

Top U.S. Open Champions–Men

Player	# of titles	Years earned
Bill Tilden	7	1913-30
Jimmy Connors	5	1973-83
John McEnroe	4	1977-92
Pete Sampras	4	1990-97
Fred Perry	3	1933-36

SOURCE: Based on data from United States Tennis Association

Top U.S. Open Champions–Women

Player	# of titles	Years earned
Molla Mallory	8	1915-26
Helen Wills Moody	7	1923-38
Chris Evert	6	1974-86
Margaret Court	5	1960-75
Steffi Graf	5	1987-96

SOURCE: Based on data from United States Tennis Association

Top Grand Slam Champions—Men

Through 1997, only five men have won over ten total grand slam, or major, tournaments. The majors are the Australian Open, the French Open, Wimbledon, and the U.S. Open.

Player	# of titles	Years earned
Roy Emerson	12	1959-71
Bjorn Borg	11	1975-81
Rod Laver	11	1959-71
Pete Sampras	10	1990-97
Bill Tilden	10	1913-30

SOURCE: Based on data from United States Tennis Association

Top Grand Slam Champions—Women

Through 1997, only six women have won over ten total grand slam, or major, tournaments. The majors are the Australian Open, the French Open, Wimbledon, and the U.S. Open.

Player	# of titles	Years earned
Margaret Court	24	1960-75
Steffi Graf	21	1987-96
Chris Evert	18	1974-86
Martina Navratilova	18	1974-95
Billie Jean King	12	1961-81
Suzanne Lenglen	12	1919-26

SOURCE: Based on data from United States Tennis Association

Pro Sports

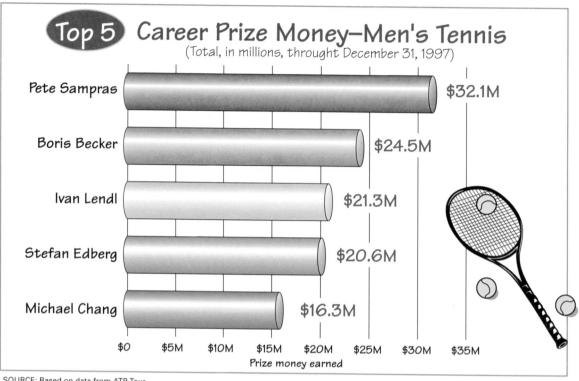

Top 5 Career Prize Money—Men's Tennis
(Total, in millions, throught December 31, 1997)

Pete Sampras — $32.1M
Boris Becker — $24.5M
Ivan Lendl — $21.3M
Stefan Edberg — $20.6M
Michael Chang — $16.3M

$0 $5M $10M $15M $20M $25M $30M $35M

Prize money earned

SOURCE: Based on data from ATP Tour

Top 5 Career Prize Money—Women's Tennis
(Total, in millions, through December 31, 1997)

Martina Navratilova — $20.3M
Steffi Graf — $20.1M
Arantxa Sanchez Vicario — $12.5M
Monica Seles — $9.9M
Chris Evert — $8.9M

$0 $5M $10M $15M $20M $25M

Prize money earned

SOURCE: Based on data from Corel WTA Tour

Pro Sports

Which Pros Do Kids Like Best?
Top 10 Most Popular Pro Athletes
(Ranked by TRU*SCORES of Teenage Research Unlimited)

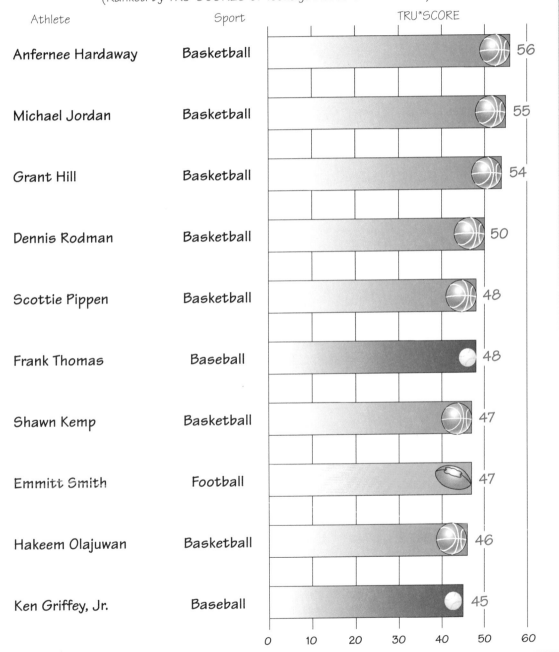

Athlete	Sport	TRU*SCORE
Anfernee Hardaway	Basketball	56
Michael Jordan	Basketball	55
Grant Hill	Basketball	54
Dennis Rodman	Basketball	50
Scottie Pippen	Basketball	48
Frank Thomas	Baseball	48
Shawn Kemp	Basketball	47
Emmitt Smith	Football	47
Hakeem Olajuwan	Basketball	46
Ken Griffey, Jr.	Baseball	45

Pro Sports

SOURCE: Based on data from Teenage Research Unlimited, Inc.

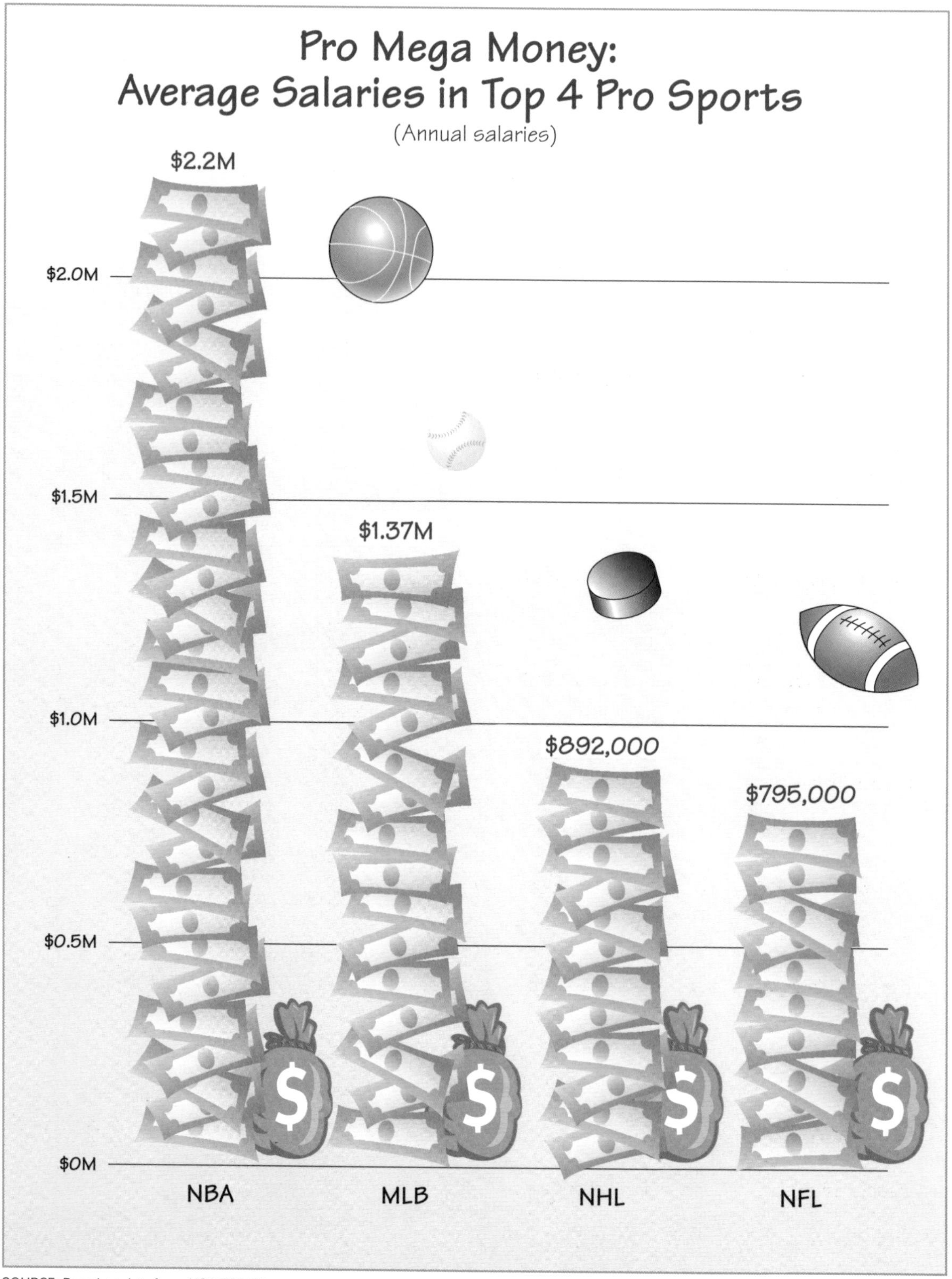

Pro Mega Money:
Average Salaries in Top 4 Pro Sports
(Annual salaries)

$2.2M

$2.0M

$1.5M

$1.37M

$1.0M

$892,000

$795,000

$0.5M

$0M

| NBA | MLB | NHL | NFL |

Pro Sports

SOURCE: Based on data from *USA TODAY*

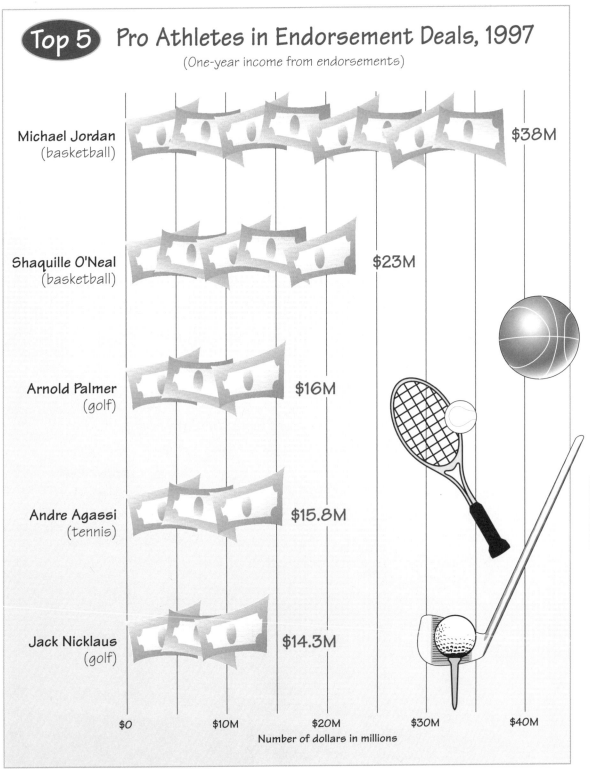

Top 5 Pro Athletes in Endorsement Deals, 1997

(One-year income from endorsements)

Michael Jordan
(basketball) — $38M

Shaquille O'Neal
(basketball) — $23M

Arnold Palmer
(golf) — $16M

Andre Agassi
(tennis) — $15.8M

Jack Nicklaus
(golf) — $14.3M

$0 $10M $20M $30M $40M

Number of dollars in millions

Pro Sports

SOURCE: Based on data from The Sports Marketing Letter estimates

Pets

Look in an American home and you're likely to see a cat snoozing on a couch or a dog sleeping on the carpet. More than half of all households in America include at least one pet. Most of these homes have either dogs or cats—or both dogs and cats. But many other kinds of animals are also kept as pets, including birds, fish, rabbits, guinea pigs, hamsters, gerbils, ferrets, horses— even pot-bellied pigs!

More homes have dogs than cats. But there are more pet cats than any other kind of pet—more than 59 million felines were counted at the end of 1996. Most cat-owning homes—52 percent— have more than one cat, while less than 38% of dog owners have more than one dog. If you live in the midwest, chances are good you own a dog; on average that region has 37% to 47.9% of all households owning dogs. If you live in the northwest, chances are you own a cat. Between 30.6% and 42.7% of all households in that region contain at least one cat.

Kidbits Tidbits

- More than 58 million homes in the U.S. have at least one pet.
- About 13% of U.S. homes include both dogs and cats.
- Dogs have been the #1 pet in the White House; 23 presidents have had dogs.
- "First Pet" Millie, an English springer spaniel that lived with President and Mrs. Bush, made almost $1 million for charity by "authoring" *Millie's Book* with Mrs. Bush in 1990.
- The last president to have a pet reptile was John Quincy Adams, who owned an alligator.

Though it's often the children in a home who eagerly want a pet, it's most often the mother who has the main responsibility for caring for the animals, including taking them to veterinarians for vaccinations and other health care. The average cost for veterinary care depends on the type of pet. In 1996, the average yearly veterinary medical expenditure for a dog was $129, compared with $81 for a cat and under $6 for a bird.

Veterinary bills are only part of the cost of owning a pet. Other costs include food, grooming, toys, housing, and so on. For example, Americans spend about $4 billion on dog food each year, and $2.5 billion on cat food.

Many people obtain their pets for little or no cost, often from neighbors or animal shelters. Other people pay hundreds or even thousands of dollars for pedigreed animals—that is, animals that have been carefully bred and for whom there is a written record of parents, grandparents, etc. These animals are often shown professionally—they compete in judged events, such as dog shows and cat shows.

Ask a pet owner if the costs of owning an animal are worth it, and the answer is most likely to be a loud "yes!" Pets add fun, companionship, and love to people's lives. They are even beneficial to people's health. For example, research shows that owning a pet can lower a person's blood pressure and decrease chances of having a heart attack.

Kidbits Tidbits

- The great majority of Americans believe that pets play a positive role in people's lives.
- About 90% of cat and dog owners consider the animals to be members of the family.
- Labrador retrievers rank #1 in registrations with the American Kennel Club, followed by rottweilers and German shepherds.
- The Cat Fanciers Association recognizes 36 breeds, of which Persians are #1 in number of registrations.

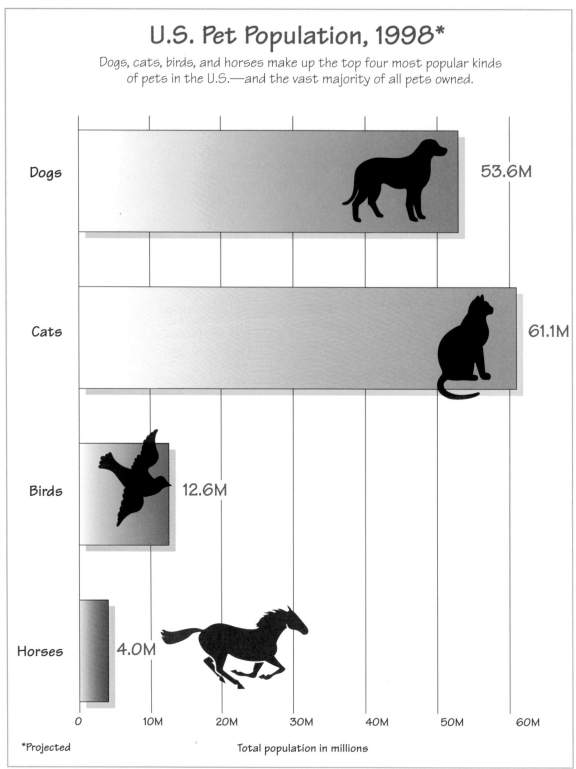

U.S. Pet Population, 1998*

Dogs, cats, birds, and horses make up the top four most popular kinds of pets in the U.S.—and the vast majority of all pets owned.

Dogs — 53.6M

Cats — 61.1M

Birds — 12.6M

Horses — 4.0M

0   10M   20M   30M   40M   50M   60M

*Projected

Total population in millions

Pets

SOURCE: Based on data from American Veterinary Medical Association - Center for Information Management, 1997

U.S. Pet Ownership Declines

Between 1987 and 1996 U.S. pet ownership of the top four varieties of pets declined an average of about 13%. Horse ownership saw a 40% decline. Percentage of all U.S. households with selected pets, 1987 vs. 1996:

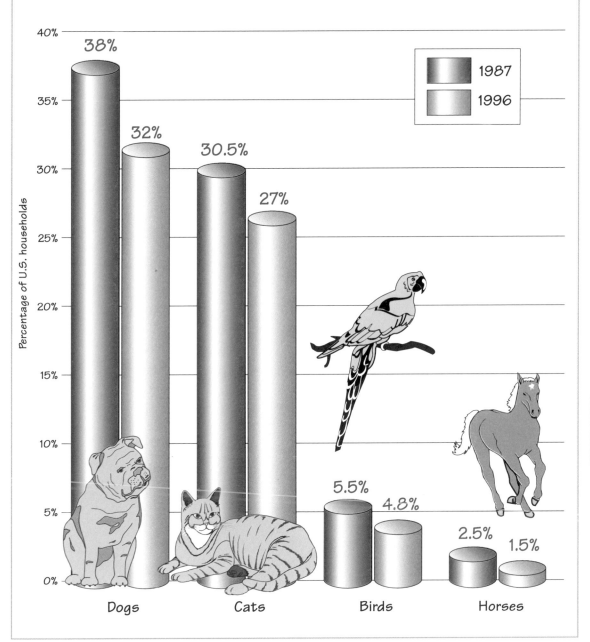

Pets

SOURCE: Based on data from American Veterinary Medical Association - Center for Information Management, 1997

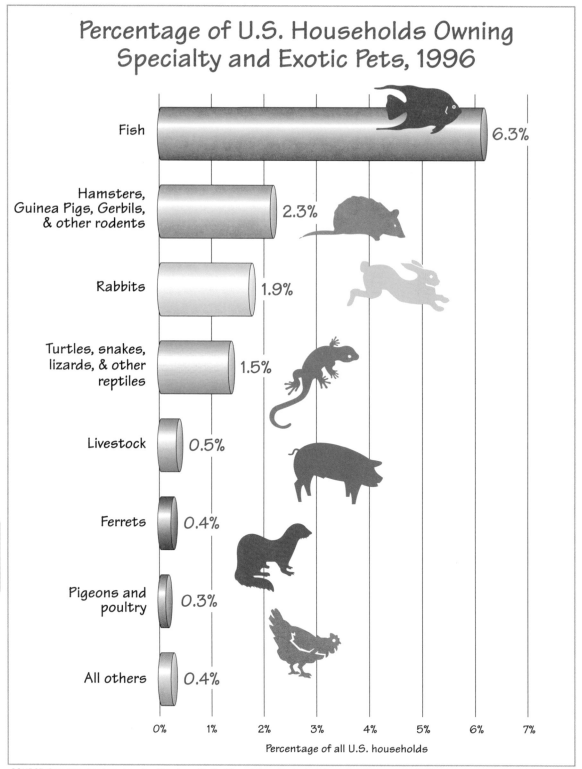

Percentage of U.S. Households Owning Specialty and Exotic Pets, 1996

Fish — 6.3%

Hamsters, Guinea Pigs, Gerbils, & other rodents — 2.3%

Rabbits — 1.9%

Turtles, snakes, lizards, & other reptiles — 1.5%

Livestock — 0.5%

Ferrets — 0.4%

Pigeons and poultry — 0.3%

All others — 0.4%

0% 1% 2% 3% 4% 5% 6% 7%

Percentage of all U.S. households

SOURCE: Based on data from American Veterinary Medical Association - Center for Information Management, 1997

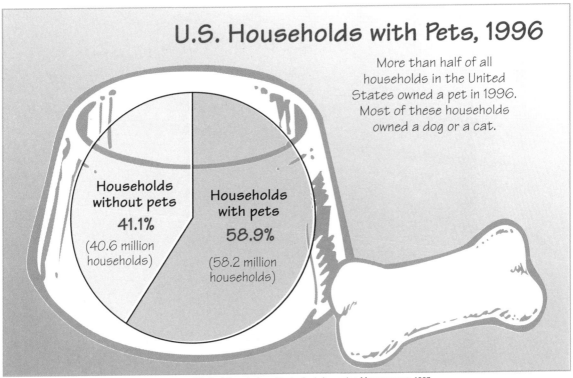

U.S. Households with Pets, 1996

More than half of all households in the United States owned a pet in 1996. Most of these households owned a dog or a cat.

Households without pets
41.1%
(40.6 million households)

Households with pets
58.9%
(58.2 million households)

SOURCE: Based on data from American Veterinary Medical Association - Center for Information Management, 1997

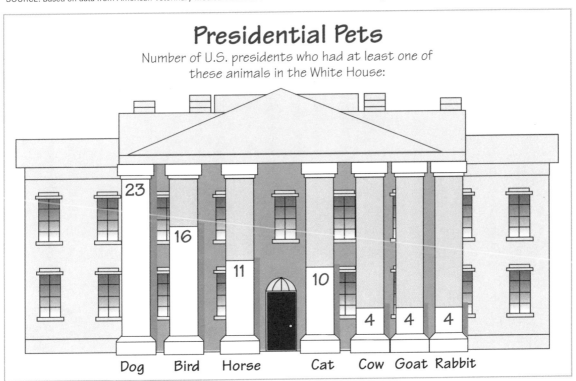

Presidential Pets

Number of U.S. presidents who had at least one of these animals in the White House:

Dog	Bird	Horse	Cat	Cow	Goat	Rabbit
23	16	11	10	4	4	4

SOURCE: Based on data from *Presidential Pets* by Niall Kelly

Pets

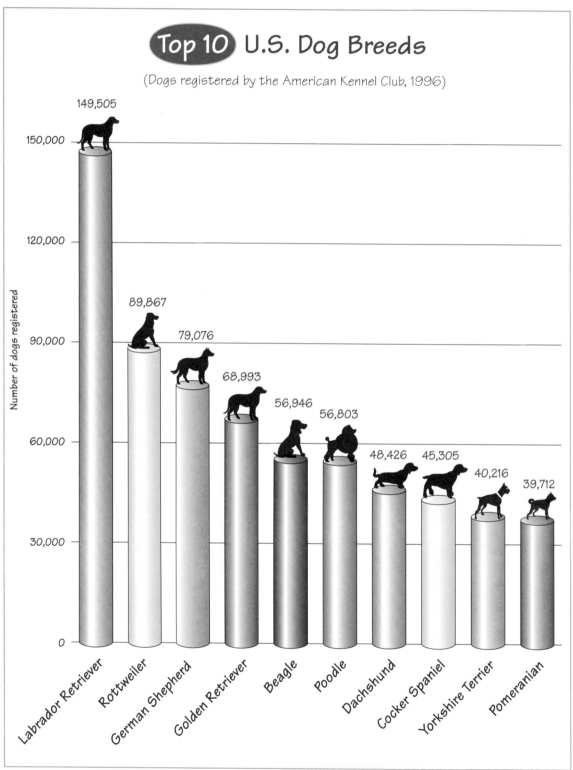

Top 10 U.S. Dog Breeds

(Dogs registered by the American Kennel Club, 1996)

Number of dogs registered

149,505
89,867
79,076
68,993
56,946
56,803
48,426
45,305
40,216
39,712

150,000
120,000
90,000
60,000
30,000
0

Labrador Retriever
Rottweiler
German Shepherd
Golden Retriever
Beagle
Poodle
Dachshund
Cocker Spaniel
Yorkshire Terrier
Pomeranian

Pets

SOURCE: Based on data from American Veterinary Medical Association - Center for Information Management, 1997

Top Dog-Loving States
(States where percentage of all households with dogs is between 37% and 47.9%)

SOURCE: Based on data from American Veterinary Medical Association - Center for Information Management, 1997

Number of Dogs Owned per U.S. Dog-Owning Household, 1996
The vast majority of U.S. dog owners own only one dog.

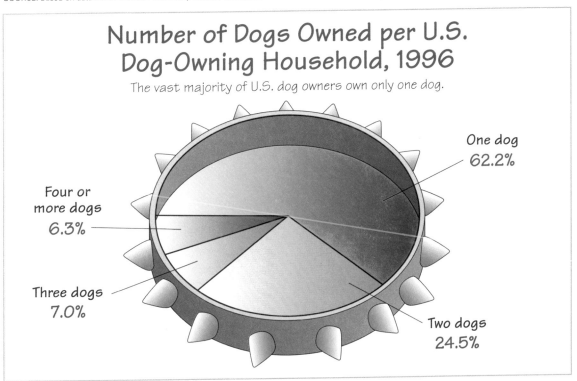

One dog
62.2%

Four or more dogs
6.3%

Three dogs
7.0%

Two dogs
24.5%

SOURCE: Based on data from American Veterinary Medical Association - Center for Information Management, 1997

Top 10 U.S. Cat Breeds

Persians are nearly 10 times more popular
than the second most-popular cat breed.
(Cats registered by the Cat
Fanciers Association, 1996)

Number of cats registered

42,578

40,000

30,000

20,000

10,000

4,747

2,865

2,383

1,981

1,371

1,264

1,032

933

868

0

Persian

Maine Coon

Siamese

Abyssinian

Exotic

Oriental

Scottish Fold

American Shorthair

Birman

Ocicat

Pets

SOURCE: Based on data from American Veterinary Medical Association - Center for Information Management, 1997

Top Cat-Loving States

(States where percentage of all households with
cats is between 30.6% and 42.7%)

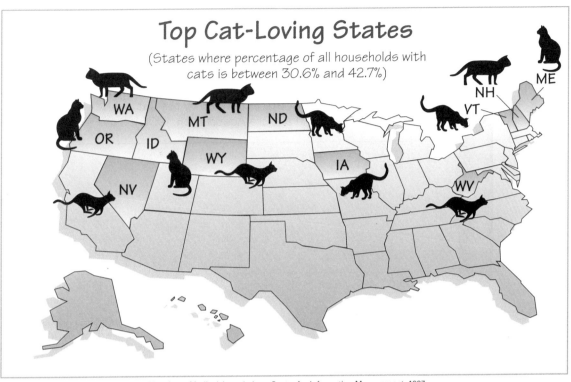

SOURCE: Based on data from American Veterinary Medical Association - Center for Information Management, 1997

Number of Cats Owned per U.S. Cat-Owning Household, 1996

The vast majority of U.S. cat owners own only one cat.

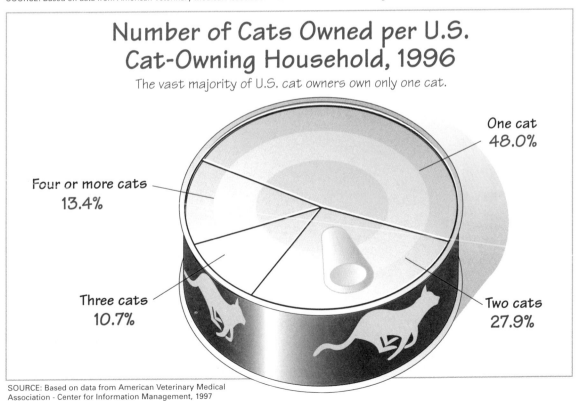

One cat
48.0%

Four or more cats
13.4%

Three cats
10.7%

Two cats
27.9%

Pets

SOURCE: Based on data from American Veterinary Medical
Association - Center for Information Management, 1997

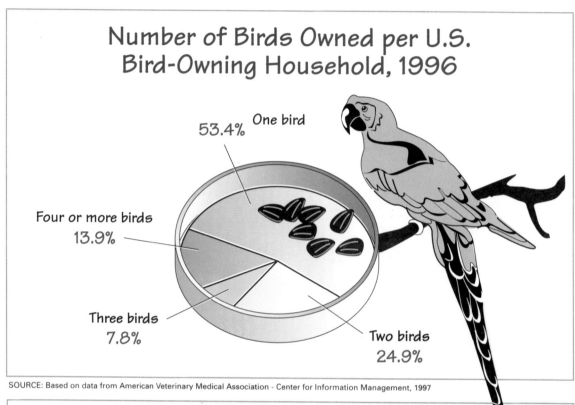

Number of Birds Owned per U.S. Bird-Owning Household, 1996

53.4% One bird

Four or more birds
13.9%

Three birds
7.8%

Two birds
24.9%

SOURCE: Based on data from American Veterinary Medical Association - Center for Information Management, 1997

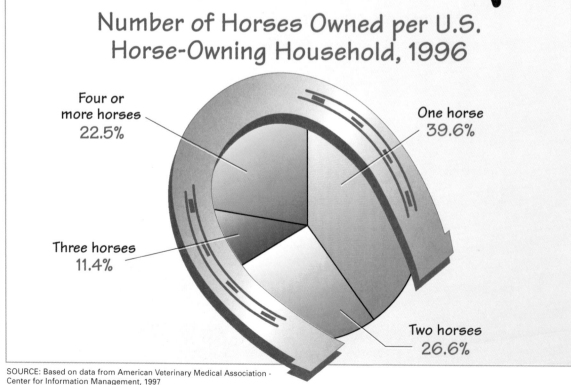

Number of Horses Owned per U.S. Horse-Owning Household, 1996

Four or more horses
22.5%

One horse
39.6%

Three horses
11.4%

Two horses
26.6%

Pets

SOURCE: Based on data from American Veterinary Medical Association - Center for Information Management, 1997

How Are Pets Combined?

U.S. horse owners are the most likely to also own dogs and cats.
Percentage of U.S. pet-owning households with pet combinations, 1996:

Dog-owning households that also own:

Cat-owning households that also own:

Bird-owning households that also own:

Horse-owning households that also own:

Cats
42.0%
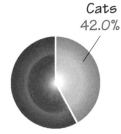

Dogs
48.5%
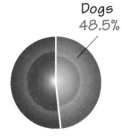

Dogs
63.0%
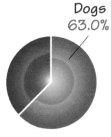

Dogs
81.3%
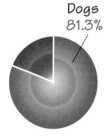

Birds
9.2%
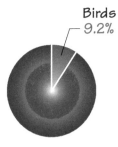

Birds
8.0%
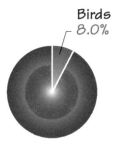

Cats
47.5%
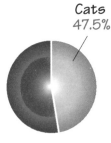

Cats
69.1%
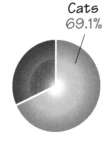

Horses
3.9%
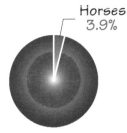

Horses
3.9%
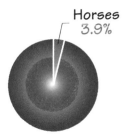

Horses
4.8%
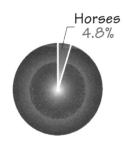

Birds
14.6%
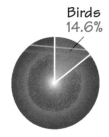

Pets

SOURCE: Based on data from American Veterinary Medical Association - Center for Information Management, 1997

Percentage of All U.S. Households with Dogs and Cats or Both, 1996

Combination of dogs and cats owned:

Owned dogs
without cats
18.3%

Owned both
dogs and cats
13.3%

Owned cats
without dogs
14.1%

Owned either dogs,
or cats, or both
45.7%

SOURCE: Based on data from American Veterinary Medical Association - Center for Information Management, 1997

Pets

Who Takes Care of Our Pets?

When it comes to caring for a pet in the U.S., nearly three-quarters of caregivers are women. More than half of caregivers are between 30- to 49-years-old.

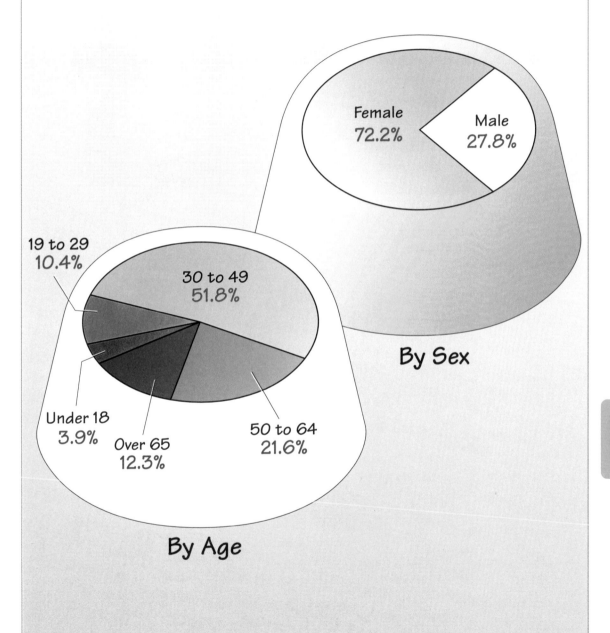

Female
72.2%

Male
27.8%

By Sex

19 to 29
10.4%

30 to 49
51.8%

Under 18
3.9%

Over 65
12.3%

50 to 64
21.6%

By Age

SOURCE: Based on data from American Veterinary Medical Association - Center for Information Management, 1997

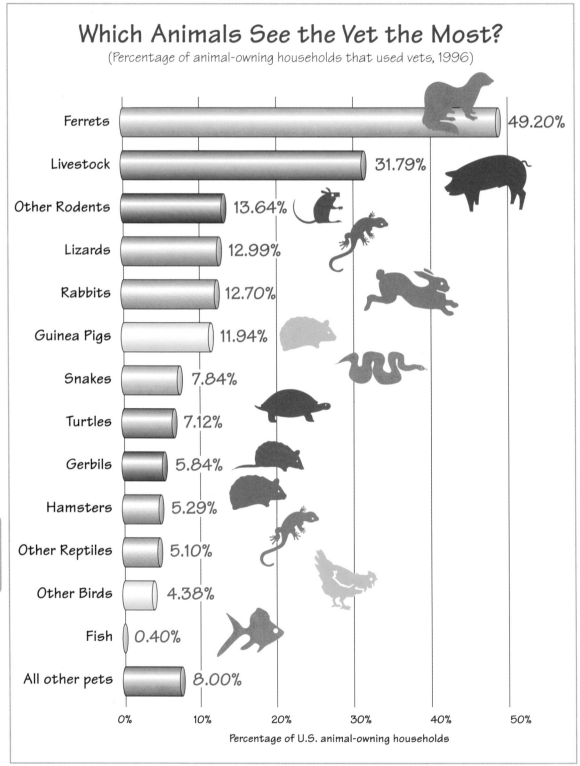

Which Animals See the Vet the Most?

(Percentage of animal-owning households that used vets, 1996)

Animal	Percentage
Ferrets	49.20%
Livestock	31.79%
Other Rodents	13.64%
Lizards	12.99%
Rabbits	12.70%
Guinea Pigs	11.94%
Snakes	7.84%
Turtles	7.12%
Gerbils	5.84%
Hamsters	5.29%
Other Reptiles	5.10%
Other Birds	4.38%
Fish	0.40%
All other pets	8.00%

Percentage of U.S. animal-owning households

SOURCE: Based on data from American Veterinary Medical Association - Center for Information Management, 1997

Average Yearly Cost for Veterinary Care, per Animal-Owning Household

U.S. horse owners spend the most on vets each year, but dog owners spend only 16.8% less.
(By selected animal)

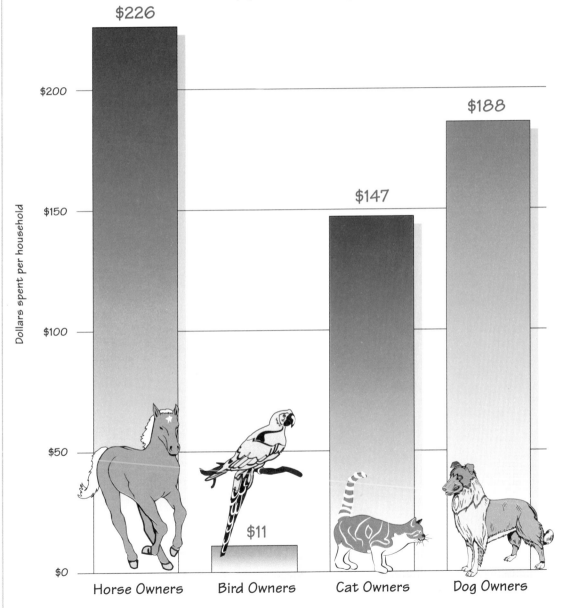

Dollars spent per household

$226 Horse Owners
$11 Bird Owners
$147 Cat Owners
$188 Dog Owners

Pets

SOURCE: Based on data from American Veterinary Medical Association, *U.S. Pet Ownership and Demographics Sourcebook*, 1997

Average Cost for Veterinary Care, per Visit

(By selected animal)

Dollars spent per household

$100

$80

$67

$74

$56

$100

$80

$60

$40

$20

$0

Horse Owners   Bird Owners   Cat Owners   Dog Owners

SOURCE: Based on data from American Veterinary Medical Association, *U.S. Pet Ownership and Demographics Sourcebook,* 1997

Pets

Average Yearly Cost for Veterinary Care, per Animal

On an animal-by-animal basis, dogs cost the most in medical care—nearly 25% more than horses and about 37% more than cats.
(By selected animal)

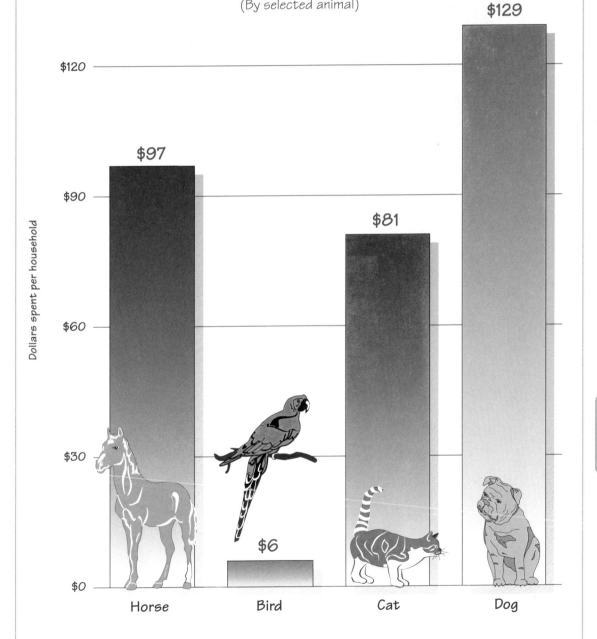

Dollars spent per household

$120
$90
$60
$30
$0

$97 — Horse
$6 — Bird
$81 — Cat
$129 — Dog

Pets

SOURCE: Based on data from American Veterinary Medical Association, *U.S. Pet Ownership and Demographics Sourcebook*, 1997

Pet-Owning Households: What Kind of Home?

Americans living in houses are the vast majority of pet owners.
(Percentage of U.S. households, 1996)

Legend:
- All U.S. households
- Pet-owning households
- Dog-owning households
- Cat-owning households
- Bird-owning households
- Horse-owning households

Percentage of U.S. households

Type of residence: House, Apartment, Mobile Home, Condominium

SOURCE: Based on data from American Veterinary Medical Association - Center for Information Management, 1997

Pet-Owning Households: Average Yearly Household Income

U.S. households with incomes greater than $25,000 own the most pets.
(Percentage of U.S. households, 1996)

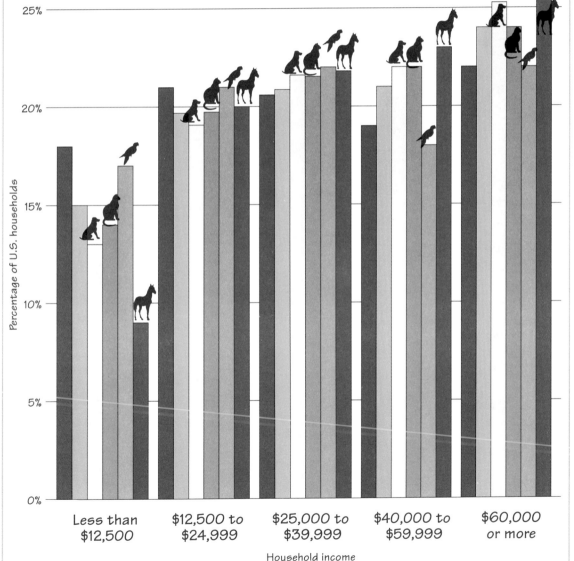

Pets

SOURCE: Based on data from American Veterinary Medical Association - Center for Information Management, 1997

Dog Dues

Owning a typical dog in the U.S. today costs an
average $14,600 over an average 11-year lifespan.
Here's where the money goes:

Other
$1,400

Food
$4,020

Training
$1,220

Veterinary
(including
spay/neuter)
$3,930

Flea and tick
treatment
$1,070

Grooming, toys,
equipment, house
$2,960

Total: $14,600
Note: Does not include any cost
of initial purchase of animal.

SOURCE: Based on data from American Kennel Club, *USA TODAY* research

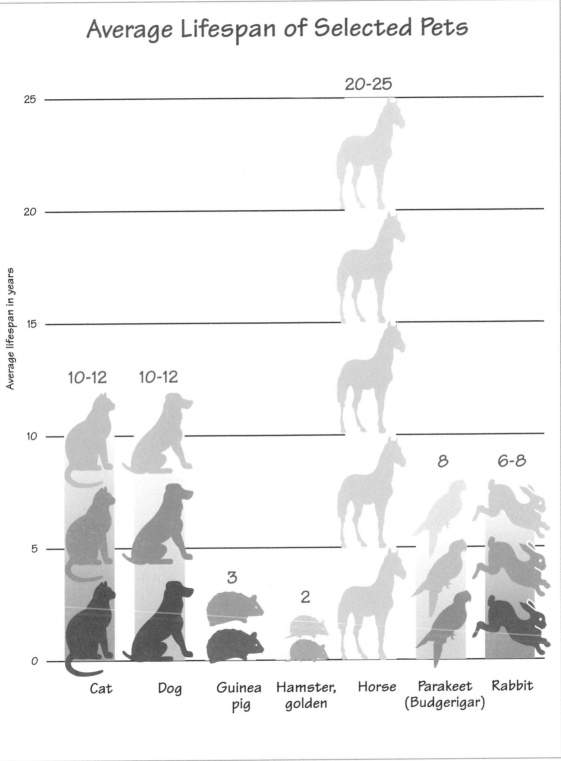

Average Lifespan of Selected Pets

Average lifespan in years

20-25

25

20

15

10-12   10-12

10

8   6-8

5

3
2

0

Cat   Dog   Guinea   Hamster,   Horse   Parakeet   Rabbit
pig   golden   (Budgerigar)

Pets

SOURCE: Based on data from James G. Doherty, General Curator, The Wildlife Conservation Society

The Environment

The world around us constantly changes. Many of the changes result from human activities. All too often, these changes are harmful. Oil spills from giant ships kill birds and mess up beaches. Gases from cars and factories dirty the air and blacken people's lungs. Cutting down forests and draining wetlands destroys the homes and food supplies of endangered animals.

One problem of great concern to many scientists is the gradual warming of Earth's atmosphere. This occurs as certain gases in the atmosphere prevent sunlight from being reflected from Earth's surface back out into space. As the amount of these "greenhouse gases" increases, the atmosphere traps more and more heat—like a greenhouse traps heat. Most scientists believe that carbon dioxide and other gases released by vehicles and factories are the main cause for the temperature increase. The United States accounts for more than 20% of the world's greenhouse gas emissions. As temperatures continue to rise, climates will change, the sea level will rise, and many plants and animals will have difficulty surviving in their current homes.

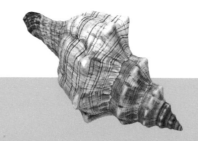

Kidbits Tidbits

- The first Earth Day was held in 1970.
- 1997 was the warmest year on record for the planet since records were first kept in the mid-1800s.
- The United States emits 4.8 billion tons of carbon dioxide a year. In second place is China, which emits 2.6 billion tons.
- Microscopic organisms in tap water cause 900,000 illnesses in the U.S. each year.
- At least 20% of the world's people do not have access to safe drinking water.

Another serious problem is the effect of air pollution on people's health. People with lung and heart disease are very sensitive to air pollution. So, too, are children and elderly people. The U.S. government measures air quality in approximately 3,000 places. In 1995, Los Angeles,California, had 103 days when there was so much pollution that the air was classified as unhealthy (L.A. is consistently the worst). Houston, Texas, had 54 unhealthy days and Bakersfield, California, had 45 unhealthy days.

Some people are taking action to solve environmental problems. Engineers have designed cars and home appliances that use less energy. Homes are better insulated, so that less energy is needed for heating and cooling. Parks around the world have been established, where wild animals and their homes are protected. Communities have recycling programs that enable us to reuse paper, plastic, glass, and other materials. This all saves energy and other valuable natural resources. It also limits pollution.

Many kids take part in projects that improve the environment. They clean up local parks and start school recycling programs. Most importantly, they spread the word about the environment's three R's: reduce, reuse, and recycle.

Kidbits Tidbits

- More than 1 million acres of U.S. wetlands were destroyed from 1985 to 1995.
- A car gets up to 20% better gas mileage at 55 miles per hour than at 70 miles per hour.
- In 1995, Americans created 208 million tons of wastes—4.3 pounds per person per day. Twenty-seven percent of the wastes were recycled. Americans recycled about 40% of their paper and paperboard wastes and more than 60% of the aluminum containers they used.
- By 1996, a total of 957 U.S. species were classified as endangered or threatened.
- Recycled plastic soda bottles can be made into sweaters. Recycled telephone books can be made into book covers.

The Environment

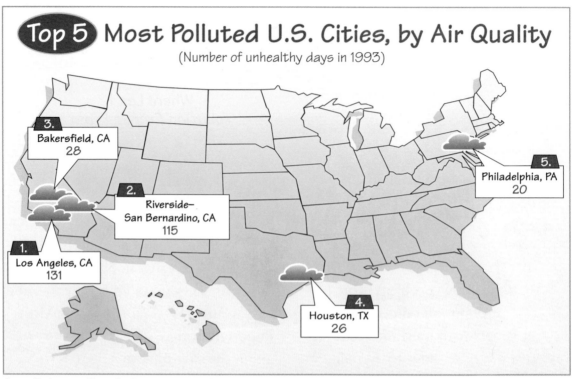

Top 5 Most Polluted U.S. Cities, by Air Quality
(Number of unhealthy days in 1993)

3.
Bakersfield, CA
28

5.
Philadelphia, PA
20

2.
Riverside–
San Bernardino, CA
115

1.
Los Angeles, CA
131

4.
Houston, TX
26

Source: Environmental Protection Agency, *National Air Quality and Emissions Trends Report, October 1994*

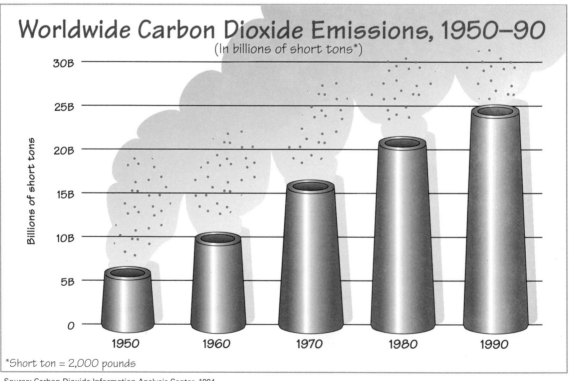

Worldwide Carbon Dioxide Emissions, 1950–90
(In billions of short tons*)

Billions of short tons

30B
25B
20B
15B
10B
5B
0

1950 1960 1970 1980 1990

*Short ton = 2,000 pounds

Source: Carbon Dioxide Information Analysis Center, 1994

The Environment

Where Carbon Monoxide & Lead Pollution Come From

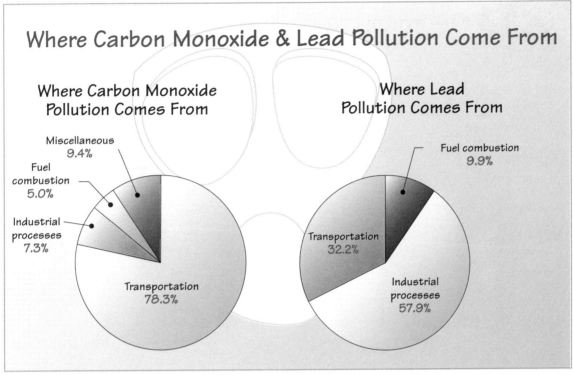

Where Carbon Monoxide Pollution Comes From

Miscellaneous
9.4%

Fuel
combustion
5.0%

Industrial
processes
7.3%

Transportation
78.3%

Where Lead Pollution Comes From

Fuel combustion
9.9%

Transportation
32.2%

Industrial
processes
57.9%

Source: Environmental Protection Agency

Emissions of Greenhouse Gases, by Type*

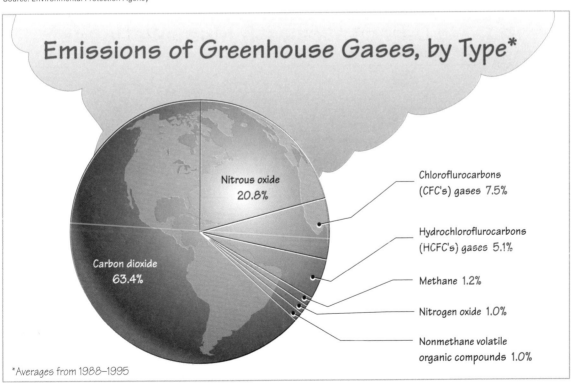

Nitrous oxide
20.8%

Chloroflurocarbons
(CFC's) gases 7.5%

Hydrochloroflurocarbons
(HCFC's) gases 5.1%

Methane 1.2%

Nitrogen oxide 1.0%

Nonmethane volatile
organic compounds 1.0%

Carbon dioxide
63.4%

*Averages from 1988–1995

Source: U.S. Energy Information Administration

Forest Lost, 1980–1990
(In millions of hectares*)

Millions of hectares

- 2.0M
- 1.5M
- 1.0M
- 0.5M
- 0

Forest area 1980
Forest area 1990

Latin America   Asia   Africa   Total

*Hectare = 2.47 acres

Source: World Resources Institute, *World Resources 1992–93*

Top 5 U.S. States with Most Wetlands*
(In total acres and percent of total area)

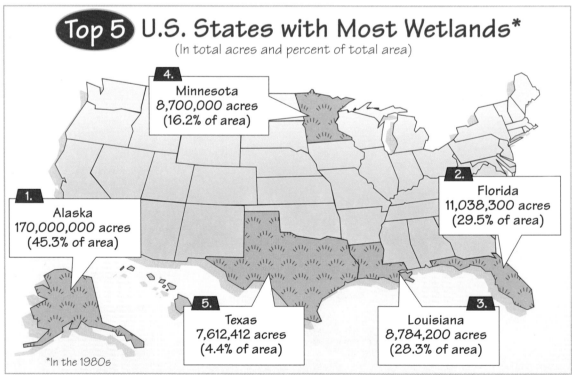

4. Minnesota
8,700,000 acres
(16.2% of area)

1. Alaska
170,000,000 acres
(45.3% of area)

2. Florida
11,038,300 acres
(29.5% of area)

5. Texas
7,612,412 acres
(4.4% of area)

3. Louisiana
8,784,200 acres
(28.3% of area)

*In the 1980s

Source: U.S. Dept. of the Interior, Fish and Wildlife Service: *Wetlands in the United States*

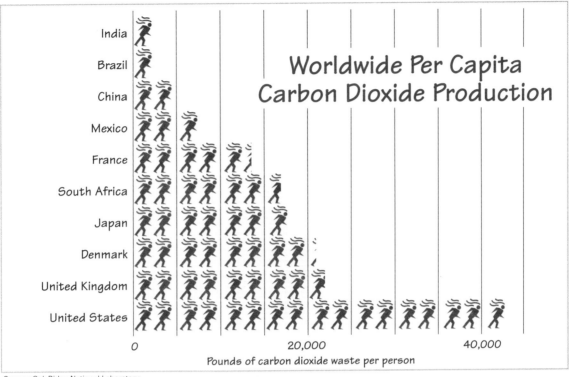

Worldwide Per Capita Carbon Dioxide Production

Pounds of carbon dioxide waste per person

Source: Oak Ridge National Laboratory

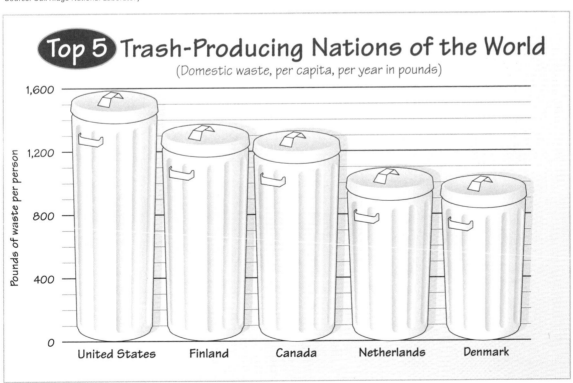

Top 5 Trash-Producing Nations of the World

(Domestic waste, per capita, per year in pounds)

Pounds of waste per person

United States   Finland   Canada   Netherlands   Denmark

Source: Based on information given in *The Top 10 of Everything 1997*

The Environment

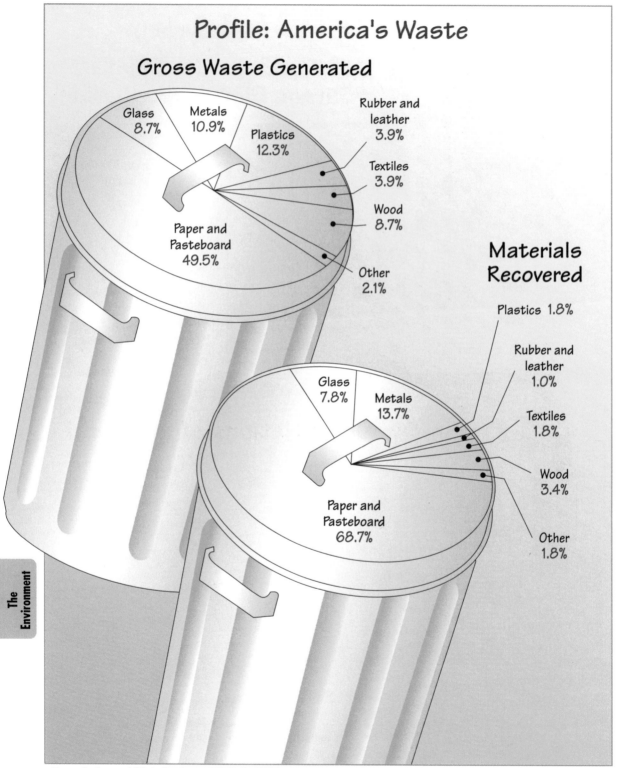

Profile: America's Waste

Gross Waste Generated

Glass
8.7%

Metals
10.9%

Plastics
12.3%

Rubber and
leather
3.9%

Textiles
3.9%

Wood
8.7%

Paper and
Pasteboard
49.5%

Other
2.1%

Materials Recovered

Plastics 1.8%

Rubber and
leather
1.0%

Textiles
1.8%

Wood
3.4%

Other
1.8%

Glass
7.8%

Metals
13.7%

Paper and
Pasteboard
68.7%

The Environment

Source: Environmental Protection Agency, 1994 Update (1995)

How Much Trash Gets Recycled?

On average, Americans create about 208 million tons of trash each year. That averages out to about 4.3 pounds of garbage created per person, per day. (Percentage of total trash, by type)

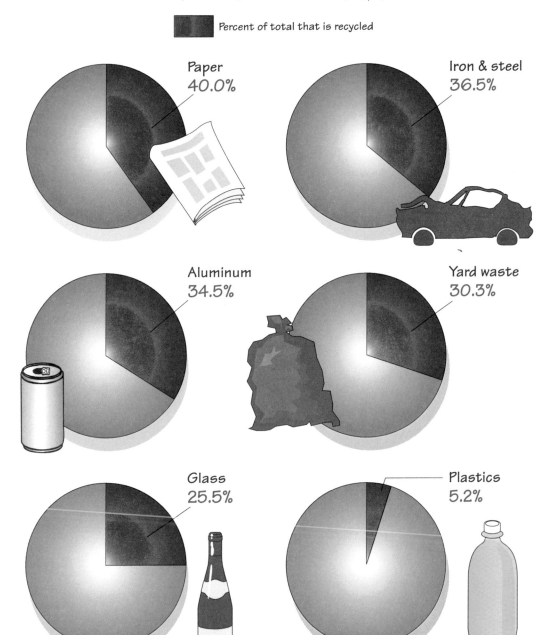

Percent of total that is recycled

Paper
40.0%

Iron & steel
36.5%

Aluminum
34.5%

Yard waste
30.3%

Glass
25.5%

Plastics
5.2%

Source: Environmental Protection Agency

The Environment

Top 5 U.S. States with Most Hazardous Waste Sites, 1995

3. California 96 Sites

2. Pennsylvania 103 Sites

4. New York 81 Sites

5. Michigan 78 Sites

1. New Jersey 108 Sites

Source: Environmental Protection Agency

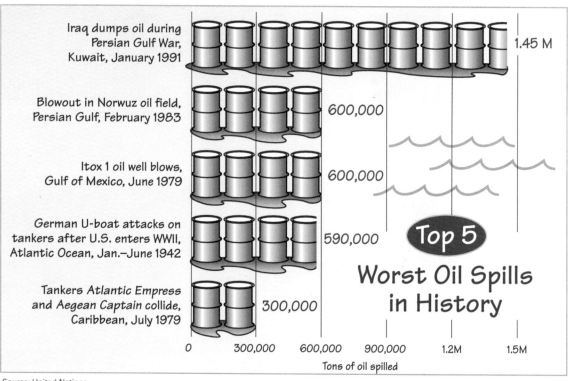

Iraq dumps oil during Persian Gulf War, Kuwait, January 1991 — 1.45 M

Blowout in Norwuz oil field, Persian Gulf, February 1983 — 600,000

Itox 1 oil well blows, Gulf of Mexico, June 1979 — 600,000

German U-boat attacks on tankers after U.S. enters WWII, Atlantic Ocean, Jan.–June 1942 — 590,000

Tankers Atlantic Empress and Aegean Captain collide, Caribbean, July 1979 — 300,000

Top 5 Worst Oil Spills in History

0   300,000   600,000   900,000   1.2M   1.5M

Tons of oil spilled

Source: United Nations

Top 10 U.S. Producers of Toxic Wastes, by Industry
(In millions and billions)

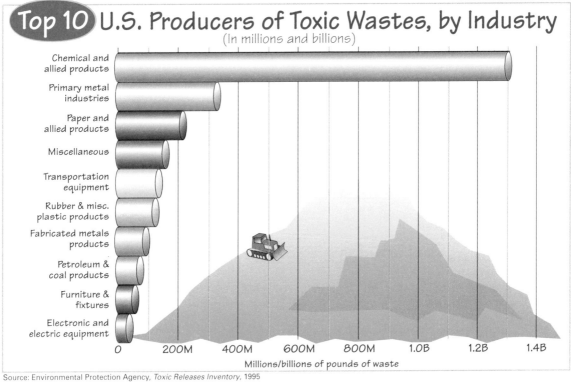

Source: Environmental Protection Agency, *Toxic Releases Inventory*, 1995

Nations with the Most Species of Threatened Mammals and Birds

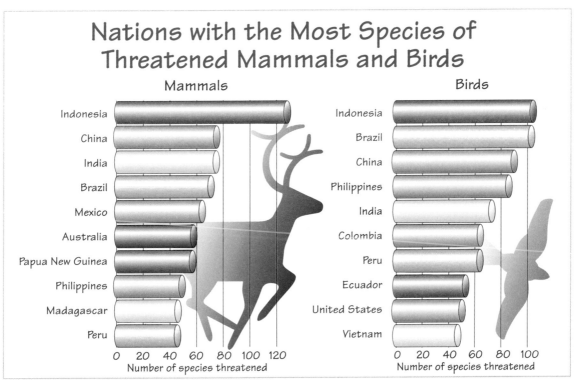

Source: IUCN Species Survival Commission

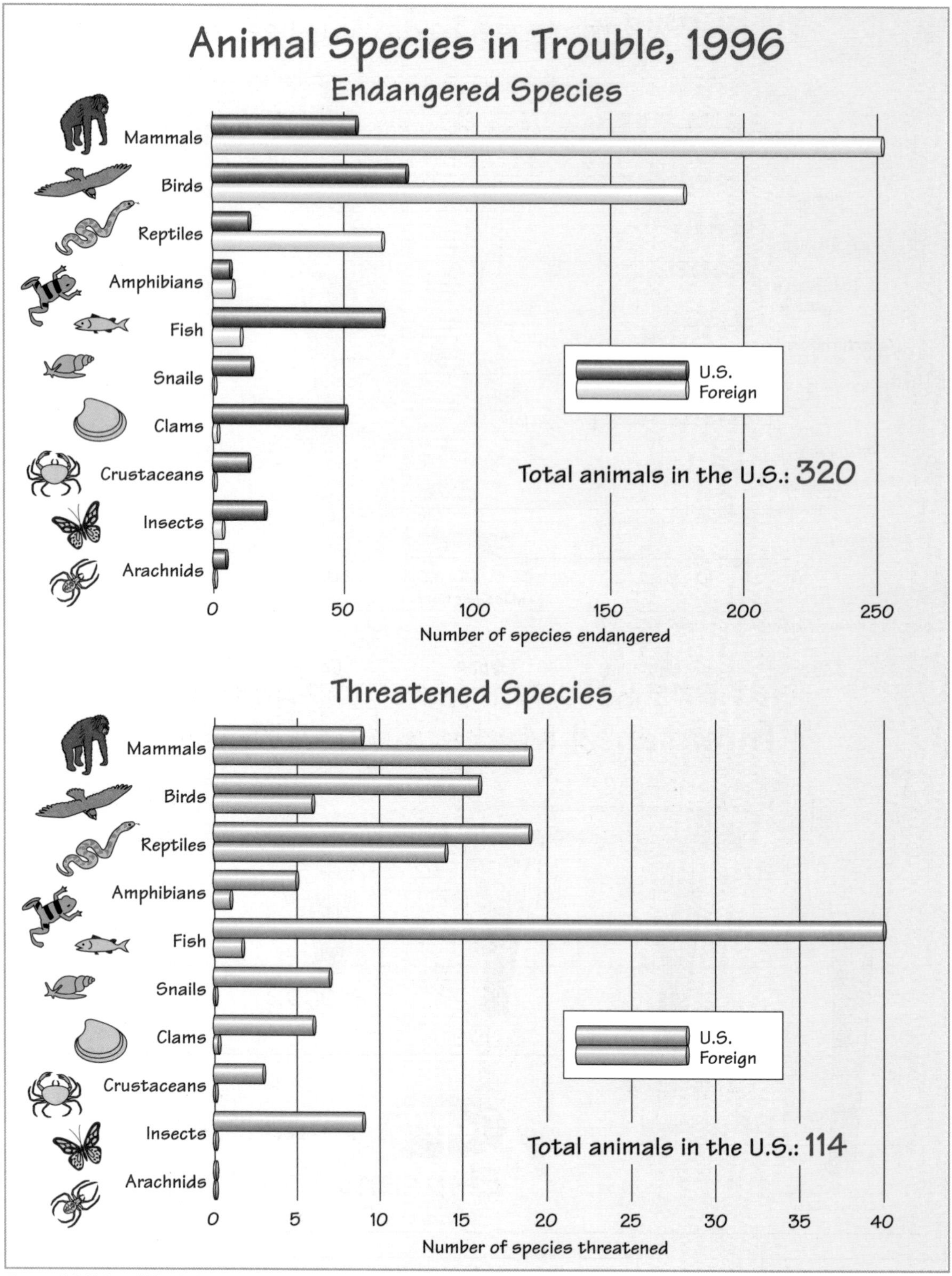

Animal Species in Trouble, 1996

Endangered Species

Total animals in the U.S.: 320

Number of species endangered

Threatened Species

Total animals in the U.S.: 114

Number of species threatened

Source: U.S. Fish and Wildlife Service, *List of Endangered and Threatened Species*, April 30, 1996

The Environment

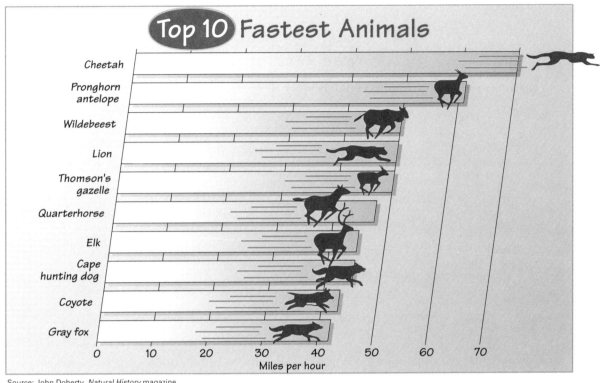

Source: John Doherty, *Natural History* magazine

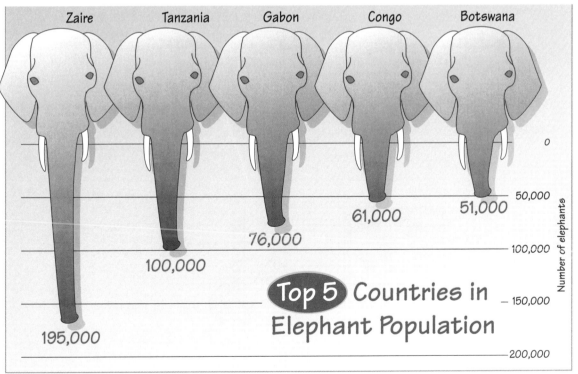

Source: Based on information given in *The Top 10 of Everything 1997*

Attitudes

So what do you think about fashion, politics, religion, dating, music, drinking, and a zillion other things? What's your favorite cereal, hobby, TV show? What are your attitudes toward people who cheat, people of different races, elderly people?

Who—and what—influences your opinions? Your parents, teachers, or friends? What you see on television or read in books?

How quickly do you form opinions? What does it take to make you change your attitude toward something, or someone? Are you willing to consider the facts and listen to reason?

Everyone has opinions on a wide range of issues. These opinions are important. Town officials want to know what issues are important to taxpayers. Jacket manufacturers want to know what brands are "in" with teenage buyers. Politicians want to know for whom people of different ages are planning to vote—and why.

Research companies are constantly taking surveys to find out

Kidbits Tidbits

- A 1998 report found that Americans strongly favored a voluntary program to test academic achievement of 4th and 8th graders.
- Americans are nearly split down the middle on having babies without being married. A total of 47% of American adults say it is wrong to have a child out of wedlock; 50% say it is not wrong.
- 89% of parents think they're doing a good job raising their kids, giving themselves an "A" or "B."
- About 60% of parents says they're spending more time with their kids than their parents spent with them.
- About 63% of Americans say they are affiliated with a religious group.

what people think, what they like, and what they plan to do. For instance, one survey of teenagers ages 15 through 18 found that their main concern was getting a good job. A survey of pre-teens found that more 7 to 12 year olds preferred to play outside than to go to a sports event. Another survey found that kids think playing sports is more fun that going to the movies—and much, much more fun than watching TV!

Opinions can differ widely depending on age, sex, education, economic status, and other factors. For example, romance books are more popular with girls than with boys, but science fiction tales are favorites of more boys than girls. Men say a person's eyes are the first thing they notice when they meet someone; women are most likely to notice a person's smile and teeth when they're first introduced. College graduates are more likely than high school dropouts to support women's right to have abortions.

Many surveys suggest that young people are more tolerant than older people. For example, there are indications that teenagers are more tolerant than adults of racial diversity. Young adults also seem to be more accepting than older adults of single parenthood.

Kidbits Tidbits

- In a 1997 survey, 63% of parents of families with children under age 18 said their family said grace or gave thanks to God before meals.
- In 1996, 54% of teenagers considered marijuana risky, a decline from 63% in 1994.
- A survey of 1,157 adolescents found that 78% of 12-year-olds—but only 26% of 17-year-olds—would report someone selling illegal drugs at school.
- The great majority of Americans believe that pets play a positive role in people's lives.
- About 90% of cat and dog owners consider the animals to be members of the family.
- 88% of adults said they do not believe that the difference of opinion between supporters and opponents of abortion will ever be resolved.

Attitudes

What Teens Like Most About School

More than three-quarters of all kids say their favorite thing about school is seeing their friends.

Percentage of teens surveyed

- Friends — 79%
- Assemblies/field trips — 43%
- Sports — 34%
- Seeing boyfriend/girlfriend — 32%
- Extra-curricular activities — 25%
- Free periods — 23%
- Learning — 22%
- Lunch — 20%
- Being away from home — 18%
- Other students — 14%
- Gossip — 12%
- Teachers — 12%
- Clubs — 11%
- Grades — 11%
- Classes — 10%
- Just being there — 9%

SOURCE: Based on data from Teenage Research Unlimited, Inc.

Attitudes

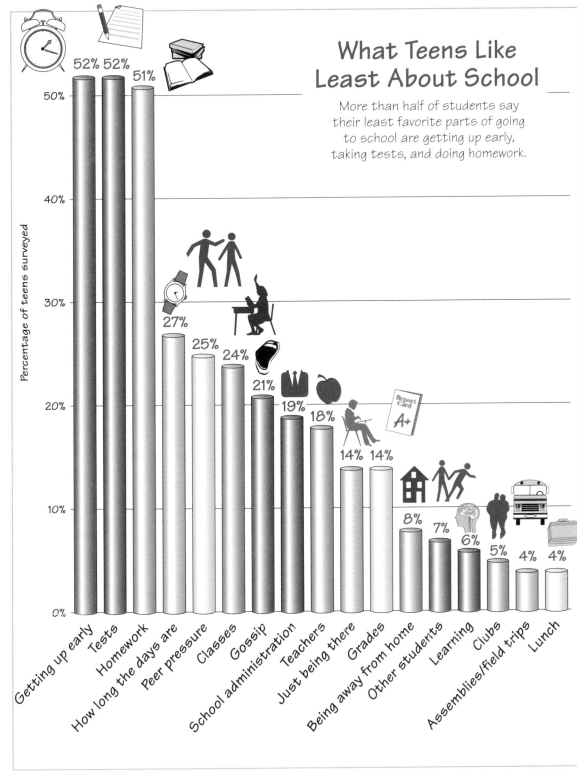

What Teens Like Least About School

More than half of students say their least favorite parts of going to school are getting up early, taking tests, and doing homework.

Percentage of teens surveyed

52% Getting up early
52% Tests
51% Homework
27% How long the days are
25% Peer pressure
24% Classes
21% Gossip
19% School administration
18% Teachers
14% Just being there
14% Grades
8% Being away from home
7% Other students
6% Learning
5% Clubs
4% Assemblies/field trips
4% Lunch

SOURCE: Based on data from Teenage Research Unlimited, Inc.

Attitudes

Top Social Issues for Teens

Issue	Percentage
Education	41%
AIDS	34%
Prejudice/racism	26%
Child abuse	25%
Violence in schools	20%
Abortion	20%
Drinking & driving	19%
The environment	17%
Drug abuse	16%
Animal rights	12%
Unplanned pregnancy	12%
Economy	10%
War	9%

0%   10%   20%   30%   40%

Percentage of teens surveyed

Teens ranked what they felt were the top three most important social issues. Education was the biggest concern.

Attitudes

SOURCE: Based on data from Teenage Research Unlimited, Inc.

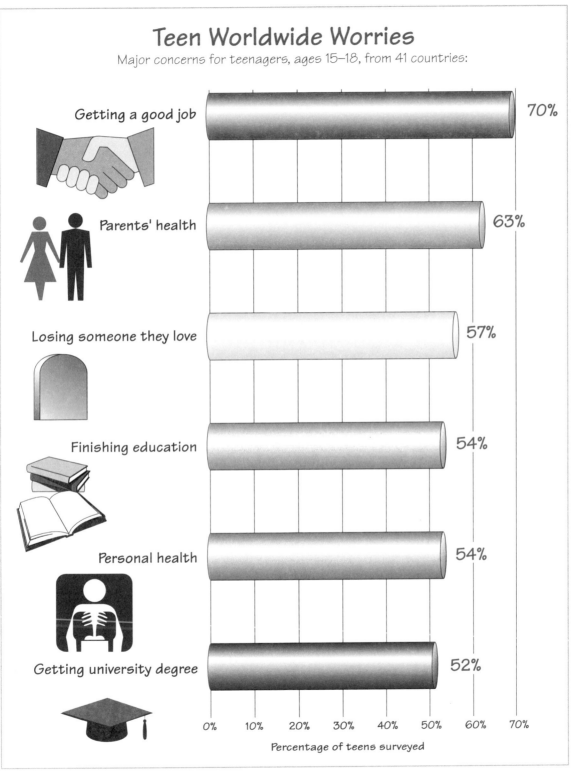

Teen Worldwide Worries

Major concerns for teenagers, ages 15–18, from 41 countries:

Getting a good job — 70%

Parents' health — 63%

Losing someone they love — 57%

Finishing education — 54%

Personal health — 54%

Getting university degree — 52%

0% 10% 20% 30% 40% 50% 60% 70%

Percentage of teens surveyed

Attitudes

SOURCE: Based on data from BrainWaves Group's New World Teen Study

Teachers Think Less of Students

Percentage of teachers who think their students have
declined over the years because students today are:

Attitudes

Less respectful of authority — 81%

Less ethical/moral — 73%

Less responsible — 65%

More self-centered — 60%

Less studious — 57%

0%   20%   40%   60%   80%

Percentage of teachers

SOURCE: Based on data from Educational Communications for *Who's Who Among America's Teachers*

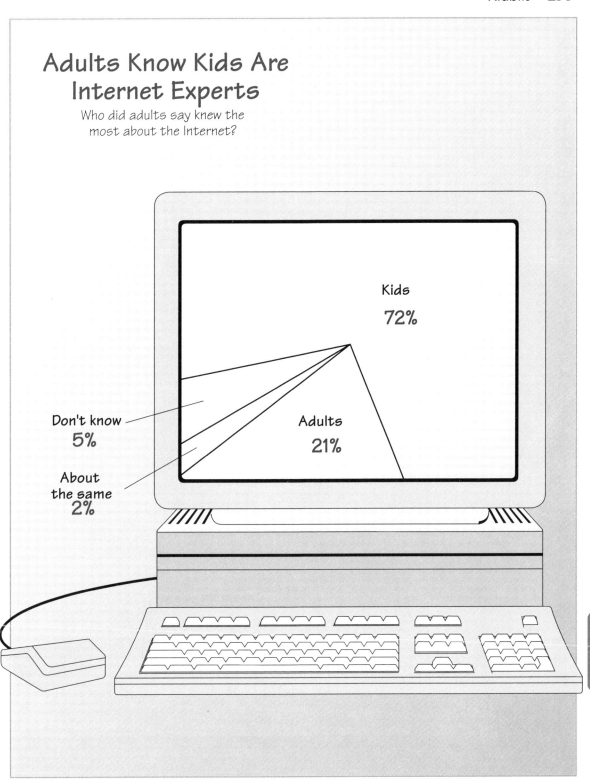

Adults Know Kids Are Internet Experts

Who did adults say knew the most about the Internet?

Kids
72%

Adults
21%

Don't know
5%

About
the same
2%

SOURCE: Based on data from The Direct Marketing Association

What Are the Best Influences on Kids?

The most important positive influences on
kids growing up, according to adults.
(Choices were other than parents.)

Men Women

Percentage of adults

41%

30%

25%

24%

19%

18%

13%

11%

5%

3%

5%

6%

40%

30%

20%

10%

0%

Religious
faith

Good
schools

Having right
kind of friends

Drug-free
environment

Family income

Not sure

Attitudes

SOURCE: Based on data from Lutheran Brotherhood

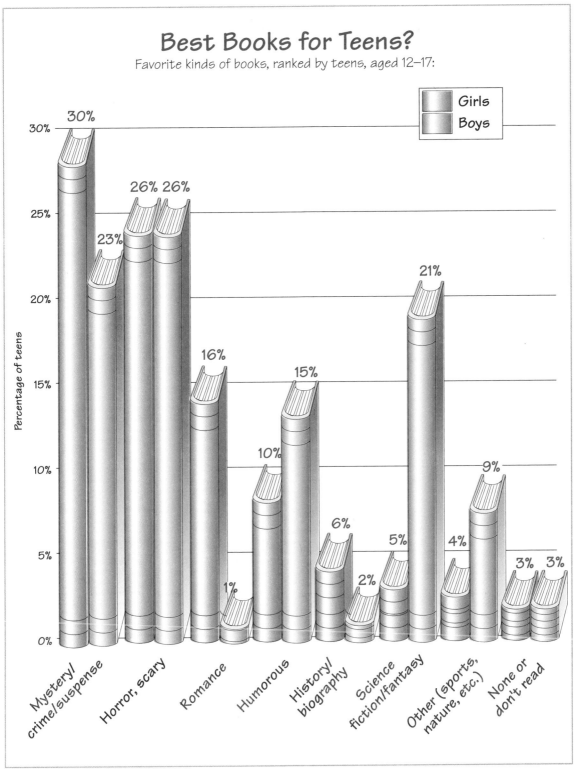

Best Books for Teens?

Favorite kinds of books, ranked by teens, aged 12–17:

Girls
Boys

Percentage of teens

30% — Mystery/crime/suspense

26% 26% — Horror, scary

23%

16% — Romance

1%

10% 15% — Humorous

6% — History/biography

2%

5% 21% — Science fiction/fantasy

4% 9% — Other (sports, nature, etc.)

3% 3% — None or don't read

Mystery/crime/suspense · Horror, scary · Romance · Humorous · History/biography · Science fiction/fantasy · Other (sports, nature, etc.) · None or don't read

Attitudes

SOURCE: Based on data from International Communications Research for Hewlett-Packard

Attitudes

Still Want to Play More Than "Surf"

The percentage of kids under 18 who think the following activities are more fun than using the Internet:

Percentage of kids under 18

Activity	Percentage
Playing sports	90%
Seeing movies	79%
Spending time with friends	55%
Talking on the phone	26%
Watching TV	8%
Reading	2%

SOURCE: Based on data from Jupiter Communications' *1997 Online Kids Report*

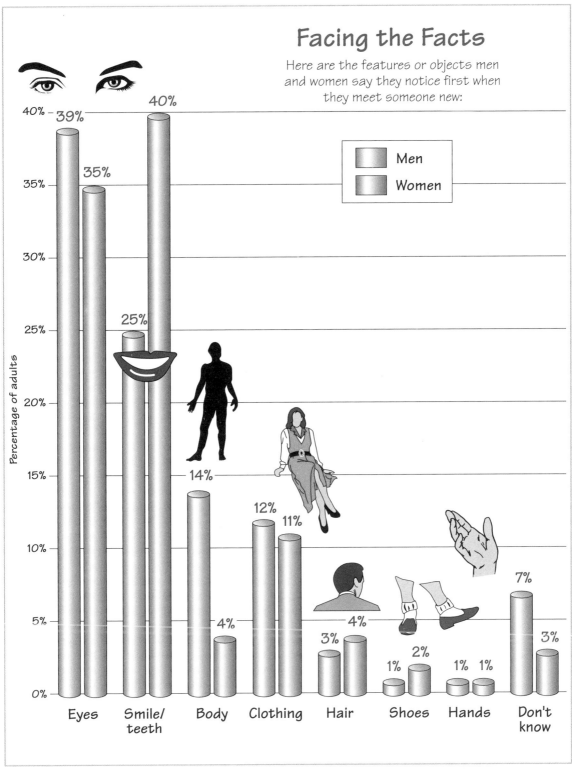

Facing the Facts

Here are the features or objects men and women say they notice first when they meet someone new:

Percentage of adults

Men
Women

	Eyes	Smile/teeth	Body	Clothing	Hair	Shoes	Hands	Don't know
Men	39%	40%	14%	12%	3%	1%	1%	7%
Women	35%	25%	4%	11%	4%	2%	1%	3%

Attitudes

SOURCE: Based on data from Opinion Research for Bausch & Lomb

Food

Food gives you energy, helps you grow, and keeps you healthy. It can also give you lots of pleasure. A meal of your favorite foods is always a treat. So, too, are those after-school snacks!

It's important to eat lots of fruit, veggies, and whole-grain starchy foods, such as bread and pasta. You should eat meat only in moderation. And, by proportion, you should eat very little fat. Many Americans do not follow this advice. They eat more cheese than lettuce, more fatty beef than lean chicken, more pepperoni pizzas than pizzas topped with vegetables. A diagram called a food pyramid shows which foods make up a healthy diet (look on page 297—or you can usually find one on your favorite cereal box or loaf of bread). But a recent study found that only 1% of American children met the food pyramid's guidelines.

Many factors influence what we eat. These include where we live, our religious beliefs, the amount of money we have, and how much time we have to prepare and eat meals.

People in different places have different food favorites. People in Philadelphia, for example, like pepper pot soup. In New

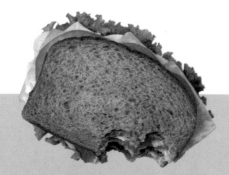

Kidbits Tidbits

- On average, Americans eat 350 slices of pizza every second.
- In 1995, U.S. restaurants served 5.2 billion hamburgers and cheeseburgers.
- On Super Bowl Sunday in 1996, Domino's Pizza delivered 829,765 pizzas, including some to the White House!
- On Thanksgiving, Americans eat about 535 million pounds of turkey.
- Coca-Cola sold 14.9 billion cases of soda worldwide in 1997. Each case equaled 24 eight-ounce servings.
- An average American eats 1,400 chickens, 21 cows, 14 sheep, and 12 pigs during his or her lifetime.

Orleans, French onion soup is the favorite. In New York and New England people prefer white cheddar cheese. Elsewhere in the U.S., yellow cheddar is the hands-down favorite. The popularity of brands also varies from region to region. For example, people who live in the South prefer one brand of peanut butter. On the West Coast, another brand is much more popular.

People in different countries also have different eating habits. Rice is the basic starchy food in Asia, while potatoes fill this role in northern Europe. Fish is the main source of protein in Japan, but in Argentina—which has broad plains for raising live-stock—beef is the main source of protein.

Cow milk is drunk in Canada, sheep and goat milk in Turkey, and reindeer milk is a staple in Finland.

Advertising plays a role in food preferences, too. A large supermarket may carry 20,000 different items, including dozens of brands of bread, breakfast cereal, cookies, and frozen desserts. Advertising helps persuade buyers to select a certain brand or item. Kellogg spent $410 million advertising its products in 1996; General Mills was close behind at $401 million. Coca-Cola spent $335 million, but McDonald's was the top spender at $599 million.

Kidbits Tidbits

- Each day, an average of about 1.2 million boxes of Jell-O are bought in the U.S. Strawberry is the overall Jell-O favorite.
- In 1996, Americans consumed 24.3 pounds of candy per person—up from 18.4 pounds in 1986. On average, each American ate 11.7 pounds of chocolate in 1996.
- Americans' favorite grain food is bread, followed by cereal, rice, and pasta.
- Each year more than 10 billion doughnuts are made in the U.S.
- Vanilla is the most popular ice cream flavor. On average, each American consumes about 47 pints of ice cream each year.

Food

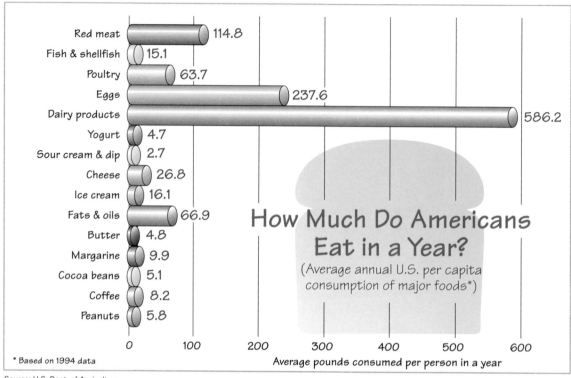

How Much Do Americans
Eat in a Year?
(Average annual U.S. per capita
consumption of major foods*)

Food	Pounds
Red meat	114.8
Fish & shellfish	15.1
Poultry	63.7
Eggs	237.6
Dairy products	586.2
Yogurt	4.7
Sour cream & dip	2.7
Cheese	26.8
Ice cream	16.1
Fats & oils	66.9
Butter	4.8
Margarine	9.9
Cocoa beans	5.1
Coffee	8.2
Peanuts	5.8

* Based on 1994 data

Average pounds consumed per person in a year

Source: U.S. Dept. of Agriculture

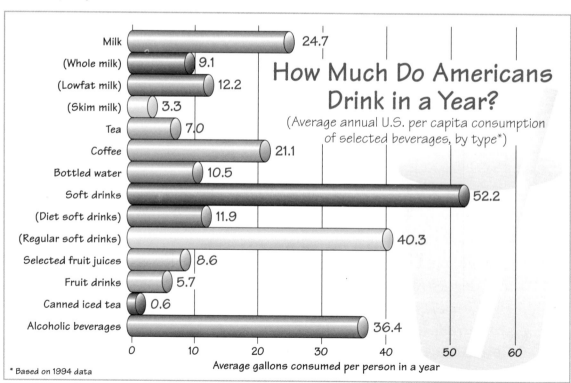

How Much Do Americans
Drink in a Year?
(Average annual U.S. per capita consumption
of selected beverages, by type*)

Beverage	Gallons
Milk	24.7
(Whole milk)	9.1
(Lowfat milk)	12.2
(Skim milk)	3.3
Tea	7.0
Coffee	21.1
Bottled water	10.5
Soft drinks	52.2
(Diet soft drinks)	11.9
(Regular soft drinks)	40.3
Selected fruit juices	8.6
Fruit drinks	5.7
Canned iced tea	0.6
Alcoholic beverages	36.4

* Based on 1994 data

Average gallons consumed per person in a year

Source: U.S. Dept. of Agriculture

Food

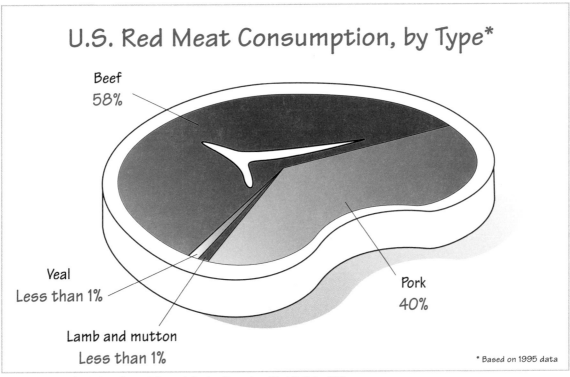

U.S. Red Meat Consumption, by Type*

Beef
58%

Veal
Less than 1%

Lamb and mutton
Less than 1%

Pork
40%

* Based on 1995 data

Source: U.S. Dept. of Agriculture, Economic Research Service, *Livestock and Meat Statistics, 1995*

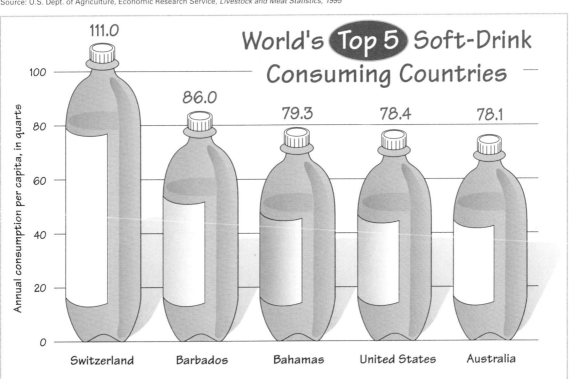

World's (Top 5) Soft-Drink Consuming Countries

Annual consumption per capita, in quarts

111.0	86.0	79.3	78.4	78.1
Switzerland	Barbados	Bahamas	United States	Australia

Source: Beverage Marketing Corporation

Food

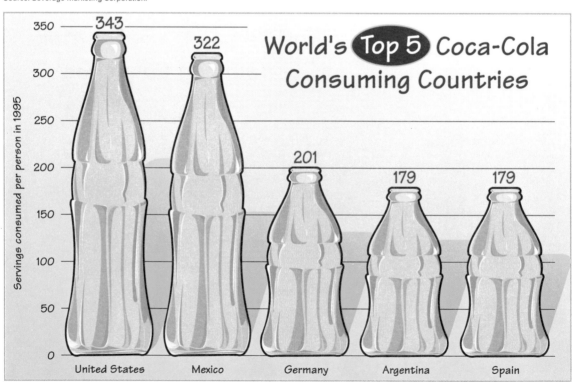

Top 5 U.S. Soft Drinks*

The U.S. consumes an average total of 13 billion gallons of soft drinks each year.

Billions of gallons consumed each year

- 2.6 B — Coca-Cola Classic
- 2.1 B — Pepsi
- 1.3 B — Diet Coke
- 768 M — Dr. Pepper
- 760 M — Diet Pepsi

Wholesale sales, based on 1994 data

Source: Beverage Marketing Corporation.

World's Top 5 Coca-Cola Consuming Countries

Servings consumed per person in 1995

- 343 — United States
- 322 — Mexico
- 201 — Germany
- 179 — Argentina
- 179 — Spain

Source: Beverage Marketing Corporation

Food

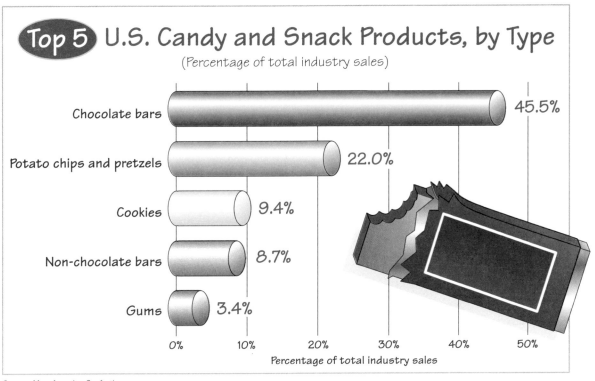

Top 5 U.S. Candy and Snack Products, by Type
(Percentage of total industry sales)

- Chocolate bars — 45.5%
- Potato chips and pretzels — 22.0%
- Cookies — 9.4%
- Non-chocolate bars — 8.7%
- Gums — 3.4%

Percentage of total industry sales
(0% 10% 20% 30% 40% 50%)

Source: *Manufacturing Confectioner*

America's Favorite Snack Sensations
(Percentage of total industry sales)

- Potato chips 31.9%
- Other 22.0%
- Popcorn 8.1%
- Snack nuts 8.4%
- Pretzels 8.6%
- Tortilla chips 21.4%

Source: Snack Food Association

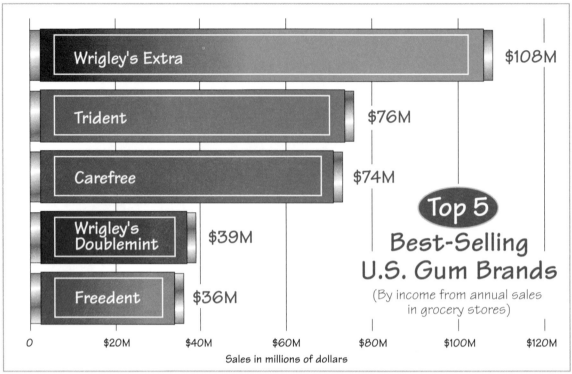

Wrigley's Extra — $108M

Trident — $76M

Carefree — $74M

Wrigley's Doublemint — $39M

Freedent — $36M

Top 5
Best-Selling
U.S. Gum Brands
(By income from annual sales in grocery stores)

0    $20M $40M $60M $80M $100M $120M

Sales in millions of dollars

Source: Information Resources, Inc.

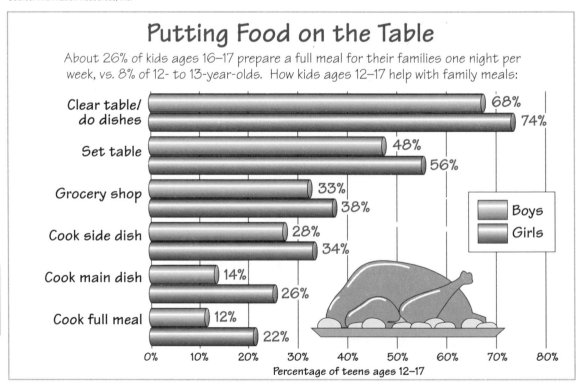

Putting Food on the Table

About 26% of kids ages 16–17 prepare a full meal for their families one night per week, vs. 8% of 12- to 13-year-olds. How kids ages 12–17 help with family meals:

Clear table/do dishes — 68% / 74%

Set table — 48% / 56%

Grocery shop — 33% / 38%

Cook side dish — 28% / 34%

Cook main dish — 14% / 26%

Cook full meal — 12% / 22%

Boys
Girls

0%   10%   20%   30%   40%   50%   60%   70%   80%

Percentage of teens ages 12–17

SOURCE: Based on data from Bruskin-Goldring for the National Pork Producers Council

Food

Top 5 Ice Cream-Consuming Countries in the World

The average American eats about 47 pints of ice cream each year.

Pints per capita, annual consumption

United States	47.0
New Zealand	37.7
Denmark	36.0
Australia	32.7
Belgium/Luxembourg	31.5

Source: International Ice Cream Association

Ben & Jerry's Top 10 Ice Cream/Frozen Yogurt Flavors

1. Chocolate Chip Cookie Dough
2. Cherry Garcia
3. Chocolate Fudge Brownie
4. New York Super Fudge Chunk
5. Cherry Garcia Frozen Yogurt
6. Chunky Monkey
7. Chocolate Fudge Brownie Frozen Yogurt
8. English Toffee Crunch
9. Peanut Butter Cup
10. Chubby Hubby

Source: Ben & Jerry's Homemade

Food

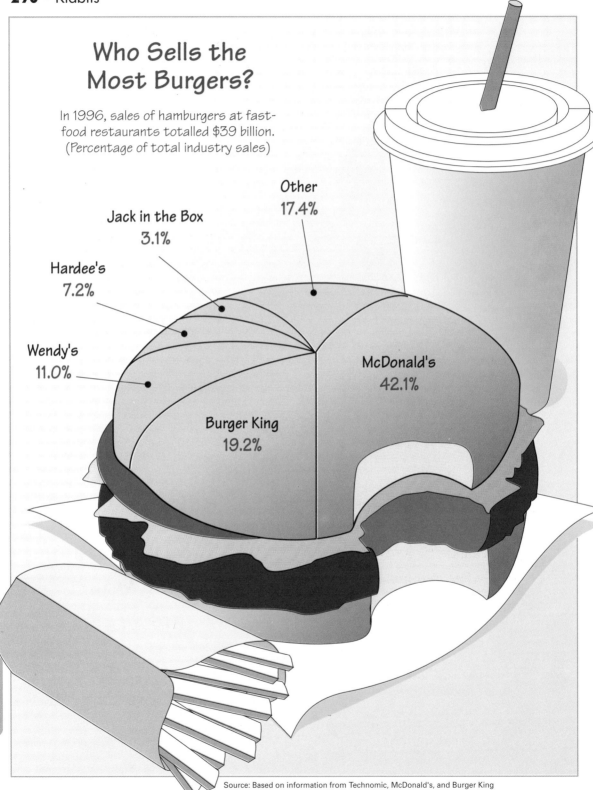

Who Sells the Most Burgers?

In 1996, sales of hamburgers at fast-food restaurants totalled $39 billion. (Percentage of total industry sales)

Other
17.4%

Jack in the Box
3.1%

Hardee's
7.2%

Wendy's
11.0%

McDonald's
42.1%

Burger King
19.2%

Food

Source: Based on information from Technomic, McDonald's, and Burger King

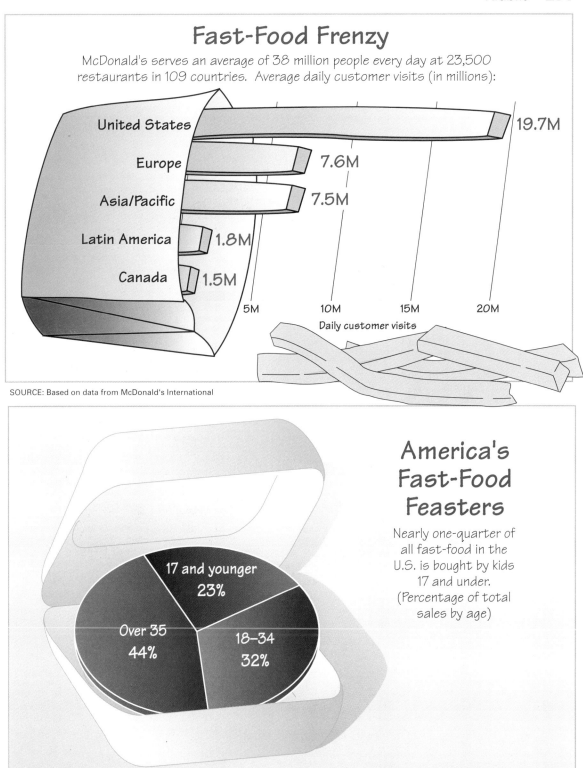

Fast-Food Frenzy

McDonald's serves an average of 38 million people every day at 23,500 restaurants in 109 countries. Average daily customer visits (in millions):

- United States — 19.7M
- Europe — 7.6M
- Asia/Pacific — 7.5M
- Latin America — 1.8M
- Canada — 1.5M

Daily customer visits

SOURCE: Based on data from McDonald's International

America's Fast-Food Feasters

Nearly one-quarter of all fast-food in the U.S. is bought by kids 17 and under. (Percentage of total sales by age)

- 17 and younger 23%
- Over 35 44%
- 18–34 32%

Food

What Tops Pizza?

(Most requested toppings,
by percentage of all pizzas sold)

Pepperoni
43%

Onions
4%

Others
7%

Vegetables
13%

Mushrooms
14%

Sausage
19%

Source: Based on data from *USA Today*

Top 10 Products in the Grocery Store

(Average annual grocery sales in dollars)

$1.8B — Coke Classic
$1.7B — Pepsi
$1.2B — Campbell's soup
$936M — Kraft cheese
$927M — Folgers coffee
$846M — Diet Coke
$810M — Snackwell's
$759M — Marlboro Lights
$750M — Budweiser beer
$681M — Tropicana Pure Premium orange juice

Sales in millions/billions of dollars

$1.5B
$1B
$500M
0

Food

Source: Based on data from *USA Today*

How $100 Gets Checked-Out

How U.S. consumers spent $100 at the grocery store in 1996:

Perishables
(In-store bakery, dairy, deli, produce, frozen foods, meat, seafood, etc.) — **$50.21**

$9.56 Miscellaneous groceries
(Baby foods, spices, baking needs, canned fruits and vegetables, etc.)

$9.53 Beverages
(Beer and wine, coffee, tea, juices, soft drinks, etc.)

$9.12 Nonedible groceries
(Household supplies, paper, pet foods, etc.)

$5.59 Snack foods
(Candy, cookies, nuts, etc.)

$5.07 Main courses/entrees
(Prepared foods, pasta, breakfast foods, etc.)

$4.01 Health and beauty care

$3.94 General merchandise

$2.97 Other

$0 $10 $20 $30 $40 $50

Average dollars spent at the grocery store

Food

SOURCE: Based on data from *USA Today*

Top 10 Grocery Products in Sales Growth, 1986-1996

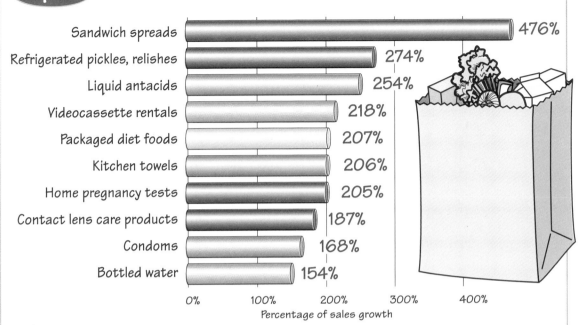

Product	Percentage
Sandwich spreads	476%
Refrigerated pickles, relishes	274%
Liquid antacids	254%
Videocassette rentals	218%
Packaged diet foods	207%
Kitchen towels	206%
Home pregnancy tests	205%
Contact lens care products	187%
Condoms	168%
Bottled water	154%

Percentage of sales growth

Top 10 Grocery Products in Sales Decline, 1986-1996

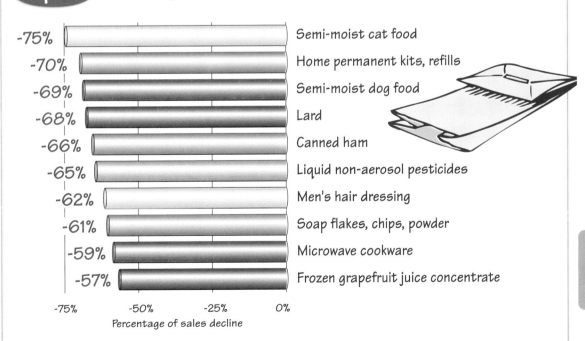

Percentage	Product
-75%	Semi-moist cat food
-70%	Home permanent kits, refills
-69%	Semi-moist dog food
-68%	Lard
-66%	Canned ham
-65%	Liquid non-aerosol pesticides
-62%	Men's hair dressing
-61%	Soap flakes, chips, powder
-59%	Microwave cookware
-57%	Frozen grapefruit juice concentrate

Percentage of sales decline

Food

SOURCE: Based on data from *USA Today*

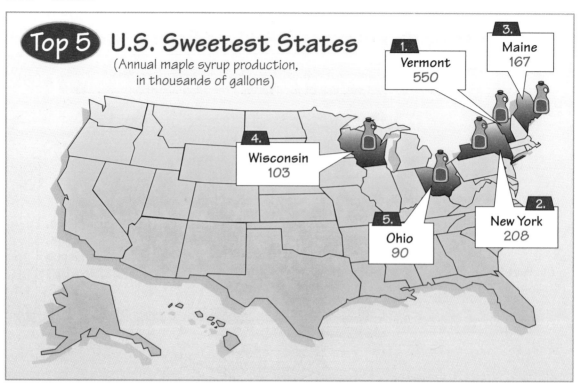

Top 5 U.S. Sweetest States

(Annual maple syrup production, in thousands of gallons)

1. Vermont 550
2. New York 208
3. Maine 167
4. Wisconsin 103
5. Ohio 90

Source: U.S. Agricultural Statistics Service

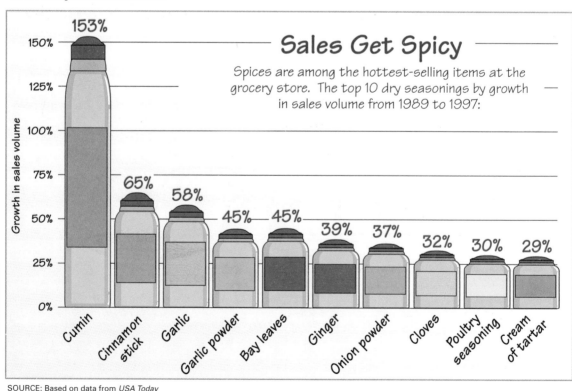

Sales Get Spicy

Spices are among the hottest-selling items at the grocery store. The top 10 dry seasonings by growth in sales volume from 1989 to 1997:

Growth in sales volume

- Cumin 153%
- Cinnamon stick 65%
- Garlic 58%
- Garlic powder 45%
- Bay leaves 45%
- Ginger 39%
- Onion powder 37%
- Cloves 32%
- Poultry seasoning 30%
- Cream of tartar 29%

SOURCE: Based on data from *USA Today*

Food

The Food Pyramid

The U.S. Department of Agriculture (USDA) has created this
recommended balance of food groups for good nutrition.

Fats, Oils, & Sweets
USE SPARINGLY

Meat, Poultry, Fish,
Dry Beans, Eggs,
& Nuts Group
2–3 SERVINGS
DAILY

Milk, Yogurt,
& Cheese Group
2–3 SERVINGS
DAILY

Vegetable Group
3–5 SERVINGS
DAILY

Fruit Group
2–4 SERVINGS
DAILY

Bread, Cereal, Rice, & Pasta Group
6–11 SERVINGS DAILY

Food

SOURCE: U.S. Department of Agriculture

Computers

• •

It's hard to believe that digital computers have only been around since 1946. And, considering where we are with laptops and PDAs, it's hard to imagine that the first computer was a huge monster that weighed 30 tons!

It didn't have transistors, integrated circuits, disk drives, not even a keyboard or a monitor. Those things hadn't been invented yet! It couldn't do word processing or play games or send e-mail. In fact, a $40 calculator today has more total computer power than that first computer!

Today, computers are everywhere. In only a short period of time, they have become as much a part of everday American life as televisions, microwaves, and telephone answering machines. PCs sit on desktops and are carried in briefcases and backpacks. Tiny computers are installed in cars, stoves, and hundreds of other products. People of every age, and in every kind of job, use computers. In general, young people are more comfortable with using computers than are older people. Today's kids have grown up with computers. In fact, many young people are finding that their computer skills can be a great source of extra money. Lots of

teens make money writing computer programs, maintaining computer bulletin boards, repairing computers, even teaching old folks how to zip around the World Wide Web!

One of the most popular uses of computers is to go "online." Surfing the Net, you can visit people and places all over the world, including sports teams, museums, parks, and schools. You can search encyclopedias, dictionaries, newspapers, and other reference sources, (a great way to do research for school and business reports!). You can "chat" with friends, movie stars, musicians, and politicians.

The best way to explore the Internet is via the World Wide Web. The Web is a collection of standards that make it easier to navigate the Internet and access information. The Web displays information in interconnected "pages" that are linked to one another by key words or phrases that are highlighted. Point to a highlighted word, click the mouse, and you instantly jump to another page. Each page has an address. For example, the Web address for the White House is: *http://www.whitehouse.gov*

Going online also lets you send e-mail from your computer to someone else's computer. You can shop for everything from candy to Cadillacs. You can make plane reservations and find recipes. You can download games and other programs to your own computer. You can even take a virtual tour of Mars, go inside the eye of a hurricane, or "chat" with some of the world's most famous people!

Computers

Profile: Teen Use of Technology
(Kids in 7th through 12th grades)

Computer Use vs. Other
Average number of hours a week teens spend:

Watching TV	18
Talking on the phone	7
Using a computer	4

Number of hours

Daily Use
Percentage of teens who use the following at least once a day:

Stereo	85%
Calculator	67%
Telephone answering machine	46%
Computer	44%
Video/computer games	40%
VCR	39%

Percentage of teens

Computer Use
Percentage of teens who have used a computer to:

Play computer games	93%
Write school report	89%
Use Internet for school report	56%
Chat on Internet/send e-mail	48%

Percentage of teens

Computers

SOURCE: Based on data from Gallup Organization

Do I Really Need a Computer?

Percentage of teens who say they could easily live without:

Video/computer games — 82%

VCR — 49%

Phone answering machine — 38%

Stereo — 31%

Calculator — 29%

TV — 28%

Computer — 23%

0% 20% 40% 60% 80%

Percentage of teens

SOURCE: Based on data from Gallup Organization

Computers

Teen Use of the Internet and Online Services

(By location of use)

Net: Used any service
- 54%
- 40%
- 27%

Internet/World Wide Web
- 38%
- 29%
- 16%

America Online
- 37%
- 22%
- 18%

Prodigy
- 17%
- 10%
- 8%

CompuServe/WOW!
- 13%
- 9%
- 5%

Microsoft Network
- 5%
- 3%
- 3%

Used Anywhere
Used at School
Used at Home

0% 10% 20% 30% 40% 50%
Percentage of teens

SOURCE: Based on data from Teenage Research Unlimited, Inc.

Computers

Profile: Teen Online Preferences, by Gender

(Percentage of users in gender group)

Males	Females

Who Checks Out Internet Sites More?

56%

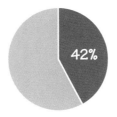 42%

Who Chats More Online?

 50%

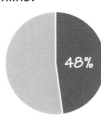 48%

Who Does More Research Online?

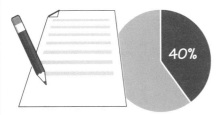 40%

 47%

Who E-mails More Online?

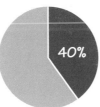 40%

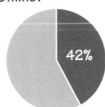 42%

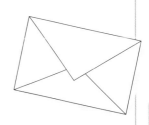

Computers

SOURCE: Based on data from Teenage Research Unlimited, Inc.

Profile: Teen Online Preferences, by Gender

(Percentage of users in gender group)

Males	Females

Who Says Entertainment Sites Are Best?

52%   48%

Who Says Sports Sites Are Best?

47%   23%

Who Says Music Sites Are Best?

48%   58%

Who Says Game Sites Are Best?

44%   31%

Computers

SOURCE: Based on data from Teenage Research Unlimited, Inc.

Online At Home

Most common activities of people with home
computers and online access:

Activity	Percentage
Write Letters to friends/family	81%
Play computer games	79%
Run educational software	76%
E-mail friends/family	74%
Do work from job	69%
Keep finances in order	66%
E-mail business colleagues	66%

Percentage of online usage

SOURCE: Based on data from Roper Starch for Lexmark

Computers

Kiddin' Online

Most kids ages 9–13 know about the Internet and more than half of them have gone online. The most popular activities of kids online:

Chat with others — 45%

Play games — 40%

Information for fun — 38%

Information for school — 28%

E-mail — 20%

Other — 10%

Don't know — 1%

0%   10%   20%   30%   40%   50%

Percentage of Internet usage

Computers

SOURCE: Based on data from *Sports Illustrated for Kids* Omnibus

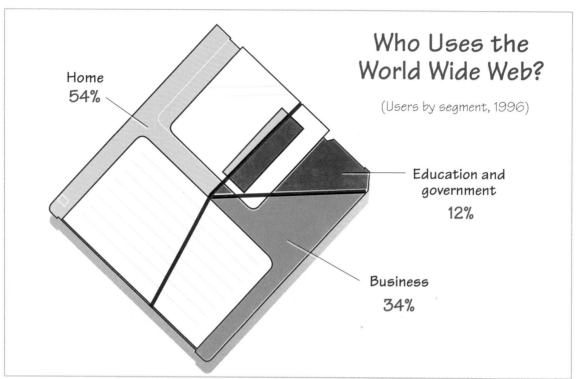

Who Uses the World Wide Web?

(Users by segment, 1996)

Home
54%

Education and government
12%

Business
34%

SOURCE: Based on data from Internet Program, International Data Corporation, 1996

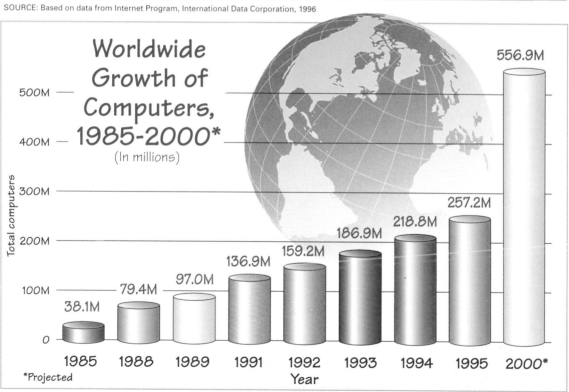

Worldwide Growth of Computers, 1985-2000*

(In millions)

Total computers

500M

400M

300M

200M

100M

0

556.9M

257.2M

218.8M

186.9M

159.2M

136.9M

97.0M

79.4M

38.1M

1985 1988 1989 1991 1992 1993 1994 1995 2000*

*Projected

Year

SOURCE: Based on data from Karen Petska-Juliussen and Egil Juliussen, *8th Annual Computer Industry Almanac*

Computers

Top 10 PC Companies in the U.S. Market

Since 1992, the rankings of the top-selling companies in the U.S.
PC market have changed. IBM and Apple have lost their top
positions to Compaq and Packard Bell.

U.S. Shipments
(In millions)

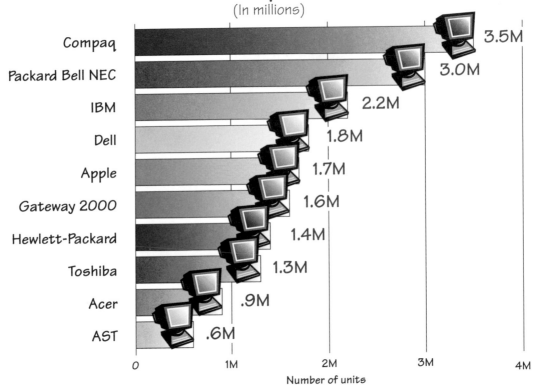

Compaq	3.5M
Packard Bell NEC	3.0M
IBM	2.2M
Dell	1.8M
Apple	1.7M
Gateway 2000	1.6M
Hewlett-Packard	1.4M
Toshiba	1.3M
Acer	.9M
AST	.6M

Number of units

U.S. Market Share

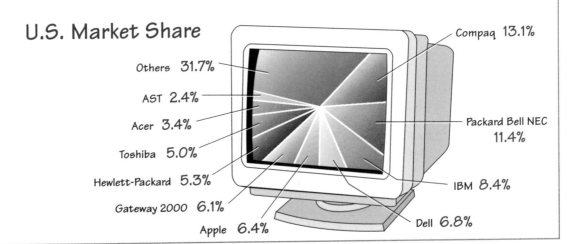

Others 31.7%
AST 2.4%
Acer 3.4%
Toshiba 5.0%
Hewlett-Packard 5.3%
Gateway 2000 6.1%
Apple 6.4%
Compaq 13.1%
Packard Bell NEC 11.4%
IBM 8.4%
Dell 6.8%

SOURCE: Based on data from International Data Corp.

Computers

Top 10 PC Companies in the Worldwide Market

Worldwide Shipments
(In millions)

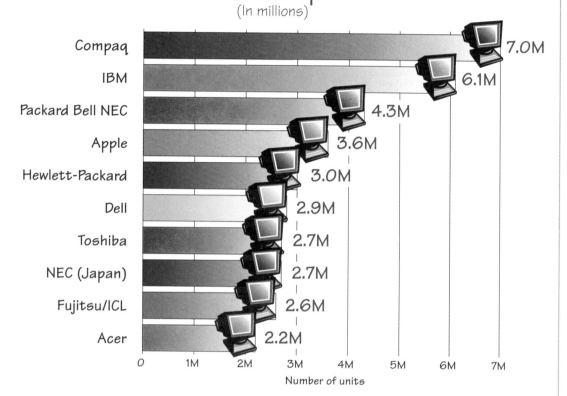

Company	Shipments
Compaq	7.0M
IBM	6.1M
Packard Bell NEC	4.3M
Apple	3.6M
Hewlett-Packard	3.0M
Dell	2.9M
Toshiba	2.7M
NEC (Japan)	2.7M
Fujitsu/ICL	2.6M
Acer	2.2M

Number of units

Worldwide Market Share

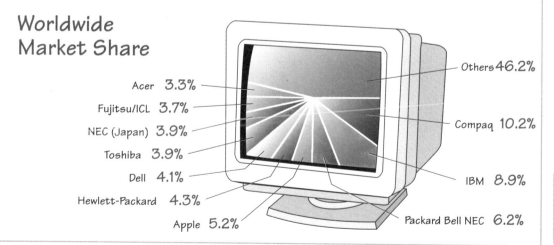

- Acer 3.3%
- Fujitsu/ICL 3.7%
- NEC (Japan) 3.9%
- Toshiba 3.9%
- Dell 4.1%
- Hewlett-Packard 4.3%
- Apple 5.2%
- Others 46.2%
- Compaq 10.2%
- IBM 8.9%
- Packard Bell NEC 6.2%

Computers

SOURCE: Based on data from International Data Corp.

Top 10 Best-Selling PC Games

1	Warcraft II	Davidson
2	Myst	Brøderbund
3	Civilization 2	MicroProse
4	Microsoft Flight Simulator	Microsoft
5	Duke Nukem 3D	Formgen
6	Mechwarrior II	Activision
7	Command & Conquer	Virgin
8	Doom II	GT Interactive
9	Ultimate Doom Thy Flesh	GT Interactive
10	Star Wars Rebel Assault II	LucasArts

SOURCE: Based on data from PC Data, Reston, VA

Top 10 Best-Selling Mac Games

1	Myst	Brøderbund
2	Top Ten Pack	Electronic Arts
3	Warcraft II	Davidson
4	Links Pro	Access
5	X-Wing Collector's CD	LucasArts
6	FA-18 Hornet	Graphic Simulations
7	Doom II	GT Interactive
8	Star Wars Rebel Assault II	LucasArts
9	Ultimate Doom Thy Flesh	GT Interactive
10	The Archives I	LucasArts

SOURCE: Based on data from PC Data, Reston, VA

Computers

Top 10 Online Advertisers, 1996

Researchers estimate that advertisers spent $300 million online in the U.S. in 1996. About $260 million of that money went to Web sites, and the rest went to non-Web publishers such as America Online and PointCast. That represents more than a 500% increase over 1995 spending.
(In millions)

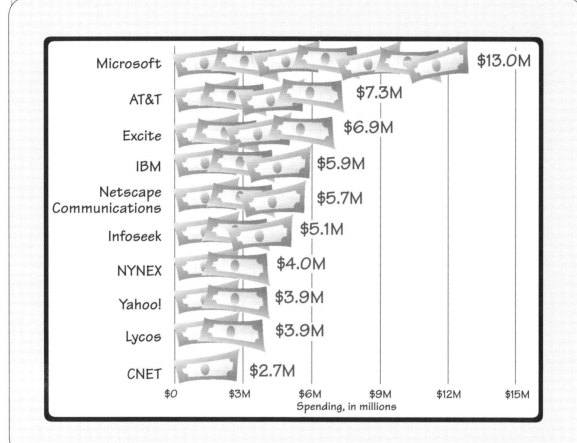

Advertiser	Spending
Microsoft	$13.0M
AT&T	$7.3M
Excite	$6.9M
IBM	$5.9M
Netscape Communications	$5.7M
Infoseek	$5.1M
NYNEX	$4.0M
Yahoo!	$3.9M
Lycos	$3.9M
CNET	$2.7M

$0 $3M $6M $9M $12M $15M
Spending, in millions

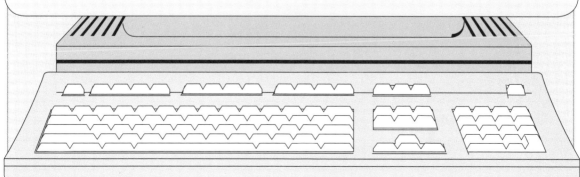

SOURCE: Based on data from Jupiter Communications

Computers

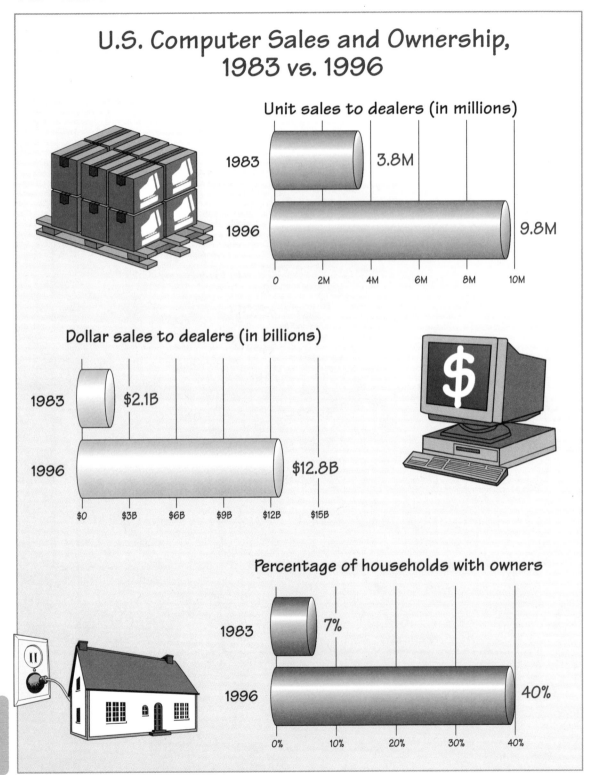

U.S. Computer Sales and Ownership, 1983 vs. 1996

Unit sales to dealers (in millions)

1983 — 3.8M
1996 — 9.8M

0 2M 4M 6M 8M 10M

Dollar sales to dealers (in billions)

1983 — $2.1B
1996 — $12.8B

$0 $3B $6B $9B $12B $15B

Percentage of households with owners

1983 — 7%
1996 — 40%

0% 10% 20% 30% 40%

SOURCE: Based on data from Electronic Industries Association, Arlington, VA

The Growth of Personal Computer Shipments and Revenues, 1983 to 1998

Shipments
(In millions of units)

Number of units

- U.S. shipments
- Worldwide shipments

100M

80M

60M

40M

20M

0

6.2M — 1983

11.1M

9.3M — 1989

21.3M

18.6M — 1994

47.9M

34.6M — 1998*

98.4M

Year

Revenues
(In millions of U.S. dollars)

Millions of U.S. dollars

- U.S. revenue
- Worldwide revenue

$200M

$150M

$100M

$50M

$0

$217.4M

$94.5M

$81.9M

$40.4M

$37.3M

$11.0M
$6.5M — 1983

$19.7M — 1989

1994

1998*

Year

*1998 Estimate

SOURCE: Based on data from Dataquest

Top 10 Countries with the Most Computers Per Person, Estimated for 2000

Country	Number of computers per 1,000 people
United States	580.0
Australia	525.7
Norway	515.4
Canada	511.9
Denmark	510.2
Sweden	508.9
Finland	505.0
New Zealand	499.2
The Netherlands	450.3
Switzerland	443.7

Number of computers per 1,000 people

SOURCE: Based on data from Karen Petska-Juliussen and Egil Juliussen, *8th Annual Computer Industry Almanac*

Computers

Index

I N D E X